Presented to

a Faithful
Hope Partner
II Corinthians 9: 7, 8

Heralds of Hope, Inc
J Ousleyda

1990

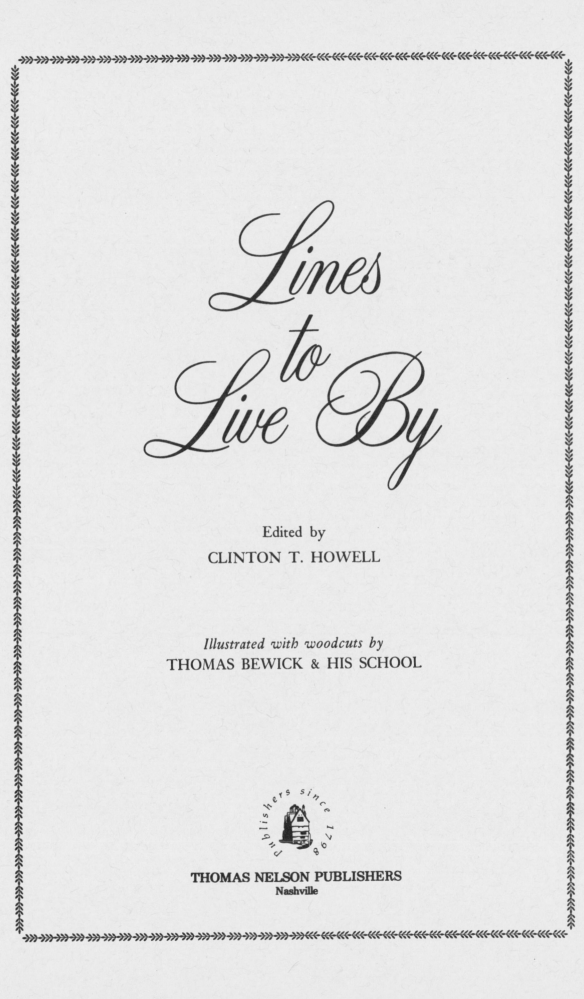

Lines
to
Live By

Edited by
CLINTON T. HOWELL

Illustrated with woodcuts by
THOMAS BEWICK & HIS SCHOOL

Publishers since 1798

THOMAS NELSON PUBLISHERS
Nashville

To those authors, representatives, and publishers who have allowed us to use their work without charge; to those who allowed us special arrangement—and to those whose work is now in the public domain, we are deeply grateful.

Some, after diligent search, we were unable to contact. Should there be such—whose work appears here without proper arrangement or acknowledgement—please allow us to make such in the next printing. It is not our desire or intention to use anyone's material without permission or proper credit.

The editor has also made every effort to trace the authorship of all selections. When no name appears the authorship is unknown.

Acknowledgement is made to the following who have, through special arrangement, granted permission to use copyrighted material:

DODD, MEAD AND COMPANY, INC., for "The House of Christmas" by Gilbert Keith Chesterton, from THE COLLECTED POEMS OF G. K. CHESTERTON, copyright 1932. Copyright renewed. "Walk Slowly" by Adelaide Love, from THE SLENDER SINGING TREE, copyright 1933, 1961 by Adelaide Love. "Just Think" from THE COMPLETE POEMS OF ROBERT SERVICE. Copyright 1940 by Robert Service.

DOUBLEDAY AND COMPANY, INC., for "If" by Rudyard Kipling, from REWARDS AND FAIRIES copyright 1910 by Rudyard Kipling. Selection from "Roofs" by Joyce Kilmer, Copyright 1915 by Current Literature Publishing Co.; Selection from "Love's Lantern" by Joyce Kilmer, copyright 1914 by George H. Doran Company, from POEMS, ESSAYS AND LETTERS by Joyce Kilmer. Reprinted by permission of Doubleday and Company, Inc.

NORMA MILLAY ELLIS for "God's World" and the conclusion of "Renasence" by Edna St. Vincent Millay, from COLLECTED POEMS OF EDNA ST. VINCENT MILLAY copyright 1913, 1940. Published by Harper and Row.

FIRST CHURCH OF CHRIST, SCIENTIST, Maywood, Illinois, for "The Journey" by Thomas Curtis Clark.

HENRY REGNERY COMPANY for "Lord, Make a Regular Man Out of Me," "It Couldn't Be Done," "Success," "Myself," "My Creed," "Sermons We See," "Your Name," "The Nurse," "At Christmas," "The Layman," "Home," "Equipment," from THE COLLECTED VERSE OF EDGAR A. GUEST, copyright 1934, Reilly and Lee Company.

HOLT, RINEHART AND WINSTON, INC. for "Tears" by Lizette Woodworth Reese.

HOUGHTON MIFFLIN COMPANY. "The Butterfly," from THE MARRIAGE CYCLE by Alice Freeman Palmer, Houghton Mifflin Company, Publisher.

THE MACMILLAN COMPANY for "The Seekers" and selections from "Everlasting Mercy" by John Masefield.

"Barter" by Sara Teasdale from THE COLLECTED POEMS OF SARA TEASDALE, Copyright 1957 by The Macmillan Company.

CHARLOTTE BAKER MONTGOMERY, Literary Executor for "Let Me Grow Lovely," by Karle Wilson Baker.

W. W. NORTON AND COMPANY for "Stubborn Ounces" from HANDS LAID UPON THE WIND by Bonaro W. Overstreet. Copyright 1955.

THE SUNDAY SCHOOL BOARD of the Southern Baptist Convention for "Country Church" by Ethel H. Bailey from THE SIGNATURE OF GOD. Copyright 1967.

YALE UNIVERSITY PRESS for "God" by Gamaliel Bradford from SHADOW VERSES.

Acknowledgement is made to the following for permission to use the listed materials:

ABINGDON PRESS for "The Parson's Prayer" by Ralph S. Cushman from PRACTICING THE PRESENCE.

THE BOBBS-MERRILL COMPANY for "Let Something Good Be Said," "The Enduring" and "He Is Not Dead" by James Whitcomb Riley; from The Biographical Edition of THE COMPLETE WORKS OF JAMES WHITCOMB RILEY, Copyright 1913 by James Whitcomb Riley; 1940 by Lesley Payne, Elizabeth Eitel Miesse and Edmund H. Eitel. Reprinted by permission of the publishers, The Bobbs-Merrill Company, Inc.

DOUBLEDAY AND COMPANY, INC., for "The Explorer," "L'Envoi" and "Recessional" by Rudyard Kipling from RUDYARD KIPLING'S VERSE: DEFINITIVE EDITION.

EPWORTH PRESS, London for "The Unseen Bridge" by Thomas Gilbert.

HOUGHTON MIFFLIN COMPANY for "Io Victis" by William Wetmore Storey; "My Wage" by Jessie B. Rittenhouse.

MISS THEODORA OXENHAM for kind permission to use the following poems by her father John Oxenham (1852-1941): "How-When-Where," "The Ways," "Great Heart," "Your Place," "The Shadow," "The Cross at the Crossways," "Credo," "The Sacrament of Work," "After Work," "A Dieu and Au Revoir."

RAND McNALLY AND COMPANY for "Worth While," "Emphasis," "Friendship," "The Winds Of Fate," "Lifting and Learning," "I Will Not Doubt," "Fortitude," "Those We Love The Best," "Growing Old," "The Beyond," "Purpose," "The Goal," by Ella Wheeler Wilcox.

CHARLES SCRIBNER'S SONS for "America For Me," "These Are The Gifts I Ask," "Aspiration," "Peace," "Four Things," "A Mile With Me," by Henry Van Dyke, from THE POEMS OF HENRY VAN DYKE, copyright 1911, and copyright 1939 by Tertius Van Dyke.

ISBN 0-8407-7191-6

Fourteenth printing   Library of Congress Catalog Card Number—72-5249

Contents

AGE   9

It is magnificent to grow old, if one keeps young.

      —HARRY EMERSON FOSDICK

BEAUTY   15

The gates are open on the road
That leads to beauty and to God.

      —CHARLES SORLEY

BOOKS   21

When we are collecting books, we are collecting happiness.

      —VINCENT STARRETT

CHALLENGE   27

Once to every man and nation comes the moment to decide—

      —JAMES RUSSELL LOWELL

CHARACTER   37

It is not what he has, nor even what he does, which directly affects the worth of a man; but what he is.

      —HENRI-FREDERIC AMIEL

CONSOLATION   45

Heaven knows we need never be ashamed of our tears, for they are rain upon the blinding dust of earth, overlying our hard hearts.

      —CHARLES DICKENS

CONTENTMENT   53

The great essentials in life are something to do, something to love, something to hope for.

      —THOMAS CHALMERS

COURAGE   61

One man with courage makes a majority.

      —ANDREW JACKSON

DAYS   67

Remember the week day, and keep it holy, too.

DEATH   75

Death is the golden key that opens the palace of eternity.

      —JOHN MILTON

DEFEAT   85

There is always another chance . . . This thing that we call "failure" is not falling down, but staying down.

      —MARY PICKFORD

FAITH   91

Faith is to believe what we do not see, and the reward of this faith is to see what we believe.

      —ST. AUGUSTINE

FRIENDSHIP   97

Art thou lonely, O my brother?
Share thy little with another!
Stretch a hand to one unfriended,
And thy loneliness is ended.

      —JOHN OXENHAM

GRATITUDE   113

Gratitude is the fairest blossom which springs from the soul.

      —BALLOU

HAPPINESS   117

Happiness is a perfume you cannot pour on others without getting a few drops on yourself.

HOME   123

He is happiest, be he king or peasant, who finds peace in his home.

      —GOETHE

HOPE   131

Hope is like the sun, which, as we journey toward it, casts the shadow of our burden behind us.

HUMILITY 135

And whosoever will be chief among you, let him be your servant.
—MATTHEW 20:27

LIFE 141

Life is measured not by accumulation but by outlay; not by how much saved, but by how much expended; not by distance traveled, but by the road taken.

LOVE 105

Love is friendship set to music.
—POLLOCK

MEMORY 147

When time, which steals our years away,
Shall steal our pleasures too;
The memory of the past will stay
And half our joys renew.

MUSIC 151

What joy to capture song from sound and send it throbbing through the hearts of men.
—EMILY SELINGER

OPPORTUNITY 155

The greatest achievement of the human spirit is to live up to one's opportunities and make the most of one's resources.
—VAUVENARGUES

PATIENCE 159

Patience is bitter, but its fruit sweet.
—JEAN J. ROUSSEAU

PATRIOTISM 163

Gold is good in its place, but living, brave, patriotic men are better than gold.
—ABRAHAM LINCOLN

RELIGION 169

The study of God's word for the purpose of discovering God's will is the secret discipline which has formed the greatest characters.
—J. W. ALEXANDER

STRUGGLE 177

Amid my list of blessings infinite,
Stands this the foremost,
"That my heart has bled."
—EDWARD YOUNG

SUCCESS 183

Men were born to succeed, not to fail.
—HENRY DAVID THOREAU

YOUTH 189

You can never have a greater or less dominion than that over yourself.
—LEONARDO DA VINCI

INDEX 195

To

Miss Theodora Oxenham
with abiding appreciation.

"*Some there are,*
By their good works exalted, lofty minds
And meditative, authors of delight
And happiness, which to the end of time
Will live, and spread, and kindle."

WORDSWORTH

Preface

It is as unseeing to ask what is the use of poetry as it would be to ask what is the use of religion.

The uses of poetry are many. The poet should stand beside the preacher in his work of restoring to mankind faith in God and in the heart of Man, in this terrible age when the only faith seems to belong to the gray and murderous creeds.

Emerson said of Plato: "He, from the sunlike centrality and reach of his vision, had a faith without cloud." This is true of the great poet. It was true in the past, it is true now, in this age when so many, because of the outer circumstances of the world and their lives, suffer from a tragic weakening or total loss of faith. Poetry will help keep us immovably centered.

Seeing the immense design of the world, one image of wonder mirrored by another image of wonder—the pattern of fern and of feather echoed by the frost on the window pane, the six rays of the snowflake mirrored by the rock-crystal's six-rayed eternity, I ask myself "Were those shapes moulded blindness? Who, then, shall teach me doubt?"

The poet speaks to all men of that other life of theirs which they have smothered and forgotten. The poet helps his brother men to be more merciful to each other, remembering the words, "Little children, love one another." To Shakespeare, for instance, even the meanest thing that lives is worthy of the light of the sun.

One of the purposes of poetry is to show the dimensions of man that are, as Sir Arthur Eddington said, "mid-way in scale between the atom and the star,"—and to make all the days of our life, each moment of our life, holy to us.

Poetry is the light of the Great Morning wherein the beings whom we see passing in the street are transformed for us into the epitome of all beauty, or of all joy, or of all sorrow.

This volume is intended to be a treasury of strength, courage, confidence, beauty and inspiration.

It is believed that *Lines to Live By* will give everyone a lift, when a lift is needed and bring forth in all "divine feeling kindred with the skies."

These preferred selections by the great poets, philosophers and writers of all the ages, will help us all better "to live in pulses stirred to generosity, in deeds of darting rectitude, in scorn for miserable aims that end with self, in thoughts sublime that . . . urge man's search to vaster issues."

There are souls, in these noise-tired times, that turn aside into unfrequented lanes, where the deep woods have harbored the fragrances of many a blossoming season. Here the light, filtering through perfect forms, arranges itself in lovely patterns for those who perceive beauty.

It is the purpose of this volume to enrich, ennoble, encourage.

Age

Let me grow lovely, growing old—
So many fine things do;
Laces, and ivory, and gold,
And silks need not be new;
And there is healing in old trees,
Old streets a glamour hold;
Why may not I, as well as these,
Grow lovely, growing old?

—KARLE WILSON BAKER

MY WAGE

I bargained with Life for a penny,
And Life would pay no more,
However I begged at evening
When I counted my scanty store;

For Life is a just employer,
He gives you what you ask,
But once you have set the wages,
Why, you must bear the task.

I worked for a menial's hire,
Only to learn, dismayed,
That any wage I had asked of Life,
Life would have paid.

—JESSIE B. RITTENHOUSE

THE NEVER OLD

They who can smile when others have hate,
Nor bind the heart with frosts of fate,
Their feet will go with laughter bold,
The green roads of the Never Old.

They who can let the spirits shine,
And keep the heart a lifted shrine,
Their feet will glide with fire-of-gold,
The bright road of the Never Old.

They who can put self aside
And in Love's saddle leap and ride,
Their eyes will see the gates unfold,
To glad roads of the Never Old.

I am done with the years that were, I am quits,
I am done with the dead and the old!
They are mines worked out, I delved in their
    pits,
I have saved their grain of gold.

Now I turn to the future for wine and bread,
I have bidden the past adieu,
I laugh, and lift hands to the years ahead:
"Come on, I am ready for you!"

—EDWIN MARKHAM

For age is opportunity no less
Than youth itself, though in another dress,
And as the evening twilight fades away
The sky is filled with stars, invisible by day.

—HENRY WADSWORTH LONGFELLOW

When I was young I was amazed at Plutarch's statement that the elder Cato began at the age of eighty to learn Greek. I am amazed no longer. Old age is ready to undertake tasks that youth shirked because they would take too long.

—W. SOMERSET MAUGHAM

AS I GROW OLD

God keep my heart attuned to laughter
    When youth is done;
When all the days are gray days, coming after
    The warmth, the sun.
God keep me then from bitterness, from
    grieving,
    When life seems cold;
God keep me always loving and believing
    As I grow old.

NOT GROWING OLD

They say that I am growing old,
I've had them tell it times untold
In language plain and bold.
But I'm not growing old.
This frail shell in which I dwell
Is growing old I know full well,

But I am not the shell.
What if my hair is turning gray?
Gray hairs are honorable, they say.
What if my eyesight's growing dim?
I still can see to follow Him
Who sacrificed His life for me
Upon the cross of Calvary.
What should I care if Time's old plow
Has left its furrow on my brow?
Another house not made with hand
Awaits me in the Glory Land.
What though I falter in my walk,
What though my tongue refuse to talk,
I still can tread the narrow way,
I can still watch and praise and pray—
Now growing old!

You can't live wrong and die right.

Hardening of the heart ages people more quickly than hardening of the arteries.

—FRANKLIN FIELD

If I stoop into a dark, tremendous sea of
   cloud,
It is but for a time;
I press God's lamp close to my heart,
Its splendours soon or late will pierce the
   gloom,
I shall emerge somewhere.

THE SERMON OF LIFE

Our birth is text. Youth the introduction. During manhood we lay down a few propositions and prove them. Some passages are dull and some sprightly. Then some Inferences and Application. At seventy we say, "Fifthly and lastly." The Doxology is sung. The Benediction is pronounced. The book is closed. It is getting cold. Frost on the window pane. Audience gone. Shut up the church. Sexton goes home with the key on his shoulder.

—T. DeWitt Talmage

Grow old along with me!
  The best is yet to be,
The last of life for which the first was made;
  Our times are in His hand
  Who saith: "A whole I planned—
Youth shows but half; trust God, see all nor
   be afraid."

—Robert Browning

It is magnificent to grow old, if one keeps
  young.

—Harry Emerson Fosdick

There is nothing more beautiful in this world than a healthy wise old man.

—Lin Yutang

Brief life is here our portion;
Brief sorrow, short-lived care:
The life that knows no ending,
The tearless life is there.
The morning shall awaken,
The shadows shall decay,
And each true-hearted servant
Shall shine as doth the day.
There God, our King and Portion,
In fullness of his grace,
Shall we behold for ever,
And worship face to face.

The flower unblown; a book unread;
A tree with fruit unharvested;
A path untrod; a house whose rooms
Lack yet the heart's divine perfumes;
A landscape whose wide border lies
In silent shade beneath the skies;
A wondrous fountain yet unsealed;
A casket with its gifts concealed—
This is the year that for you waits
Beyond tomorrow's mystic gates.

—Horatio Nelson Powers

As I grow old, the winds of life
Die down, the hate, the hurt, the strife.
The waters calm, the waves are still.
I want no triumph, wish no ill
To any man. Now from my heart
The ancient angers all depart.
New friends I know, new songs are sung
New joys are mine—Yes, I grow young
As I grow old!

—Douglas Malloch

I shall not mind
* The whiteness of my hair,*
Or that slow steps falter
* On the stair,*
Or that young friends hurry
* As they pass,*
Or what strange image
* Greets me in the glass—*
If I can feel,
* As roots feel in the sod,*
That I am growing old to bloom
* Before the face of God.*

Here at Stoke-by-Nayland once lived a wealthy miser who pulled down crows' nests for fuel and got the usual reward of suchlike thrift in having half a million of money half a minute before he died, and nothing half a minute later.

To be seventy years young is sometimes far more cheerful and hopeful than to be forty years old.

—Oliver Wendell Holmes

What matter if I stand alone?
* I wait with joy the coming years;*
My heart shall reap where it has sown,
* And garner up its fruit of tears.*

—John Burroughs

YOUTH

Youth is not a time of life . . . it is a state of mind. It is not a matter of ripe cheeks, red lips and supple knees . . . it is a temper of the will, a quality of the imagination, a vigor of the emotions . . . it is a freshness of the deep springs of life.

Youth means a temperamental predominance of courage over timidity, of the appetite for adventure over love of ease. This often exists in a man of fifty more than a boy of twenty.

Nobody grows old merely living a number of years; people grow old only by deserting their ideals. Years wrinkle the skin, but to give up enthusiasm wrinkles the soul. Worry, doubt, self-distrust, fear and despair . . . these are the long, long years that bow the head and turn the growing spirit back to dust.

Whether seventy or sixteen, there is in every being's heart the love of wonder, the sweet amazement of the stars and star-like things and thoughts, the undaunted challenge of events, the unfailing child-like appetite for what next, and the joy and game of life.

You are as young as your faith, as old as your doubt; as young as your self-confidence, as old as your fear; as young as your hope, as old as your despair.

In the central place of your heart there is a wireless station; so long as it receives messages of beauty, hope, cheer, courage, grandeur and power from the earth, from men and from the Infinite, so long are you young.

When the wires are all down and all the central place of your heart is covered with the snows of pessimism and the ice of cynicism, then are you grown old indeed and may God have mercy on your soul.

Beautiful young people are accidents of nature. But beautiful old people are works of art.

—Marjorie Barstow Greenbie

A PETITION TO TIME

Touch us gently, Time!
  Let us glide adown thy stream
Gently, as we sometimes glide
  Through a quiet dream.
Humble voyagers are we,
Husband, wife, and children three.
(One is lost—an angel, fled
To the azure overhead!)

Touch us gently, Time!
  We've not proud nor soaring wings,
Our ambition, our content,
  Lies in simple things.
Humble voyagers are we,
O'er Life's dim, unsounded sea,
Seeking only some calm clime;
Touch us gently, gentle Time!

—BRYAN WALLER PROCTER

The greatest comfort of my old age, and that which gives me the highest satisfaction, is the pleasing remembrance of the many benefits and friendly offices I have done to others.

—CATO

For, as I like a young man in whom there is something of the old, so I like an old man in whom there is something of the young; and he who follows this maxim, in body will possibly be an old man, but he will never be an old man in mind.

—CICERO

GROWING OLDER

A little more tired at the close of day,
A little less anxious to have our way,
A little less ready to scold and blame,
A little more care for a brother's name;
And so we are nearing the journey's end,
Where time and eternity meet and blend.

A little less care for bonds or gold,
A little more zeal for the days of old;

A broader view and a saner mind,
And a little more love for all mankind;
And so we are faring down the way
That leads to the gates of a better day.

A little more love for the friends of youth,
A little more zeal for established truth,
A little more charity in our views,
A little less thirst for the daily news;
And so we are folding our tents away
And passing in silence at close of day.

A little more leisure to sit and dream,
A little more real the things unseen,
A little nearer to those ahead,
With visions of those long loved and dead;
And so we are going where all must go—
To the place the living may never know.

A little more laughter, a few more tears,
And we shall have told our increasing years.
The book is closed and the prayers are said,
And we are part of the countless dead;
Thrice happy, then, if some soul can say,
"I live because of their help on the way."

—R. G. WELLS

Walter Savage Landor wrote his "Imaginary Conversations," picturing the love of Pericles and Aspasia, at eighty-five. Izaak Walton went a-fishing and wrote fiction about his luck at ninety. Fontenelle was as light-hearted at ninety-eight as at forty; Cornaro enjoyed better health at ninety-five than at thirty, and Sir Isaac Newton at eighty-five was still smoking the pipe that cost him his lady-love. Simon Cameron went to the Bermudas at ninety to investigate the resources of the Islands.

Whatever crazy sorrow saith,
No life that breathes with human breath
Has ever truly long'd for death.
'Tis life, whereof our nerves are scant,
O, life, not death, for which we pant;
More life, and fuller, that I want.

—ALFRED LORD TENNYSON

And more than once in days
Of doubt and cloud and storm, when
    drowning hope
Sank all but out of sight, I heard His voice,
"Be not cast down. I lead thee by the hand,
Fear not." And I shall hear His voice again—
I know that He has led me all my life;
I am not yet too old to work His will. . . .

Lo, as some venturer from his stars receiving
    Promise and presage of the great emprise,
Ever thereafter wears the seal of his believing
    Deep in the dark of solitary eyes;
Ever thereafter in palace or in prison
    Fashions his fancies of the realm to be. . . .

—ALFRED LORD TENNYSON

GROWING OLD

The days grow shorter, the nights grow
    longer;
    The headstones thicken along the way;
And life grows sadder, but love grows
    stronger
    For those who walk with us day by day.
The tear comes quicker, the laugh comes
    slower;
    The courage is lesser to do and dare;
And the tide of joy in the heart falls lower,
    And seldom covers the reefs of care.
But all true things in the world seem truer,
    And the better things of earth seem best,
And friends are dearer, as friends are fewer,
    And love is all as our sun dips west.
Then let us clasp hands as we walk together,
    And let us speak softly in low, sweet tone,
For no man knows on the morrow whether
    We two pass on—or but one alone.

—ELLA WHEELER WILCOX

Some day the silver cord will break,
    And I no more as now shall sing;
But oh, the joy when I shall wake
    Within the palace of the King!
And I shall see Him face to face . . .

THOSE HILLS OF LONG AGO

Remember that time, long, long ago
When your heart was full of sorrow;
When every day weighed down your grief
And made you fear tomorrow.

    Was it someone dear to you
    That grim death took away;
    Did your best friend prove untrue—
    Oh, weren't you sad that day.

Your love? A heartache there—
That romance? You remember?
As you hear the strains of an old sweet song,
It kindles every ember.

    Every memory is revived
    Each heartache reappears;
    But only for a moment
    Your eyes are dim with tears.

For all these disappointments
Have mellowed with age.
You scan your book of memories
And turn another page.

    Yes, every hill you've climbed in life
    Looked impossibly high—
    When you were at the bottom
    And looked up toward the sky.

But once life's hills surmounted
They level backward—so
You sigh—and then in time forget
Those Hills of Long Ago.

—DON MCNEILL

FROM APPARENT FAILURE

It's wiser being good than bad;
    It's safer being meek than fierce:
It's fitter being sane than mad.
    My own hope is, a sun will pierce
The thickest cloud earth ever stretched;
    That, after Last, returns the First,
Though a wide compass round be fetched;
    That what began best, can't end worst,
Nor what God blessed once, prove accurst.

—ROBERT BROWNING

Beauty

Never lose an opportunity of seeing anything that is beautiful, for beauty is
God's handwriting—a wayside sacrament.
Welcome it in every fair face, in every fair
sky, in every flower, and thank God for it as
a cup of blessing.

—RALPH WALDO EMERSON

A LITTLE TE DEUM

For all things beautiful, and good, and true;
For things that seemed not good, yet turned
*   to good;*
For all the sweet compulsions of Thy will
That chased, and tried, and wrought us to
*   Thy shape;*
For things unnumbered that we take of right,
For value first when first they are withheld;
For light and air; sweet sense of sound and
*   smell;*
For ears to hear the heavenly harmonies;
For eyes to see the unseen in the seen;
For vision of The Worker in the work;
For hearts to apprehend Thee everywhere;
*   We thank Thee, Lord!*

—JOHN OXENHAM

The most natural beauty in the world is honesty and moral truth.—For all beauty is truth.—True features make the beauty of the face; true proportions, the beauty of architecture; true measures, the beauty of harmony and music.

—SHAFTESBURY

There are two worlds: the world that we can measure with line and rule, and the world that we feel with our hearts and imagination.

—LEIGH HUNT

A THING OF BEAUTY

A thing of beauty is a joy for ever:
Its loveliness increases; it will never
Pass into nothingness; but still will keep
A bower quiet for us, and a sleep
Full of sweet dreams, and health, and quiet
*   breathing.*
Therefore, on every morrow, are we
*   wreathing*
A flowery band to bind us to the earth,
Spite of despondence, of the inhuman dearth
Of noble natures, of the gloomy days,
Of all the unhealthy and o'er-darkened ways
Made for our searching: yes, in spite of all,
Some shape of beauty moves away the pall
From our dark spirits. Such the sun, the
*   moon,*
Trees old and young, sprouting a shady boon
For simple sheep; and such are daffodils
With the green world they live in; and clear
*   rills*
That for themselves a cooling covert make
'Gainst the hot season; the mid-forest brake,
Rich with a sprinkling of fair musk-rose
*   blooms:*
And such too is the grandeur of the dooms
We have imagined for the mighty dead;
All lovely tales that we have heard or read:
An endless fountain of immortal drink,
Pouring unto us from the heaven's brink.
Nor do we merely feel these essences
For one short hour; no, even as the trees
That whisper round a temple become soon
Dear as the temple's self, so does the moon,
The passion poesy, glories infinite,
Haunt us till they become a cheering light
Unto our souls, and bound to us so fast,
That, whether there be shine, or gloom
*   o'ercast,*
They always must be with us, or we die.

—JOHN KEATS

Every year of my life I grow more convinced that it is wisest and best to fix our attention on the beautiful and the good, and dwell as little as possible on the evil and the false.

—CECIL

WHO WALKS WITH BEAUTY

Who walks with Beauty has no need of fear;
The sun and moon and stars keep pace with
him;
Invisible hands restore the ruined year,
And time itself grows beautifully dim.
One hill will keep the footprints of the moon
That came and went a hushed and secret
hour;
One star at dusk will yield the lasting boon;
Remembered beauty's white immortal flower.

Who takes of Beauty wine and daily bread
Will know no lack when bitter years are lean;
The brimming cup is by, the feast is spread;
The sun and moon and stars his eyes have
seen
Are for his hunger and the thirst he slakes:
The wine of Beauty and the bread he breaks.

—DAVID MORTON

The gates are open on the road
That leads to beauty and to God.

—CHARLES SORLEY

THE BEAUTY OF JESUS IN ME

My life touched yours for a very brief space,
And what, oh, what did you see?
A hurried, a worried and anxious face,
Or the beauty of Jesus in me?

Was I steeped so deep in the ways of the
world
That you couldn't detect one thing
That would set me apart and show that my
heart
Belonged to the Heavenly King?

Did I carry no banner for Jesus my Lord,
Not one thing at all that could show
Whose side I am on in this glorious fight?
I am His! But you wouldn't know.

Forgive me! And if we should e'er meet again
Upon earth, oh, I pray you will see
No mark of this world, but His banner
unfurled,
And the beauty of Jesus in me!

—ALICE HANSCHE MORTENSON

RESURRECTION

Beauty they thought was dead, was dead that
day,
They sealed the Master in his new-wrought
tomb,
And wondered that along the dusty way,
White lilies of delight were all in bloom.

Dear Christ, so long ago, so long ago,
And men have dreamed again that Gladness
dies,
Chanted her requiem and laid her low—
And turned to meet the smiling of her
eyes!
Truth answers not; it does not take offense:
But with mighty silence bides its time.
As some great cliff that braves the elements,
And lifts through all the storms its head
sublime,
So truth, unmoved, it puny foes defies,
And never dies.

FLOWERS

How the universal heart of man blesses flowers! They are wreathed round the cradle, the marriage-altar and the tomb. The Persian in the Far East delights in their perfume, and writes his love in nosegays; while the Indian child of the Far West claps his hands with glee as he gathers the abundant blossoms—the illuminated scriptures of the prairies. The Cupid of the ancient Hindoos tipped his arrows with flowers, and orange-flowers are a bridal crown with us, a nation of yesterday.

Flowers garlanded the Grecian altar, and hung in votive wreath before the Christian shrine. All these are appropriate uses. Flowers should deck the brow of the youthful bride, for they are in themselves a lovely type of marriage. They should twine round the tomb, for their perpetually renewed beauty is a symbol of the resurrection. They should festoon the altar, for their fragrance and their beauty ascend in perpetual worship before the most High.

—L. M. CHILD

ROSES

Roses, that briefly live,
Joy is your dower—
Blest be the Fates that give
One perfect hour:—

And, though, too soon you die,
In your dust glows
Something the passer-by
Knows was a Rose.

—Louise Chandler Moulton

BEAUTIFUL THOUGHTS

The thought that is beautiful is the thought to cherish. The word that is beautiful is worthy to endure. The act that is beautiful is eternally and always true and right. Only beware that your appreciation of beauty is just and true; and to that end, I urge you to live intimately with beauty of the highest type, until it has become a part of you, until you have within you that fineness, that order, the calm, which puts you in tune with the finest things of the universe, and which links you with that spirit that is the enduring life of the world.

—Bertha Bailey

THE STARRY HEAVENS

Ye quenchless stars! so eloquently bright,
Untroubled sentries of the shadowy night,
While half the world is lapped in downy
*   dreams,*
And round the lattice creep your midnight
*   beams,*
How sweet to gaze upon your placid eyes,
In lambent beauty looking from the skies!
And when, oblivious of the world, we stray
At dead of night along some noiseless way,
How the heart mingles with the moonlit hour,
As if the starry heavens suffused a power!
Full in her dreamy light, the moon presides,
Shrined in a halo, mellowing as she rides;
And far around, the forest and the stream
Bathe in the beauty of her emerald beam.

—Robert Montgomery

BEAUTY

Beauty is an all-prevading presence. It unfolds to the numberless flowers of the Spring; it waves in the branches of the trees and in the green blades of grass; it haunts the depths of the earth and the sea, and gleams out in the hues of the shell and the precious stone. And not only these minute objects, but the ocean, the mountains, the clouds, the heavens, the stars, the rising and the setting sun all overflow with beauty. The universe is its tèmple; and those men who are alive to it can not lift their eyes without feeling themselves encompassed with it on every side. Now, this beauty is so precious, the enjoyment it gives so refined and pure, so congenial without tenderest and noblest feelings, and so akin to worship, that it is painful to think of the multitude of men as living in the midst of it, and living almost as blind to it as if, instead of this fair earth and glorious sky, they were tenants of a dungeon. An infinite joy is lost to the world by the want of culture of this spiritual endowment. The greatest truths are wronged if not linked with beauty, and they win their way most surely and deeply into the soul when arrayed in this their natural and fit attire.

—William Ellery Channing

TRUTH NEVER DIES

Truth never dies. The ages come and go;
*   The mountains wear away; the seas retire;*
Destruction lays earth's mighty cities low;
*   And empires, states, and dynasties expire;*
But caught and handed onward by the wise,
*   Truth never dies.*

Though unreceived and scoffed at through
*   the years;*
*   Though made the butt of ridicule and jest;*
Though held aloft for mockery and jeers,
*   Denied by those of transient power*
*   possessed,*
Insulted by the insolence of lies,
*   Truth never dies.*

Did it ever strike you that goodness is not merely a beautiful thing, but by far the most beautiful thing in the whole world? So that nothing is to be compared for value with goodness; that riches, honor, power, pleasure, learning, the whole world and all in it, are not worth having in comparison with being good; and the utterly best thing for a man is to be good, even though he were never to be rewarded for it.

—CHARLES KINGSLEY

I DIED FOR BEAUTY

I died for beauty, but was scarce
Adjusted in the tomb,
When one who died for truth was lain
In an adjoining room.

He questioned softly why I failed?
"For beauty," I replied.
"And I for truth,—the two are one;
We brethren are," he said.

And so, as kinsmen met a night,
We talked between the rooms,
Until the moss had reached our lips,
And covered up our names.

—EMILY DICKINSON

GOD IS BEAUTIFUL

Oh, Thou art beautiful! and Thou dost
    bestow
  Thy beauty on this stillness: still as sheep
  The hills lie under Thee; the waters deep
Murmur for joy of Thee; the voids below
Mirror Thy strange fair vapors as they flow;
  And now, afar upon the ashen height,
  Thou sendest down a radiant look of light,
So that the still peaks glisten, and a glow
Rose-color'd tints the little snowy cloud
  That poises on the highest peak of all.
Oh, Thou art beautiful!—the hills are bowed
  Beneath Thee; on Thy name the soft winds
    call,—
The monstrous ocean trumpets it aloud,
  The rains and snows intone it as they fall.

—ROBERT BUCHANAN

THANK GOD FOR LITTLE THINGS

Thank you, God, for little things
  that often come our way—
The things we take for granted
  but don't mention when we pray—
The unexpected courtesy,
  the thoughtful, kindly deed—
A hand reached out to help us
  in the time of sudden need—
Oh make us more aware, dear God,
  of little daily graces
That come to us with "sweet surprise"
  from never-dreamed-of places.

—HELEN STEINER RICE

Give us grace and strength to persevere. Give us courage and gaiety and the quiet mind. Spare to us our friends and soften to us our enemies. Give us the strength to encounter that which is to come, that we may be brave in peril, constant in tribulation, temperate in wrath and in all changes of fortune, and down to the gates of death loyal and loving to one another.

—ROBERT LOUIS STEVENSON

There is no more potent antidote to low sensuality than the adoration of beauty. —All the higher arts of design are essentially chaste.—They purify the thoughts, as tragedy, according to Aristotle, purifies the passions.

—SCHLEGEL

We are living in a world of beauty but how few of us open our eyes to see it! What a different place this would be if our senses were trained to see and hear! We are the heirs of wonderful treasures from the past: treasures of literature and of the arts. They are ours for the asking—all our own to have and to enjoy, if only we desire them enough.

—LORADO TAFT

THE WHIRLPOOL

He was caught in the whirl of the pool of
　dismay,
By a thoughtless remark he had said;
He had injured a friend in a nonchalant way,
And the love they had cherished lay dead.

To his mirror he went, in its glass to confide,
And his face was both haggard and pale,
And he asked of the glass, "Should I swallow
　the pride,
That is pinning me down like a nail?

Should I go to my friend with remorse on
　my face,
A remorse that I honestly feel?
Should I beg him this whirlpool of shame to
　erase,
In a soul-stirring voice of appeal?"

"As your heart so dictates," said a voice from
　the glass,
"I advise you to follow its path,
And remember 'twill pay you to keep off
　the grass,
That is bordered with ill words and wrath."

So he went to his friend, and he asked most
　sincere,
To be taken again to his heart
And the whirlpool of friendship once more
　does endear
These friends who had drifted apart.

If there's someone you know, whom you
　treated that way,
And your heart is both heavy and blue,
Seek and find him again without further
　delay,
Don't wait until he comes to you.

You'll find that the whirlpool of Love will
　replace,
Every misunderstanding and strife,
It will give you the courage to meet face
　to face,
The changeable Whirlpool of Life.

W here words fail, music speaks.

　　　　　　　　—HANS CHRISTIAN ANDERSEN

Let me go where'er I will
I hear a sky-born music still:
It sounds from all things old,
It sounds from all things young,
From all that's fair, from all that's foul,
Peals out a cheerful song.

It is not only in the rose,
It is not only in the bird,
Not only where the rainbow glows,
Nor in the song of woman heard,
But in the darkest, meanest things
There alway, alway something sings.

'Tis not in the high stars alone,
Nor in the cup of budding flowers,
Nor in the red-breast's mellow tone,
Nor in the bow that smiles in showers,
But in the mud and scum of things
There alway, alway something sings.

　　　　　　　　—RALPH WALDO EMERSON

WISDOM IN A PHRASE

W hen President Eliot, of Harvard, was asked how he accounted for his good health and vigorous mind at his advanced age (he was then 88, and lived 8 years longer) he included in his reply this significant phrase:

"A calm temperament expectant of good."

Here is a phrase of only six words, but one of concentrated wisdom. Others have expressed the same idea differently but none so felicitously as did Harvard's famous president. This phrase is an inclusive definition of optimism, for the optimist calmly looks on the bright side of things, and the bright side is expected to bring forth good.

To be sure, a calm temperament is denied to many, and it is difficult to acquire, but anyone, if he choose, can live his daily life "expectant of good."

Dr. Eliot clothed an old idea in new words, and the more they are pondered the more effective they appear, the more worth while to be stored in one's mind. Old age cannot be prevented, but its unpleasant mental manifestations may be retarded to a degree, without doubt, by "a calm temperament expectant of good."

Books

O for a Booke and a Shadie Nooke
Eyther in-a-doore or out;
With the greene leaves whispering overhede,
Or the Streete cries all aboute,
Where I maie reade all at my ease,
Bothe of the Newe and Olde,
For a jollie goode Booke whereon to looke,
Is better to me than Golde.

—JOHN WILSON

There is no Frigate like a Book
To take us Lands away
Nor any Courses like a Page
Of prancing Poetry—
This Travel may the poorest take
Without offence of Toil—
How frugal is the Chariot
That bears the Human soul.

—EMILY DICKINSON

GOOD COMPANY

Consider what you have in the smallest chosen library.

A company of the wisest and wittiest men that could be picked out of all civilized countries in a thousand years have set in the best order the results of their learning and wisdom.

The men themselves were hid and inaccessible, solitary, impatient of interruption, fenced by etiquette; but the thought which they did not uncover to their bosom friend is here written out in transparent words to us, the strangers of another age.

—RALPH WALDO EMERSON

When you sell a man a book
You don't sell him just twelve ounces
Of paper and ink and glue—
You sell him a whole new life.

—CHRISTOPHER MORLEY

When we are collecting books, we are collecting happiness.

—VINCENT STARRETT

IMMORTALITY IN BOOKS

Since honour from the honourer proceeds,
How well do they deserve, that memorize
And leave in books for all posterities
The names of worthies and their virtuous
  deeds;
When all their glory else, like water-weeds
Without their element, presently dies,
And all their greatness quite forgotten lies,
And when and how they flourished no man
  heeds!
How poor remembrances are statues, tombs
And other monuments that men erect
To princes, which remain in closèd rooms,
Where but a few behold them, in respect
Of books, that to the universal eye
Show how they lived; the other where they
  lie!

—J. FLORIO

Every generation enjoys the use of a vast hoard bequeathed to it by antiquity, and transmits that hoard, augmented by fresh acquisitions to future ages.

—THOMAS MACAULAY

Books are strange things. Although
  untongued and dumb,
Yet with their eloquence they sway the
  world;
And, powerless and impassive as they seem,
Move o'er the impressive minds and hearts of
  men
Like fire across a prairie. Mind sparks,
  They star the else dark firmament.

Ignorance is the night of the mind, but a night without moon or star.

—CONFUCIUS

THE LAND OF MAGIC

There's a wonderful land where I go by
    myself
  Without stirring out of my chair;
I just take a book from the library shelf,
  Turn its pages, and presto! I'm there.
In that wonderful country of Yesterday,
  Where "to-morrow" is always the "now,"
Where the good ship Adventure is
    spreading her sails,
  While the sea-foam breaks white at her
    prow.

Where the desert sands burn in the African
    sun,
  Where the North shivers under the snow;
Over the mountains and valleys where
    strange rivers run,
  With hardy explorers I go.
I share, too, in the magic of fairies and
    gnomes;
  I have followed the ways of the sea;
I have studied the fish in their watery homes,
  And the bird and the ant and the bee.

I have followed the trail of the first pioneers
  Over prairie and mountain range;
I have lived with their dangers and shared
    in their fears
  In a country so new and so strange.
And then—just like magic—I'm high in the
    air
  In a glittering aeroplane!
Swooping in bird-flight now here and now
    there—
  Up, up through clouds and the rain!

O ship of adventure! your sails are spread
    wide
  As they fill with the winds of the West;
Restless and swaying, you wait for the tide
  To bear you away on your quest.
With you I will sail for a year and a day,
  To the world's most unreachable nooks,
For there's nothing to hinder the traveler's
    way
  Through the wonderful Country of Books!

                —EDITH D. OSBORNE

We should accustom the mind to keep the best company by introducing it only to the best books.

                —SYDNEY SMITH

BOOKS

If you'd move to a bygone measure,
  Or shape your heart to an ancient mould,
Maroons and schooners and buried treasure
  Wrought on a page of gold,—

Then take the book in the dingy binding,
  Still the magic comes, bearded, great,
And swaggering files of sea-thieves winding
  Back, with their ruffling cut-throat gait,
Reclaim an hour when we first went finding
  Pieces of Eight—of Eight.

           —PATRICK REGINALD CHALMERS

Except a living man there is nothing more wonderful than a book! a message to us from the dead—from human souls we never saw, who lived, perhaps, thousands of miles away. And yet these, in those little sheets of paper, speak to us, arouse us, terrify us, teach us, comfort us, open their hearts to us as brothers.

            —CHARLES KINGSLEY

Books are keys to wisdom's treasure;
Books are gates to lands of pleasure;
Books are paths that upward lead;
Books are friends, Come, let us read.

            —EMILIE POULSSON

To do things worthy the writing and to write worthy the doing thereof and thereby to make the much loved earth more lovely.

            —PHILIP SIDNEY

There is nothing so costly as ignorance.

            —HORACE MANN

We get no good
By being ungenerous, even to a book,
And calculating profits,—so much help
By so much reading. It is rather when
We gloriously forget ourselves and plunge
Soul-forward, headlong, into a book's
*   profound,*
Impassioned for its beauty and salt of truth—
'Tis then we get the right good from a book.

—ELIZABETH BARRETT BROWNING

BOOKS

The scholar only knows how dear these silent yet eloquent companions of pure thoughts and innocent hours become in the season of adversity. When all that is worldly turns to dross around us, these only retain their steady value. When friends grow cold, and the converse of intimates languishes into vapid civility and commonplace these only continue the unaltered countenance of happier days, and cheer us with that true friendship which never deceived hope nor deserted sorrow.

—WASHINGTON IRVING

I believe the poets; it is they
Who utter wisdom from the central deep,
And, listening to the inner flow of things,
Speak to the age out of eternity.

—JAMES RUSSELL LOWELL

Books won't stay banned. They won't burn. Ideas won't go to jail.

—ALFRED WHITNEY GRISWOLD

When others fail him, the wise man looks To the sure companionship of books.

—ANDREW LANG

A good book is the best of friends, the same today and forever.

—MARTIN FARQUHAR TUPPER

To be at home in all lands and all ages; to count nature a familiar acquaintance, and art an intimate friend; to gain a standard for the appreciation of other men's work and the criticism of one's own; to carry the keys to the world's library in one's pocket and feel its resources behind one in whatever task he undertakes; to make hosts of friends among the men of one's own age, who are the leaders in all walks of life; to lose one's self in generous enthusiasms, and co-operate with others for common ends; to learn manners from students who are gentlemen and to form character under professors who are Christian—These are the returns of the college for the best four years of one's life.

—WILLIAM DE WITT HYDE

THE LIBRARY A GLORIOUS COURT

That place, that does contain
My books, the best companions, is to me
A glorious court, where hourly I converse
With the old sages and philosophers.
And sometimes, for variety, I confer
With kings and emperors, and weigh their
*   counsels;*
Calling their victories, if unjustly got,
Unto a strict account: and in my fancy,
Deface their ill-planned statues. Can I then
Part with such constant pleasures, to embrace
Uncertain vanities? No: be it your care
To augment your heap of wealth; it shall
*   be mine*
To increase in knowledge. Lights there for
*   my study!*

—J. FLETCHER

We see then how far the monuments of wit and learning are more durable than the monuments of power, or of the hands. For have not the verses of Homer continued twenty-five hundred years, or more, without the loss of a syllable or letter; during which time infinite palaces, temples, castles, cities have been decayed and demolished?

—FRANCIS BACON

Some there are,
By their good works exalted, lofty minds
And meditative, authors of delight
And happiness, which to the end of time
Will live, and spread, and kindle.

—WILLIAM WORDSWORTH

Books are the legacies that a great genius leaves to mankind, which are delivered down from generation to generation, as presents to the posterity of those who are yet unborn.

—JOSEPH ADDISON

Go, little book, and wish to all
Flowers in the garden, meat in the hall—
A bit of wine, a spice of wit
A house with lawn enclosing it,
A living river by the door—
A nightingale in the sycamore.

—ROBERT LOUIS STEVENSON

We should be as careful of the books we read, as of the company we keep. The dead very often have more power than the living.

—TYRON EDWARDS

My book and heart
Shall never part.

—NEW ENGLAND PRIMER

'Tis the mind that makes the body rich.

—SHAKESPEARE

The school will teach children how to read, but the environment of the home must teach them what to read. The school can teach them how to think, but the home must teach them what to believe.

—CHARLES A. WELLS

Books are the ever-burning lamps of accumulated wisdom.

—G. W. CURTIS

WHO HATH A BOOK

Who hath a book
Has friends at hand,
And gold and gear
At his command.

And rich estates,
If he but look,
Are held by him
Who hath a book.

Who hath a book
Has but to read
And he may be
A king indeed.

His Kingdom is
His inglenook;
All this is his
Who hath a book.

—WILBUR D. NESBIT

A book is a garden, an orchard, a storehouse, a party, a company by the way, a counsellor, a multitude of counsellors.

—HENRY WARD BEECHER

We should gloat over a book, be rapt clean out of ourselves, and rise from the perusal, our mind filled with the busiest, kaleidoscopic dance of images, incapable of sleep or of continuous thought. The words, if the book be eloquent, should run thenceforward in our ears like the noise of breakers, and the story, if it be a story, repeat itself in a thousand colored pictures to the eye.

—ROBERT LOUIS STEVENSON

No man can be called friendless when he has God and the companionship of good books.

—ELIZABETH BARRETT BROWNING

If you are poor I will tell you how you can become rich—richer than any millionaire: Learn to love good books. There are treasures in books that all the money of the world cannot buy, but that the poorest laborer can have for nothing.

My heart goes out to all the great, the self-denying and the good—to the builders of homes, to the inventors, to the artists who have filled the world with beauty, to the composers of music, to the soldiers of the right, to the makers of mirth, to honest men, and to all the loving mothers of the race.

—Robert G. Ingersoll

USE OF BOOKS

He who learns and makes no use of his learning is a beast of burden with a load of books. Does the ass comprehend whether he carries on his back a library or a bundle of faggots?

—Saadia

It is a duty incumbent upon upright and credible men of all ranks, who have performed anything noble or praiseworthy, to truthfully record, in their own writing, the principal events of their lives.

—Benvenuto Cellini

To leave a monument behind, *aere perennius,* an imperishable work which might stir the thoughts, the feelings, the dreams of men, generation after generation,—this is the only glory which I could wish for, if I were not weaned even from this wish also. A book would be my ambition, if ambition were not vanity and vanity of vanities.

—Henri-Frédéric Amiel

As a writer, I have only one desire—to fill you with fire, to pour into you the distilled essence of the sun itself. I want every thought, every word, every act of mine to make you feel that you are receiving into your body, into your mind, into your soul, the sacred spirit that changes clay into men and men into gods.

—Thomas Dreier

Poetry is the grouping of words, phrases, and ideas that have always loved each other but have never gotten into that combination before.

I am the man who, when Love lectures in the heart, takes notes, and then retells the lessons to the rest of men.

—Dante Alighieri

Challenge

You say the little efforts that I make
Will do no good: they never will prevail
To tip the hovering scale
Where justice hangs in balance.
   I don't think
I ever thought they would.
But I am prejudiced beyond debate
In favor of my right to choose which side
Shall feel the stubborn ounces of my weight.

—Bonaro W. Overstreet

You cannot run away from a weakness; you must sometime fight it out or perish. And if that be so, why not now, and where you stand?

—ROBERT LOUIS STEVENSON

GREAT HEART

Where are you going, Great-Heart?
  To fight a fight with all my might,
  For Truth and Justice, God and Right,
  To grace all Life with His fair light.
    Then God go with you, Great-Heart!

Where are you going, Great-Heart?
  To lift To-day above the Past;
  To make To-morrow sure and fast;
  To nail God's colors to the mast.
    Then God go with you, Great-Heart!

Where are you going, Great-Heart?
  To set all burdened peoples free;
  To win for all God's liberty;
  To stablish His Sweet Sovereignty.
    God goeth with you, Great-Heart!

—JOHN OXENHAM

Whatever you have received more than others in health, in talents, in ability, in success, in a pleasant childhood, in harmonious conditions of home life, all this you must not take to yourself as a matter of course. You must pay a price for it. You must render an unusually great sacrifice of your life for other life.

—ALBERT SCHWEITZER

The future is a great land. . . . It is wider than the vision and has no end.

THINK

If you think you are beaten, you are;
  If you think you dare not, you don't;
If you'd like to win, but think you can't,
  It's almost a cinch you won't.

If you think you'll lose, you're lost,
  For out in the world we find
Success begins with a fellow's WILL—
  It's all in the state of mind.

If you think you're outclassed, you are;
  You've got to think high to rise.
You've just got-to-be sure of yourself
  Before you can win the prize.

Life's battles don't always go
  To the stronger or faster man,
But sooner or later the man who wins
  Is the one who THINKS HE CAN.

LOVE

Love is the sunshine of the soul. Without it we get hard and sour and we never grow into what we could be. Love sweetens the bitterness of experience and softens the core of selfishness that is inherent in human nature.

THE WINDS OF FATE

One ship drives east and another drives west
  With the selfsame winds that blow.
    'Tis the set of the sails
    And not the gales
  Which tells us the way to go.

Like the winds of the sea are the ways of fate,
  As we voyage alone through life:
    'Tis the set of a soul
    That decides its goal,
  And not the calm or the strife.

—ELLA WHEELER WILCOX

THE QUITTER

It ain't the failures he may meet
That keeps a man from winnin',
It's the discouragement complete
That blocks a new beginnin';
You want to quit your habits bad,
And, when the shadows flittin'
Make life seem worthless an' sad,
You want to quit your quittin'!

You want to quit a-layin' down
An' sayin' hope is over,
Because the fields are bare an' brown
Where once we lived in clover.
When jolted from the water cart
It's painful to be hittin'
The earth; but make another start.
Cheer up, an' quit your quittin'!

Although the game seems rather stiff
Don't be a doleful doubter;
There's always one more innin' if
You're not a down-and-outer.
But fortune's pretty sure to flee
From folks content with sittin'
Around an' sayin' life's N.G.
You've got to quit your quittin'.

Spend your time in nothing which you know must be repented of; in nothing on which you might not pray the blessing of God; in nothing which you could not review with a quiet conscience on your dying bed; in nothing which you might not safely and properly be found doing if death should surprise you in the act.

—RICHARD BAXTER

CONVICTIONS

I'm not for free trade, and I'm for protection;
I approve of them both, and to both have
objection.
In strolling through life I increasingly find
It's a terrible nuisance to make up one's mind;
So, in spite of all comment, reproaches, pre-
dictions,
I firmly adhere to unsettled convictions.

NOTHING WORTHWHILE IS FREE

There's no free gate to anything worth-while—not to skill nor health, nor to success nor friendship, nor even to the lasting love and respect of those who are nearest and dearest to us.

These are the items that make up the best income that any human being can have, and the sum of that income will be measured by the sum of what we are willing to pay to get it.

Today is your day and mine, the only day we have, the day in which we play our part. What our part may signify in the great whole we may not understand; but we are here to play it, and now is our time. This we know: it is a part of action, not of whining. It is a part of love, not cynicism. It is for us to express love in terms of human helpfulness.

—DAVID STARR JORDAN

Life is a leaf of paper white
Whereon each one of us may write
His word or two, and then comes night.

Greatly begin! though thou have time
But for a line, be that sublime,—
Not failure, but low aim, is crime.

—JAMES RUSSELL LOWELL

TEN GOOD THINGS

There are ten good things for which no
man has ever been sorry:
For doing good to all;
For speaking evil of no one;
For hearing before judging;
For thinking before speaking;
For holding an angry tongue;
For being kind to the distressed;
For asking pardon for all wrongs;
For being patient toward everybody;
For stopping the ear to the tale bearer;
For dis-believing the most of the evil
reports.

There is no moment like the present. The man who will not execute his resolutions when they are fresh upon him can have no hope from them afterwards: they will be dissipated, lost, and perish in the hurry and scurry of the world, or sunk in the slough of indolence.

—MARIA EDGEWORTH

THE DOOMED MAN

There is a time, we know not when,
A point we know not where,
That marks the destiny of men,
For glory or despair.

There is a line, by us unseen,
That crosses every path;
The hidden boundary between
God's patience and His wrath.

—JOSEPH ADDISON ALEXANDER

We are not sent into this world to do anything into which we can not put our hearts ❧ We have certain work to do for our bread and that is to be done strenuously, other work to do for our delight and that is to be done heartily; neither is to be done by halves or shifts, but with a will; and what is not worth this effort is not to be done at all.

—JOHN RUSKIN

NO STAR IS EVER LOST

Have we not all, amid life's petty strife,
Some pure ideal of a noble life
That once seemed possible? Did we not hear
The flutter of its wings and feel it near,
And just within our reach? It was. And yet

We lost it in this daily jar and fret.
But still our place is kept and it will wait,
Ready for us to fill it, soon or late.
No star is ever lost we once have seen:
We always may be what we might have
*   been.*

—ADELAIDE A. PROCTER

MORNING PRAYER

When little things would irk me, and I grow
Impatient with my dear ones, make me know
How in a moment joy can take its flight
And happiness be quenched in endless night.
Keep this thought with me all the livelong
*   day*
That I may guard the harsh words I might
*   say*
When I would fret and grumble, fiery hot,
At trifles that tomorrow are forgot—
Let me remember, Lord, how it would be
If these, my loved ones, were not here with
*   me.*

Have you ever rightly considered what the mere ability to read means? That it is the key which admits us to the whole world of thought and fancy and imagination? To the company of saint and sage, of the wisest and the wittiest at their wisest and wittiest moment? That it enables us to see with the keenest of eyes, hear with the finest ears, and listen to the sweetest voices of all time? More than that, it annihilates time and space for us.

—JAMES RUSSELL LOWELL

THE WAY TO POWER

Self-reverence, self-knowledge, self-
*   control,*
These three alone lead life to sovereign
*   power.*
Yet not for power (power of herself
Would come uncall'd for) but to live by law,
Acting the law we live by without fear;
And, because right is right, to follow right
Were wisdom in the scorn of consequence.

—ALFRED LORD TENNYSON

Let no pleasure tempt thee, no profit allure thee, no ambition corrupt thee, to do anything which thou knowest to be evil; so shalt thou always live jollily; for a good conscience is a continual Christmas.

—BENJAMIN FRANKLIN

Each day of our lives we should make it a point to do some small thing that we would rather not do. Just as a lesson in education and self-control. Then we will enter the doing of the larger tasks of life with zest and spirit.

—George Matthew Adams

GUILTY

I never cut my neighbor's throat;
   My neighbor's gold I never stole;
I never spoiled his house and land;
   But God have mercy on my soul!

For I am haunted night and day
   By all the deeds I have not done;
O unattemtped loveliness!
   O costly valor never won!

—Marguerite Wilkinson

He knows, He loves, He cares;
   Nothing this truth can dim.
He gives the very best to those
   Who leave the choice with Him.

TRUE

Refuse to open your purse, and soon you cannot open your sympathy. Refuse to give, and soon you will cease to enjoy that which you have. Refuse to love, and you lose the power to love and be loved. Withhold your affections and you become a moral paralytic. But the moment you open wider the door of your life, you let the sunshine of your life into some soul.

HORSE SENSE

A horse can't pull while kicking.
   This fact I merely mention.
And he can't kick while pulling.
   Which is my chief contention.

Let's imitate the good old horse
   And lead a life that's fitting;
Just pull an honest load, and then
   There'll be no time for kicking.

THE WELCOME MAN

There's a man in the world who is never
   turned down wherever he chances to stray;
He gets the glad hand in the populous town,
   or out where the farmers make hay;
He's greeted with pleasure on deserts of
   sand, and deep in the aisles of the woods;
Wherever he goes there's the welcoming
   hand—he's The Man Who Delivers The
   Goods.

The failures of life sit around and complain;
   the gods haven't treated them white;
They've lost their umbrellas whenever there's
   rain, and they haven't their lanterns at
   night;
Men tire of the failures who fill with their
   sighs the air of their own neighborhoods;
There's one who is greeted with lovelighted
   eyes—he's The Man Who Delivers The
   Goods.

One fellow is lazy, and watches the clock,
   and waits for the whistle to blow;
And one has a hammer, with which he will
   knock, and one tells a story of woe;
And one, if requested to travel a mile, will
   measure the perches and roods;
But one does his stunt with a whistle or smile
   —he's The Man Who Delivers The Goods.

One man is afraid that he'll labor too hard—
   the world isn't yearning for such;
And one man is always alert, on his guard,
   lest he put in a minute too much;
And one has a grouch or a temper that's bad,
   and one is a creature of moods;
So it's hey for the joyous and rollicking lad
   —for the One Who Delivers The Goods.

—Walt Mason

Do the work that's nearest,
   Though it's dull at whiles,
Helping when we meet them
   Lame dogs over stiles;

See in every hedgerow
   Marks of angels' feet.
Epics in each pebble
   Underneath our feet.

—Charles Kingsley

THE PLOUGH

Above yon sombre swell of land
   Thou seest the dawn's grave orange hue,
With one pale streak like yellow sand,
   And over that a vein of blue.

The air is cold above the woods;
   All silent is the earth and sky,
Except with his own lonely moods
   The blackbird holds a colloquy.

Over the broad hill creeps a beam,
   Like hope that gilds a good man's brow;
And now ascends the nostril-steam
   Of stalwart horses come to plough.

Ye rigid ploughmen, bear in mind—
   Your labour is for future hours,
Advance—spare not—nor look behind—
   Plough deep and straight with all your
     powers.

—R. H. HOENE

BRIDLE YOUR TONGUE

That speech—it hadn't been gone half a
  minute
Before I saw the cold black poison in it;
And I'd have given all I had, and more,
To've only safely got it back indoor.
I'm now what most folks "Well-to-do" would
  call.
I feel today as if I'd give it all,
Provided I through fifty years might reach
And kill and bury that half-minute speech.
Boys flying kites haul in their white-winged
  birds,
You can't do that when you're flying words.
Careful with fire—is good advice we know:
Careful with words—is ten times doubly so.
Thoughts unexpressed may sometimes fall
  back dead,
But God Himself can't kill them when they're
  said.

—WILL CARLETON

OBEDIENCE

The man who would lift others must be lifted himself, and he who would command others must learn to obey.

IT'S UP TO YOU

You are the fellow that has to decide
   Whether you'll do it or toss it aside,
You are the fellow who makes up your mind
   Whether you'll lead or linger behind—

Whether you'll try for the goal that's afar
   Or be contented to stay just where you are.
Take it or leave. Here's something to do,
   Just think it over. It's all up to you!

What do you wish? To be known as a shirk
   Or known as a good man who's willing
     to work,
Scorned for a loafer or praised by your chief
   Rich man or poor man or beggar or thief?

Eager or earnest or dull through the day,
   Honest or crooked? It's you who must say!
You must decide in the face of the test
   Whether you'll shirk it or give your best.

Eyes that the preacher could not school
By wayside graves are raised;
And lips say, 'God be merciful!'
That ne'er said, 'God be praised!'

—ELIZABETH BARRETT BROWNING

AM I A BUILDER?

I watched them tearing a building down,
   A gang of men in a busy town.
With a ho-heave-ho and lusty yell
   They swung a beam, and the side wall fell.
I asked the foreman. "Are these men skilled,
   And the men you'd hire if you had to
     build?"

He gave a laugh and said: "No, indeed!
   Just common labor is all I need.
I can easily wreck in a day or two
   What builders have taken a year to do?"
And I thought to myself as I went away,
   Which of these roles have I tried to play?

Am I a builder who works with care,
   Measuring life by the rule and square?
Am I shaping my deeds to a well-made plan,
   Patiently doing the best I can?
Or am I a wrecker, who walks the town
   Content with the labor of tearing down?

TO THE QUITTER . . .

The world won't care if you quit
And the world won't whine if you fail;
The busy world won't notice it,
No matter how loudly you wail.

Nobody will worry that you
Have relinquished the fight and gone down
For it's only the things that you do
That are worth while and get your renown.

The quitters are quickly forgot;
On them the world spends little time;
And a few e'er care that you've not
The courage or patience to climb.

So give up and quit in despair,
And take your place back on the shelf;
But don't think the world's going to care;
You are injuring only yourself.

KEEP YOUR OWN GATE

Have you ever watched a grower irrigate his grove, or a farmer his land? When he opens little gates to irrigation furrows there rushes in a life-giving flow of water which, in time, will result in beautiful trees and nourishing plants. Our lives are like that. Each of us is given a furrow into which flow power, wisdom, energy and health from a divine source. Like the trees and plants, we thrive—or dry up—according to the degree to which our gates are opened. But there is this tremendous difference. God lets every man be the keeper of his own gate!

THINK

Harsh words, like chickens, love to stray
But they come home to rest each day . . .
If you have angry words to say . . .
   Stop and think!
The world will judge you by your deeds;
They can be flowers? fair, or weeds . . .
Before you plant those tiny seeds . . .
   Stop and think!
God gave us each a heart for song;
A brain to reason right from wrong . . .
So, when temptation gets too strong . . .
   Stop and think!

LIFTING AND LEANING

There are two kinds of people on earth today;
Just two kinds of people, no more, I say.

Not the sinner and saint, for it's well under-
stood,
The good are half bad, and the bad are half
good.

Not the rich and the poor, for to rate a
man's wealth,
You must first know the state of his con-
science and health.

Not the humble and proud, for in life's little
span,
Who puts on vain airs, is not counted a man.

Not the happy and sad, for the swift flying
years
Bring each man his laughter and each man
his tears.

No; the two kinds of people on earth I mean,
Are the people who lift, and the people who
lean.

Wherever you go, you will find the earth's
masses
Are always divided in just these two classes.

And, oddly enough, you will find too, I
ween,
There's only one lifter to twenty who lean.

In which class are you? Are you easing the
load
Of overtaxed lifters, who toil down the road?

Or are you a leaner, who lets others share
Your portion of labor, and worry and care?

—ELLA WHEELER WILCOX

Build thee more stately mansions, O my soul,
  As the swift seasons roll!
   Leave thy low-vaulted past!
Let each new temple, nobler than the last,
Shut thee from heaven with a dome more
  vast,
   Till thou at length art free,
Leaving thine outgrown shell by life's unrest-
  ing sea!

—OLIVER WENDELL HOLMES

JUST A MINUTE

I have only just a minute
Only sixty seconds in it,
Forced upon me, can't refuse it,
Didn't seek it, didn't choose it.
But it's up to me to use it,
I must suffer if I lose it,
Give account if I abuse it,
Just a tiny little minute—
But eternity is in it.

THE BOY

A lad stood there, as I opened the door, whom I thought I'd seen somewhere before.

"What do you want, my boy?" said I, as he gazed at me with a puzzled eye.

"Excuse me," he said, "for troubling you; I'm seeking a friend that I once knew. You look like him, you bear his name, but now I see you're not the same. He used to live at this address, but he has moved away, I guess."

And turning away, he left my place with disappointment in his face. With a "Goodbye, sir," he closed the gate, and left me there disconsolate.

And then I heard, as strange it seems, a voice I'd heard in my youthful dreams. An inner voice, that said to me: "That boy is the boy you used to be! His wistful heart has a pang within, for he's seeking the man you might have been!"

—Andrew R. Marker

AS A MAN SOWETH

We must not hope to be mowers,
And to gather the ripe gold ears,
Unless we have first been sowers
And watered the furrows with tears.

It is not just as we take it,
This mystical world of ours,
Life's field will yield as we make it
A harvest of thorns or of flowers.

—Johann W. von Goethe

A MILE WITH ME

Oh, who will walk a mile with me,
Along life's merry way?
A comrade blithe and full of glee,
Who dares to laugh out loud and free,
And let his frolic fancy play,
Like a happy child, through the flowers gay
That fill the field and fringe the way,
Where he walks a mile with me.

And who will walk a mile with me,
Along life's weary way?
A friend whose heart has eyes to see
The stars shine out o'er the darkening lea,
And the quiet rest at the end of the day—
A friend who knows, and dares to say,
The brave, sweet words that cheer the way
Where he walks a mile with me.

With such a comrade, such a friend,
I fain would walk till journeys end,
Through summer sunshine, winter rain,
And then? Farewell, we shall meet again!

—Henry Van Dyke

BE STRONG

Be strong!
We are not here to play, to dream, to drift;
We have hard work to do, and loads to lift;
Shun not the struggle—fact it; 'tis God's gift.

Be strong!
Say not, "The days are evil. Who's to blame?"
And fold the hands and acquiesce—oh shame!
Stand up, speak out, and bravely, in God's name.

Be strong!
It matters not how deep intrenched the wrong,
How hard the battle goes, the day how long;
Faint not—fight on! To-morrow comes the song.

—Maltbie Davenport Babcock

It's not what you'd do with a million,
If riches should e'er be your lot,
But what are you doing at present
With the dollar and a half you've got?

Once to every man and nation comes the
 moment to decide;
In the strife of Truth with Falsehood, for
 the good or evil side;
Some great cause, God's new Messiah, offer-
 ing each the bloom or blight,
Parts the goats upon the left hand and the
 sheep upon the right,
And the choice goes by forever 'twixt that
 darkness and that light.

—JAMES RUSSELL LOWELL

The constant interchange of those thousand little courtesies which impercep-
tibly sweeten life has a happy effect upon
the features, and spreads a mellow evening
charm over the wrinkles of old age.

—WASHINGTON IRVING

THE GRANDEST PRIZE

In summing up the things to praise,
 For what they do for me,
There's one to which I give first place,
 Whose virtues plain I see.
I pay it well-earned tribute,
 For it to me doth teach
Life's greatest, noblest lesson,
 'Tis the prize beyond my reach.

It dares me come and take it,
 It says to me, "You know
By struggle and by effort
 Your strength and skill will grow;
I'll not surrender tamely,
 Tho' you wheedle and beseech,
But if you toil you'll win me,
 Tho' now beyond your reach."

And I have found that always
 Whene'er I use my skill,
My muscle and intelligence,
 My energy and will,
I'm always sure to win it,
 And sweet beyond all speech
Is the rapture of the capture
 Of the prize once out of reach.

—WILLIAM T. CARD

IF—

If you can keep your head when all about you
 Are losing theirs and blaming it on you;
If you can trust yourself when all men doubt
 you,
 But make allowance for their doubting too;
If you can wait and not be tired by waiting,
 Or, being lied about, don't deal in lies,
Or, being hated, don't give way to hating,
 And yet don't look too good, nor talk too
 wise;
If you can dream—and not make dreams your
 master;
 If you can think—and not make thoughts
 your aim;
If you can meet with triumph and disaster
 And treat those two impostors just the
 same;
If you can bear to hear the truth you've
 spoken
 Twisted by knaves to make a trap for fools,
Or watch the things you gave your life to
 broken,
 And stoop and build 'em up with wornout
 tools;
If you can make one heap of all your
 winnings
 And risk it on one turn of pitch-and-toss,
And lose, and start again at your beginnings
 And never breathe a word about your loss;
If you can force your heart and nerve and
 sinew
 To serve your turn long after they are
 gone,
And so hold on when there is nothing in you
 Except the Will which says to them:
 "Hold on";
If you can talk with crowds and keep your
 virtue,
 Or walk with kings—nor lose the common
 touch;
If neither foes nor loving friends can hurt
 you;
 If all men count with you, but none too
 much;
If you can fill the unforgiving minute
 With sixty seconds' worth of distance run—
Yours is the Earth and everything that's in it,
 And—which is more—you'll be a Man, **my**
 son!

—RUDYARD KIPLING

SELFISHNESS

Love that is hoarded, moulds at last
  Until we know some day
The only thing we ever have
  Is what we give away.

And kindness that is never used
  But hiddend all alone
Will slowly harden till it is
  As hard as any stone.

It is the things we always hold
  That we will lose some day;
The only things we ever keep
  Are what we give away.

—HAROLD CORNELIUS SANDALL

Hold fast to dreams
For if dreams die
Life is a broken-winged bird
That cannot fly.

Hold fast to dreams
For when dreams go
Life is a barren field
Frozen with snow.

—LANGSTON HUGHES

THREE GATES

If I am tempted to reveal
  A tale someone to me has told
About another, let it pass,
  Before I speak, three gates of gold.

Three narrow gates: First, is it true?
  Then, is it needful? In my mind
Give truthful answer, and the next
  Is last and narrowest, Is it kind?

And if to reach my lips at last,
  It passes through these gateways, three,
Then I may tell the tale, nor fear
  What the result of speech may be.

NOBODY ELSE BUT YOU

When you been workin' a long, long time,
A-doin' the best you can,
And you start to think about the day
When you'll be an old, old man—
When you'll want to fish and hunt and golf,
Or whatever you love to do—
Nobody goin' to save that money,
Nobody else but you!

Ain't no use to sit and dream
About that pot of gold,
Or about the things you'd like to have
When you find you're growin' old.
When the speculatin's over,
And the propaganda's through,
You know who's gonna be holdin' the bag—
Nobody else but you!

So I been smokin' and wonderin'
'Bout a lot of fancy schemes
Where I could get rich without any work—
And I'm sure they're all just dreams.
'Cause you'll find out as you go along
And see things clear on through—
Things worth while are the things that are
  earned
By nobody else but you!

—WILLIAM L. MILLER

LIFE'S MELODY

Life is like a keyboard. The Master's fingers will sweep over it, and a weary world will catch notes of melody as we go along. The life that is in tune with God is keyed to the note of love.

—J. R. MILLER

Swift to its close ebbs out life's little day;
Earth's joys grow dim, its glories pass away;
Change and decay in all around I see:
O Thou who changest not, abide with me!

If Winter comes, can Spring be far behind?

—PERCY BYSSHE SHELLEY

Character

Character is like a tree and reputation is like its shadow. The shadow is what we think of it; the tree is the real thing.

—Abraham Lincoln

The depth of one's convictions measures the breadth of his influence.

The reputation of a thousand years may be determined by the conduct of one hour.

It is not what he has, nor even what he does, which directly affects the worth of a man; but what he is.

—Henri-Frederic Amiel

MYSELF

I have to live with myself, and so
I want to be fit for myself to know,
I want to be able, as days go by,
Always to look myself straight in the eye;
I don't want to stand, with the setting sun,
And hate myself for things I have done.

I don't want to keep on a closet shelf
A lot of secrets about myself,
And fool myself, as I come and go,
Into thinking that nobody else will know
The kind of a man I really am;
I don't want to dress up myself in sham.

I want to go out with my head erect,
I want to deserve all men's respect;
But here in the struggle for fame and pelf
I want to be able to like myself.
I don't want to look at myself and know
That I'm bluster and bluff and empty show.

I can never hide myself from me;
I see what others may never see;
I know what others may never know,
I never can fool myself, and so,
Whatever happens, I want to be
Self-respecting and conscience free.

—Edgar A. Guest

THE BRIDGE-BUILDER

An old man going a lone highway
Came at the evening, cold and gray,
To a chasm vast and wide and steep,
With waters rolling cold and deep.
The old man crossed in the twilight dim,
The sullen stream had no fears for him;
But he turned when safe on the other side,
And built a bridge to span the tide.

"Old man," said a fellow pilgrim near,
"You are wasting your strength with building
   here.
Your journey will end with the ending day,
You never again will pass this way.
You've crossed the chasm, deep and wide,
Why build you this bridge at eventide?"

The builder lifted his old gray head.
"Good friend, in the path I have come," he
   said,
"There followeth after me today
A youth whose feet must pass this way.
The chasm that was as nought to me
To that fair-haired youth may a pitfall be;
He, too, must cross in the twilight dim—
Good friend, I am building this bridge for
   him."

—Will Allen Dromgoole

ALTERNATIVES

Not what we have, but what we use;
Not what we see, but what we choose—
These are the things that mar or bless
The sum of human happiness.

There are too many people praying for mountains of difficulty to be removed, when what they really need is courage to climb them.

INFLUENCE

'Twas a sheep, not a lamb, that strayed away,
  In the parable Jesus told—
A grown-up sheep that had gone astray
  From the ninety and nine in the fold.

Out in the meadows, out in the cold,
  'Twas a sheep the good shepherd sought,
And back in the flock, safe into the fold,
  'Twas a sheep the good shepherd brought.

And why for the sheep should we earnestly
    long,
  And as earnestly hope and pray?
Because there is danger, if they go wrong,
  They will lead the young lambs astray.

For the lambs will follow the sheep, you
    know,
  Wherever the sheep may stray:
If the sheep go wrong, it will not be long
  Till the lambs are as wrong as they.

And so with the sheep we earnestly plead,
  For the sake of the lambs today:
If the lambs are lost, what a terrible cost
  Some sheep will have to pay!

No man can hold another man in the gutter without remaining there himself.

—BOOKER T. WASHINGTON

THE SEVEN MODERN SINS

Policies without principles
Pleasure without conscience
Wealth without work
Knowledge without character
Industry without morality
Science without humanity
Worship without sacrifice.

What stronger breastplate than a heart un-
    tainted!
Thrice is he arm'd that hath his quarrel just,
And he is naked, though locked up in steel,
Whose conscience with injustice is corrupted.

—WILLIAM SHAKESPEARE

The greatest homage we can pay to truth is to use it.

—RALPH WALDO EMERSON

IN ANGER

When I have lost my temper
I have lost my reason too.
I'm never proud of anything
Which angrily I do.

When I have talked in anger
And my cheeks are flaming red
I have always uttered something
That I wish I hadn't said.

In anger I have never done
A kindly deed, or wise,
But many things for which I know
I should apologize.

In looking back across my life
And all I've lost or made,
I can't recall a single time
When fury ever paid.

Love of truth will bless the lover all his days; yet when he brings her home, his fair-faced bride, she comes empty-handed to his door, herself her only dower.

—THEODORE PARKER

Grief knits two hearts in closer bonds than happiness ever can, and common suffering is a far stronger link than common joy.

—ALPHONSE DE LAMARTINE

THE FOE WITHIN

None but one can harm you,
None but yourself who are your greatest foe;
He that respects himself is safe from others:
He wears a coat of mail that none can pierce.

—HENRY WADSWORTH LONGFELLOW

It is the cause and not the death, that makes the martyr.

—NAPOLEON

CONSCIENCE

I sat alone with my conscience
  In a place where time had ceased,
And we talked of my former living
  In the land where the years increased;
And I felt I should have to answer
  The question it put to me,
And to face the answer and questions
  Through all eternity.

The ghosts of forgotten actions
  Came floating before my sight,
And things that I thought were dead things
  Were alive with terrible might.
And the vision of all my past life
  Was an awful thing to face,
Alone with my conscience sitting
  In that solemnly silent place.

And I thought of a faraway warning,
  Of a sorrow that was to be mine,
In a land that was then the future,
  But now is the present time.
And I thought of my former thinking
  Of the judgment day to be;
But sitting alone with my conscience
  Seemed judgment enough for me.

And I wondered if there was a future
  To this land beyond the grave;
But no one gave me an answer,
  And no one came to save.
Then I felt that the future was present.
  And the present would never go by,
For it was but the thought of my past life
  Growing into eternity.

Then I woke from my timely dreaming,
  And the vision passed away,
And I knew that the far-off seeming
  Was a warning of yesterday;
And I pray that I may not forget it,
  In this land before the grave,
That I may not cry in the future
  And no one come to save.

And so I have learned a lesson
  Which I ought to have known before,
And which, though I learned it dreaming,
  I hope to forget no more.
So I sit alone with my conscience
  In the place where the years increase,
And I try to remember the future
  In the land where time will cease.

And I know of the future judgment,
  How dreadful soe'er it be,
That to sit alone with my conscience
  Will be judgment enough for me.

—CHARLES WILLIAM STUBBS

I love the man that can smile in trouble, that can gather strength from distress, and grow brave by reflection. 'Tis the business of little minds to shrink, but he whose heart is firm, and whose conscience approves his conduct, will pursue his principles unto death.

—THOMAS PAINE

Character is the joint product of nature and nurture.

MY CREED

To live as gently as I can;
To be, no matter where, a man;
To take what comes of good or ill
And cling to faith and honor still;
To do my best, and let that stand;
The record of my brain and hand;
And then, should failure come to me,
Still work and hope for victory.

To have no secret place wherein
I stoop unseen to shame or sin;
To be the same when I'm alone
As when my every deed is known;
To live undaunted, unafraid
Of any step that I have made;
To be without pretense or sham
Exactly what men think I am.

To leave some simple mark behind
To keep my having lived in mind;
If enmity to aught I show,
To be an honest, generous foe,
To play my little part, nor whine
That greater honors are not mine.
This, I believe, is all I need
For my philosophy and creed.

—EDGAR A. GUEST

THE GATE
AT THE END OF THINGS

Some people say the world's all a stage
  Where each plays a part in life;
While others proclaim that life is quite real,
  Its joys, its battles, its strife.
Some say it's a joke, we should laugh it along,
  Should smile at the knocks and stings;
Whatever is true just take this from me,
  There's a gate at the end of things.

Don't try to kid yourself with the thought,
  You can do as you please all the while;
Don't think you can kick the poor fellow
    who's down,
  While you climb to the top of the pile.
Don't go back on your pal, just because he
    won't know,
  Oh, in his eyes you may be a king;
Some day he will see you just as you are,
  At the gate at the end of things.

Don't think you fool all the folks all the
    while,
  You may do it sometimes, that is true;
They will find you out in the end every time,
  The only one you fool is you.
If you see a man down, why, give him a hand,
  And find how much pleasure it brings,
To know you are ready to meet all mankind,
  At the gate at the end of things.

Don't let your head swell 'cause your bank
    roll is large
  And your clothes are the latest style;
There is many a prince walking round in rags,
  May have you beaten a mile.
Just try to remember as through life you go,
  If you're square you're as good as a king,
And you won't have to crawl through a hole
    in the wall,
  At the gate at the end of things.

If you've got a wife, as most fellows have,
  Remember what she's been to you,
When prosperity smiles, treat her like a pal,
  She's the one that has stuck to you;
Don't look for the girl from the Great White
    Way,
  Who wears diamonds, fine clothes and those
    things;
Think how you'd feel to meet your little girl,

At the gate at the end of things.

Live like a man, it don't cost any more,
  To act on the square and be right.
It's reward enough to know you're a man,
  To hear people say, "He's white."
You can look everybody straight in the eye,
  And your voice has sincerity's ring;
Then you're ready to go and pass through
    with the bunch,
  At the gate at the end of things.

PROFANITY

It is no mark of a gentleman to swear. The most worthless and vile, the refuse of mankind, the drunkard and the prostitute, swear as well as the best dressed and educated gentleman. No particular endowments are requisite to give a finish to the art of cursing. The basest and meanest of mankind swear with as much tact and skill as the most refined; and he that wishes to degrade himself to the very lowest level of pollution and shame should learn to be a common swearer. Any man has talents enough to learn to curse God, and imprecate perdition on himself and his fellow men.

Profane swearing never did any man any good. No man is the richer or wiser or happier for it. It helps no one's education or manners. It commends no one to any society. It is disgusting to the refined, abominable to the good, insulting to those with whom we associate, degrading to the mind, unprofitable, needless, and injurious to society; and wantonly to profane His name, to call His vengeance down, to curse Him, and to involve His vengeance, is perhaps of all offenses the most awful in the sight of God.

—MARTIN LUTHER

WORDS

Before I knew how cruel
  Just common talk can be,
I thought that words were singing things
  With colors like the sea.

But since I've felt their caustic lash,
  And know how they can sting,
I hold my breath when words go by
  For fear they will not sing.

YOUR NAME

You got it from your father. 'Twas the best
  he had to give,
And right gladly be bestowed it—it is yours
  the while you live.
You may lose the watch he gave you and another you may claim,
But remember, when you're tempted, to be
  careful of his name.

It was fair the day you got it and a worthy
  name to wear.
When he took it from his father, there was no
  dishonor there;
Through the years he proudly wore it, to his
  father he was true,
And that name was clean and spotless when
  he passed it on to you.

Oh, there's much that he has given that he
  values not at all.
He has watched you break your playthings in
  the days when you were small,
And you've lost the knife he gave you and
  you've scattered many a game
But you'll never hurt your father if you're
  careful of his name.

It is yours to wear forever, yours to wear the
  while you live,
Yours, perhaps, some distant morning to another boy to give,
And you'll smile as did your father smile
  above that baby there,
If a clean name and a good name you are giving him to wear.

—EDGAR A. GUEST

Govern the lips as they were palace-doors, the king within; tranquil and fair and courteous be all words which from that presence win.

—SIR EDWIN ARNOLD

WATCH YOURSELF GO BY

Just stand aside and watch yourself go by;
  Think of yourself as "he" instead of "I."
Note closely as in other men you note
The bag-kneed trousers and the seedy coat.
Pick flaws; find fault; forget the man is you,
And strive to make your estimate ring true.
Confront yourself and look you in the eye—
Just stand aside and watch yourself go by.

Interpret all your motives just as though
You looked on one whose aims you did not
  know.
Let undisguised contempt surge through you
  when
You see you shirk, O commonest of men!
Despise your cowardice; condemn whate'er
You note of falseness in you anywhere.
Defend not one defect that shares your eye—
Just stand aside and watch yourself go by.

And then, with eyes unveiled to what you
  loathe,
To sins that with sweet charity you'd clothe,
Back to your self-walled tenements you'll go
With tolerance for all who dwell below.
The faults of others then will dwarf and
  shrink,
Love's chain grows stronger by one mighty
  link,
When you, with "he" as substitute for "I,"
Have stood aside and watched yourself go by.

—STRICKLAND GILLILAN

It is possible to be straight in creed, but crooked in character.

Still as of old
Men by themselves are priced—
For thirty pieces Judas sold
Himself, not Christ.

—HESTER H. CHOLMONDELEY

There is nothing that makes men rich and strong but that which they carry inside of them. Wealth is of the heart, not of the hand.

—JOHN MILTON

M en are usually down on what they are
not up to.

—Hoyt M. Dobbs

WHAT THEN?

When the great plants of our cities
  Have turned out their last finished work;
When our merchants have sold their last yard
  of silk
  And dismissed the last tired clerk;
When our banks have raked in their last
  dollar
  And paid the last dividend;
When the Judge of the earth says: "Close for
  the night,"
  And asks for a balance—WHAT THEN?

When the choir has sung its last anthem,
  And the preacher has made his last prayer,
When the people have heard their last sermon
  And the sound has died out on the air;
When the Bible lies closed on the altar
  And the pews are all empty of men
And each one stands facing his record—
  And the great Book is opened—WHAT
  THEN?

When the actors have played their last
  drama,
  And the mimic has made his last fun,
When the film has flashed its last picture,
  And the billboard displayed its last run;
When the crowds seeking pleasure have van-
  ished,
  And gone out in the darkness again—
When the trumpet of ages is sounded,
  And we stand up before Him—WHAT
  THEN?

When the bugle's call sinks into silence
  And the long marching columns stand still,
When the captain repeats his last orders,
  And they've captured the last fort and hill,
And the flag has been hauled from the mast
  head,
  And the wounded afield checked in,
And a world that rejected its Saviour,
  Is asked for a reason—WHAT THEN?

—J. Whitfield Green

BE TRUE

Thou must be true thyself
  If thou the truth wouldst teach;
Thy soul must overflow if thou
  Another's soul wouldst reach!
It needs the overflow of heart
  To give the lips full speech.

Think truly, and thy thoughts
  Shall the world's famine feed;
Speak truly, and each word of thine
  Shall be a fruitful seed;
Live truly, and thy life shall be
  A great and noble creed.

—Horatius Bonar

Fame is vapor;
Popularity is an accident.
Riches take wings and fly.
Those who cheer you to-day
May curse you and stab you to-morrow.
Then there is only one thing left—
That is: CHARACTER.

—Horace Greeley

COWARD

You have no enemies, you say?
Alas! my friend, the boast is poor—
He who has mingled in the fray
Of duty, that the brave endure,
Must have made foes! If you have none,
Small is the work that you have done;
You've hit no traitor on the hip;
You've dashed no cup from perjured lip;
You've never turned the wrong to right—
You've been a coward in the fight!

—Charles Mackey

Who steals my purse steals trash; 'tis some-
  thing, nothing;
'Twas mine, 'tis his, and has been slave to
  thousands;
But he that filches from me my good name
Robs me of that which not enriches him
And makes me poor indeed.

—William Shakespeare

A NEW START

I will start anew this morning with a higher,
   fairer creed,
I will cease to stand complaining of my ruth-
   less neighbor's greed;
I will cease to sit repining while my duty's
   call is clear;
I will waste no moment whining, and my
   heart shall know no fear.
I will look sometimes about me for the things
   that merit praise;
I will search for hidden beauties that elude
   the grumbler's gaze.
I will try to find contentment in the paths
   that I must tread;
I will cease to have resentment when another
   moves ahead.
I will not be swayed by envy when my rival's strength is shown;
I will not deny his merit, but I'll strive to
   prove my own;
I will try to see the beauty spread before me,
   rain, or shine;
I will cease to preach your duty, and be more
   concerned with mine.

We sow a thought and reap an act,
   We sow an act and reap a habit,
We sow a habit and reap a character,
   We sow a character and reap a destiny.

—William Makepeace Thackeray

JUDGED BY THE COMPANY
ONE KEEPS

One night in late October,
When I was far from sober,
Returning with my load with manly pride,
My feet began to stutter,
So I lay down in the gutter,
And a pig came near and lay down by my
   side;
A lady passing by was heard to say:
"You can tell a man who boozes,
By the company he chooses,"
And the pig got up and slowly walked away.

THE ARROW AND THE SONG

I shot an arrow into the air,
It fell to earth, I knew not where;
For, so swiftly it flew, the sight
Could not follow it in its flight.

I breathed a song into the air,
It fell to earth, I knew not where;
For who has sight so keen and strong,
That it can follow the flight of song?

Long, long afterward, in an oak
I found the arrow, still unbroke;
And the song, from beginning to end,
I found again in the heart of a friend.

—Henry Wadsworth Longfellow

GOD—LET ME BE AWARE

God—let me be aware.

Let me not stumble blindly down life's
   ways,
Just seeking somehow safely to get through
   the days,
Hand never groping for another hand,
Not even wondering why it all was planned,
Eyes to the ground, unseeking for the
   light,
Soul never longing for a wild wing flight,
Please, keep me eager just to do my share.
   God—let me be aware.

God—let me be aware.
Stab my soul fiercely with others' pain,
Let me walk seeing horror and stain.
Let my hand, groping, find other hands.
Give me the heart that divines, understands.
Give me the courage, wounded, to fight.
Fill me with knowledge and drench me with
   light.
Please—keep me eager just to do my share.
   God—let me be aware.

—Miriam Teichner

The esteem of wise and good men is the
greatest of all temporal encouragements
to virtue; and it is a mark of an abandoned
spirit to have no regard to it.

—Edmund Burke

Consolation

He knows, He loves, He cares;
  Nothing this truth can dim.
He gives the very best to those
  Who leave the choice with Him.

There is a day of sunny rest
For every dark and troubled night:
And grief may hide an evening guest,
But joy shall come with early light.

—WILLIAM CULLEN BRYANT

Believe me, every man has his secret sorrows, which the world knows not; and oftentimes we call a man cold when he is only sad.

—HENRY WADSWORTH LONGFELLOW

PEACE AFTER SORROW

There is a peace which cometh after sorrow,
  A peace of hope surrendered, not fulfilled;
A peace that looketh not upon the morrow
  But backward, on the storm already stilled.
It is the peace in sacrifice secluded,
  The peace that is from inward conflict free;
'Tis not the peace which over Eden brooded
  But that which triumphed in Gethsemane.

—JESSIE ROSE GATES

Grief can take care of itself, but to get the full value of a joy you must have somebody to divide it with.

—MARK TWAIN

FAITH

In the bitter waves of woe,
  Beaten and tossed about
By the sullen winds that blow
  From the desolate shores of doubt,
Where the anchors that faith has cast
  Are dragging in the gale,
I am quietly holding fast
  To the things that cannot fail.

Sorrow is only one of the lower notes in the oratorio of our blessedness.

—ARMISTEAD GORDON

THANK GOD!

Thank God for life!
E'en though it bring much bitterness and
    strife,
  And all our fairest hopes be wrecked and
      lost,
E'en though there be more ill than good in
    life,
  We cling to life and reckon not the cost.
    Thank God for life!

Thank God for love!
For though sometimes grief follows in its
    wake,
  Still we forget love's sorrow in love's joy,
And cherish tears with smiles for love's dear
    sake;
  Only in heaven is bliss without alloy.
    Thank God for love!

Thank God for pain!
No tear hath ever yet been shed in vain,
  And in the end each sorrowing heart shall
    find
No curse, but blessings in the hand of pain;
  Even when he smiteth, then is God most
    kind.
    Thank God for pain!

Thank God for death!
Who touches anguished lips and stills their
    breath
  And giveth peace unto each troubled breast;
Grief flows before thy touch, O blessed death;
  God's sweetest gift; thy name in heaven is
    Rest.
    Thank God for death!

Grief can take care of itself, but to get the full value of a joy you must have somebody to divide it with.

—MARK TWAIN

WE'LL UNDERSTAND

Not now, but in the coming years,
It may be in the Better Land,
We'll read the meaning of our tears,
And there, sometime, we'll understand.

We'll catch the broken threads again,
And finish what we here began;
Heaven will the mysteries explain,
And then, ah then, we'll understand.

We'll know why clouds instead of sun
Were over many a cherished plan;
Why sun has ceased, when scarce begun;
'Tis there, sometime, we'll understand.

God knows the way, He holds the key,
He guides us with unerring hand;
Sometimes with tearless eyes we'll see;
Yes, there, up there, we'll understand.

Then trust in God through all thy days;
Fear not, for he doth hold thy hand;
Though dark the way, still sing and praise;
Sometime, sometime, we'll understand.

—MAXWELL N. CORNELIUS

Let not your heart be troubled, neither let it be afraid."

—JOHN 14:27

I NEVER KNEW A NIGHT

I never knew a night so black
Light failed to follow on its track.
I never knew a storm so gray
It failed to have its clearing day.
I never knew such bleak despair
That there was not a rift, somewhere.
I never knew an hour so drear
Love could not fill it full of cheer!

—JOHN KENDRICK BANGS

God will wipe away every tear from their eyes, and death shall be no more, neither shall there be mourning nor crying nor pain any more, for the former things have passed away.

—REVELATION 21:4

THE DAY IS DONE

The day is done, and the darkness
Falls from the wings of Night,
As a feather is wafted downward
From an eagle in his flight.

I see the lights of the village
Gleam through the rain and the mist,
And a feeling of sadness comes o'er me
That my soul cannot resist.

A feeling of sadness and longing,
That is not akin to pain,
And resembles sorrow only
As the mist resembles the rain.

Come, read to me some poem,
Some simple and heartfelt lay,
That shall soothe this restless feeling,
And banish the thoughts of day.

Such songs have power to quiet
The restless pulse of care,
And come like the benediction
That follows after prayer.

Then read from the treasured volume
The poem of thy choice,
And lend to the rhyme of the poet
The beauty of thy voice.

And the night shall be filled with music,
And the cares, that infest the day,
Shall fold their tents, like the Arabs,
And as silently steal away.

—HENRY WADSWORTH LONGFELLOW

From "THE FORCE OF PRAYER"

Oh! there is never sorrow of heart
That shall lack a timely end,
If but to God we turn, and ask
Of Him to be our friend!

—WILLIAM WORDSWORTH

Silence is no certain token
That no secret grief is there;
Sorrow which is never spoken
Is the heaviest load to bear.

—FRANCES RIDLEY HAVERGAL

Heaven knows we need never be ashamed of our tears, for they are rain upon the blinding dust of earth, overlying our hard hearts.

—CHARLES DICKENS

Go, bury thy sorrow,
  The world hath its share;
Go, bury it deeply,
  Go, hide it with care.
Go, bury thy sorrow,
  Let others be blest;
Go, give them the sunshine,
  And tell God the rest.

It is dangerous to abandon oneself to the luxury of grief; it deprives one of courage, and even of the wish for recovery.

—HENRI-FREDERIC AMIEL

WHAT GOD HATH PROMISED

God hath not promised
Skies always blue,
Flower-strewn pathways
All our lives through;
God hath not promised
Sun without rain,
Joy without sorrow,
Peace without pain.

But God hath promised
Strength for the day,
Rest for the labor,
Light for the way,
Grace for the trials,
Help from above,
Unfailing sympathy,
Undying love.

—ANNIE JOHNSON FLINT

THIS PRAYER I MAKE

This prayer I make,
Knowing that Nature never did betray
The heart that loved her; 'tis her privilege,
Through all the years of this our life, to lead
From joy to joy: for she can so inform
The mind that is within us, so impress
With quietness and beauty, and so feed
With lofty thoughts, that neither evil
  tongues,
Rash judgments, nor the sneers of selfish
  men,
Nor greetings where no kindness is, nor all
The dreary intercourse of daily life,
Shall e'er prevail against us, or disturb
Our cheerful faith, that all which we behold
Is full of blessings.

—WILLIAM WORDSWORTH

Mourn not for me, for frailty is left behind. I face the next step in life's pilgrimage with the great calm with which God has so richly blessed me, knowing we are His children whether we live or die, and that our deep love which endureth all things is everlasting.

—ELSIE BUSH WOOLSEY

Yearneth thy heart for a sweet friend dead,
Sigheth thy heart for a dear day fled?
  I pity thee, my friend.

Hast known regret for a word unspoken,
When a loving heart did await some token?
  My friend, God comfort thee.

Hast spoken ungently to one now gone,
Hast lain on her grave and grieved alone?
  I know God heard thy prayer.

Hast been harshly judged, misunderstood,
By one to whom thou wished but good?
  God understood thy heart.

Has the friend of thy heart and soul false
  proved,
The friend of all the world best loved?
  Christ pities thee, poor one.

—KATE VANNAH

Some of your hurts you have cured,
   And the sharpest you still have survived,
But what torments of grief you endured
   From evils that never arrived!

              —RALPH WALDO EMERSON

Facing and accepting a loss is the first step of managing bereavement. Only the life which deliberately picks up and starts over again is victorious.

              —JAMES GORDON GILKEY

FATHER, THY WILL BE DONE!

He sendeth sun, He sendeth shower,
Alike they're needful for the flower;
And joys and tears alike are sent
To give the soul fit nourishment:
   As comes to me or cloud or sun,
   Father, Thy will, not mine, be done!

              —SARAH FLOWER ADAMS

You cannot prevent the birds of sorrow from flying over your head, but you can prevent them from building nests in your hair.

              —CHINESE PROVERB

They bid us live each day afresh,
   Trade last year's grief for a better morrow;
But happiness were flabby flesh
   If it should lack the bones of sorrow.

              —ERNESTINE MERCER

Let nothing disturb thee,
Nothing affright thee;
All things are passing;
God never changeth;
Patient endurance
Attaineth to all things;
Who God possesseth
In nothing is wanting;
Alone God sufficeth.

              —ST. THERESA

Keep your fears to yourself; share your courage with others.

Be still, my soul: the Lord is on thy side;
   Bear patiently the cross of grief or pain;
Leave to thy God to order and provide;
   In every change he faithful will remain.
Be still, my soul: thy best, thy heavenly
   Friend
Through thorny ways leads to a joyful end.

There is a destiny that makes us brothers;
   None goes his way alone:
All that we send into the lives of others
   Comes back into our own.

WORRY

The world is wide
In time and tide,
And—God is guide;
   Then do not hurry.
That man is blest
Who does his best
And leaves the rest;
   Then do not worry.

              —CHARLES F. DEEMS

THE RAINY DAY

The day is cold and dark and dreary;
It rains, and the wind is never weary;
The vine still clings to the moldering wall,
But at every gust the dead leaves fall,
   And the day is dark and dreary.

My life is cold and dark and dreary;
It rains, and the wind is never weary;
My thoughts still cling to the moldering past,
But the hopes of youth fall thick in the blast,
   And the days are dark and dreary.

Be still, sad heart! and cease repining;
Behind the clouds is the sun still shining:
Thy fate is the common fate of all:
Into each life some rain must fall,
   Some days must be dark and dreary.

         —HENRY WADSWORTH LONGFELLOW

Surely it is not true blessedness to be free from sorrow while there is sorrow and sin in the world; sorrow is then a part of love, and love does not seek to throw it off.

—GEORGE ELIOT

THESE THINGS I HAVE

*I wanted health and strength to do great
 things,
Infirmity taught patience for each day.
My strength, as fleeting as a moth's white
 wing,
Left me dependent, that I might obey.
I wanted wealth for happiness and ease,
But poverty prevailed and made me wise.
I wanted power to conquer and to please,
But weakness made me see through others'
 eyes.
I wanted leisure time to dream and plan,
But duty brought self-discipline, and while
I sought approval of my fellowman,
I found it not, but in my Saviour's smile.
And now that I have been so richly blest,
This is my daily prayer, "Give what is best."*

—JOSEPHINE STONE BREEDING

SORROW

*Count each affliction, whether light or grave,
 God's messenger sent down to thee; do
 thou
 With courtesy receive him, rise and bow;
And, ere his shadow pass thy threshold, crave
Permission first his heavenly feet to lave;
 Then lay before him all thou hast; allow
 No cloud of passion to usurp thy brow,
 Or mar thy hospitality; no wave
Of mortal tumult to obliterate
 Thy soul's marmoreal calmness.
 Grief should be
Like joy, majestic, equable, sedate,
 Confirming, cleansing, raising, making free;
Strong to consume small troubles; to
 commend
Great thoughts, grave thoughts, thoughts
 lasting to the end.*

—SIR AUDREY DE VERE

If a friend of mine . . . gave a feast, and did not invite me to it, I should not mind a bit. . . . But if . . . a friend of mine had a sorrow and refused to allow me to share it, I should feel it most bitterly. If he shut the doors of the house of mourning against me, I would move back again and again and beg to be admitted, so that I might share in what I was entitled to share. If he thought me unworthy, unfit to weep with him, I should feel it as the most poignant humiliation, as the most terrible mode for which disgrace could be inflicted on me . . . he who can look on the loveliness of the world and share its sorrow, and realize something of the wonder of both, is in immediate contact with divine things, and has got as near to God's secret as any one can get.

—OSCAR WILDE

*In this vast universe
There is but one supreme truth—
That God is our friend!
By that truth meaning is given
To the remote stars, the numberless
 centuries,
The long and heroic struggle of mankind . . .
O my Soul, dare to trust this truth!
Dare to rest in God's kindly arms,
Dare to look confidently into His face,
Then launch thyself into life unafraid!
Knowing thou art within thy Father's house,
That thou art surrounded by His love,
Thou wilt become master of fear
Lord of life, conqueror even of death!*

*Stone walls do not a prison make,
 Nor iron bars a cage;
Minds innocent and quiet take
 That for an hermitage:
If I have freedom in my love,
 And in my soul am free,
Angels alone, that soar above,
 Enjoy such liberty.*

—RICHARD LOVELACE

FOR ONE LATELY BEREFT

*Though now you are bereft and ways seem
    black,
  With emptiness and gloom on every hand;
Someday Time's healing touch will lead you
    back,
  And gradually your heart will understand
That what you bore must come to one and all,
  And Peace, the clean white flower born of
    pain,
Will slowly, surely, rise from sorrow's pall,
  And happiness will come to you again.*

—Margaret E. Bruner

From "TO A SKYLARK"

*We look before and after,
  And pine for what is not;
Our sincerest laughter
With some pain is fraught;
Our sweetest songs are those that tell of sad-
  dest thought.*

*Yet if we could scorn
  Hate and pride and fear;
If we were things born
  Not to shed a tear,
I know not how thy joy we ever should come
  near.*

—Percy Bysshe Shelley

REST

*Are you very weary? Rest a little bit.
In some quiet corner, fold your hands and sit.
Do not let the trials that have grieved you all
  the day
Haunt this quiet corner; drive them all away!
Let your heart grow empty of every thought
  unkind
That peace may hover round you, and joy
  may fill your mind.
Count up all your blessings, I'm sure they are
  not few,
That the dear Lord daily just bestows on you.
Soon you'll feel so rested, glad you stopped
  a bit,
In this quiet corner, to fold your hands and
  sit.*

THE TOWN OF DON'T YOU WORRY

*There's a town called Don't you worry
On the banks of River Smile,
Where the Cheer-up and Be-happy
Blossom sweetly all the while;
Where the Never-grumble flower
Blooms beside the fragrant Try,
And the Ne'er-give-up and Patience
Point their faces to the sky.*

*Rustic benches quite enticing
You'll find scattered here and there;
And to each a vine is clinging
Called the Frequent-earnest prayer.
Everybody there is happy
And is singing all the while,
In the town of Don't you worry
On the banks of River Smile.*

TEARS

*When I consider Life and its few years—
A wisp of fog betwixt us and the sun;
A call to battle, and the battle done
Ere the last echo dies within our ears;
A rose choked in the grass; an hour of fears;
The gusts that past a darkening shore do beat;
The burst of music down an unlistening
  street,—
I wonder at the idleness of tears.*

*Ye old, old dead, and ye of yesternight,
Chieftains, and bards, and keepers of the
  sheep,
By every cup of sorrow that you had,
Loose me from tears, and make me see aright
How each hath back what once he stayed to
  weep:
Homer his sight, David his little lad!*

—Lizette Woodworth Reese

*When some great sorrow, like a mighty river,
  Flows through your life with peace-
    destroying power,
And dearest things are swept from sight
  forever,
  Say to your heart each trying hour:
    "This, too, shall pass away."*

—Lanta Wilson Smith

THE LAND OF BEGINNING AGAIN

I wish that there were some wonderful place
  Called the Land of Beginning Again,
Where all our mistakes and all our heartaches
  And all of our poor selfish grief
Could be dropped like a shabby old coat at
    the door,
  And never be put on again.

I wish we could come on it all unaware,
  Like the hunter who finds a lost trail;
And I wish that the one whom our blindness
    had done
  The greatest injustice of all
Could be at the gates like an old friend that
    waits
  For the comrade he's gladdest to hail.
We would find all the things we intended
    to do
  But forgot, and remembered too late,
Little praises unspoken, little promises
    broken,
  And all of the thousand and one
Little duties neglected that might have
    perfected
  The day for one less fortunate.

It wouldn't be possible not to be kind
  In the Land of Beginning Again;
And the ones we misjudged and the ones
    whom we grudged
  Their moments of victory here
Would find in the grasp of our loving
    handclasp
  More than penitent lips could explain.

For what had been hardest we'd know had
    been best,
  And what had seemed loss would be gain;
For there isn't a sting that will not take wing
  When we've faced it and laughed it away;
And I think that the laughter is most what
    we're after
  In the Land of Beginning Again.
So I wish that there were some wonderful
    place
  Call the Land of Beginning Again,
Where all our mistakes and all our heartaches
  And all of our poor selfish grief
Could be dropped like a shabby old coat at
    the door,
  And never be put on again. —LOUISA FLETCHER

THE HOUSE OF CHRISTMAS

There fared a mother driven forth
Out of an inn to roam;
In the place where she was homeless
All men are at home.
The crazy stable close at hand,
With shaking timber and shifting sand,
Grew a stronger thing to abide and stand
Than the square stones of Rome.

For men are homesick in their homes,
And strangers under the sun,
And they lay their heads in a foreign land
Whenever the day is done.
Here we have battle and blazing eyes,
And chance and honour and high surprise,
But our homes are under miraculous skies
Where the yule tale was begun.

A Child in a foul stable,
Where the beasts feed and foam,
Only where He was homeless
Are you and I at home;
We have hands that fashion and heads that
    know,
But our hearts we lost—how long ago!—
In a place no chart nor ship can show
Under the sky's dome.

This world is wild as an old wives' tale,
And strange the plain things are.
The earth is enough and the air is enough
For our wonder and our war;
But our rest is as far as the fire-drake swings
And our peace is put in impossible things
Where clashed and thundered unthinkable
    wings
Round an incredible star.

To an open house in the evening
Home shall men come,
To an older place than Eden
And a taller town than Rome.
To the end of the way of the wandering star,
To the things that cannot be and that are,
To the place where God was homeless
And all men are at home.

—GILBERT K. CHESTERTON

Contentment

Banish the future; live only for the hour and its allotted work. Think not of the amount to be accomplished, the difficulties to be overcome, but set earnestly at the little task at your elbow, letting that be sufficient for the day; for surely our plain duty is "not to see what lies dimly at a distance, but to do what lies clearly at hand."

—William Osler

MY MIND TO ME A KINGDOM IS

My mind to me a kingdom is;
  Such present joys therein I find,
That it excels all other bliss
  That earth affords or grows by kind;
Though much I want which most would have,
Yet still my mind forbids to crave.

I see how plenty surfeits oft,
  And hasty climbers soon do fall;
I see that those which are aloft
  Mishap doth threaten most of all,
They get with toil, they keep with fear;
Such cares my mind could never bear.

Content to live, this is my stay;
  I seek no more than may suffice;
I press to bear no haughty sway;
  Look, what I lack my mind supplies:
Lo, thus I triumph like a king,
Content with that my mind doth bring.

Some have too much, yet still do crave;
  I little have, and seek no more:
They are but poor, though much they have,
  And I am rich with little store:
They poor, I rich; they beg, I give;
They lack, I leave; they pine, I live.

I laugh not at another's loss;
  I grudge not at another's gain;
No worldly wave my mind can toss;
  My state at one doth still remain:
I fear no foe, nor fawn on friend;
I loathe not life, nor dread my end.

My wealth is health and perfect ease;
  My conscience clear my chief defence;
I never seek by bribes to please,
  Nor by desert to give offence.
Thus do I live, thus will I die;
Would all did so as well as I!

—EDWARD DYER

THE DAFFODILS

I wandered lonely as a cloud
That floats on high o'er vales and hills,
When all at once I saw a crowd,
A host, of golden daffodils;
Beside the lake, beneath the trees,
Fluttering and dancing in the breeze.

Continuous as the stars that shine
And twinkle in the milky way,
They stretched in never-ending line
Along the margin of a bay:
Ten thousand saw I at a glance,
Tossing their heads in sprightly dance.

The waves beside them danced; but they
Out-did the sparkling waves in glee:
A poet could not but be gay,
In such a jocund company:
I gazed—and gazed—but little thought
What wealth the show to me had brought.

For oft, when on my couch I lie
In vacant or in pensive mood,
They flash upon that inward eye
Which is the bliss of solitude;
And then my heart with pleasure fills,
And dances with the daffodils.

—WILLIAM WORDSWORTH

Blessed is the man who, seeing his own face as in a mirror and haunted with a divine discontent at the manner of man he is, goes on to perfection.

From "LOVE'S LANTERN"

Because the way was steep and long,
And through a dark and dreary land,
God set upon her lips a song
And placed a lantern in her hand.

—JOYCE KILMER

The day is always his who works in it with serenity and great aims.

—Ralph Waldo Emerson

RED GERANIUMS

Life did not bring me silken gowns,
Nor jewels for my hair,
Nor signs of gabled foreign towns
In distant countries fair,
But I can glimpse, beyond my pane, a green
⠀⠀and friendly hill,
And red geraniums aflame upon my window
⠀⠀sill.

The brambled cares of everyday,
The tiny humdrum things,
May bind my feet when they would stray,
But still my heart has wings
While red geraniums are bloomed against my
⠀⠀window glass,
And low above my green-sweet hill the
⠀⠀gypsy wind-clouds pass.

And if my dreamings ne'er come true,
The brightest and the best,
But leave me lone my journey through,
I'll set my heart at rest,
And thank God for home-sweet things, a
⠀⠀green and friendly hill,
And red geraniums aflame upon my window
⠀⠀sill.

—Martha Haskell Clark

TODAY

Every day is a gift I receive from Heaven. Let me enjoy today that which it bestows on me. It belongs not more to the young than to the old, and tomorrow belongs to no one.

—Mancroix

Peace I leave with you, my peace I give unto you: not as the world giveth, give I unto you. Let not your heart be troubled, neither let it be afraid.

—John 14:27

INSIGHT

Often when it seemed I found
Goodness here, there, all around,
I saw, on closer scrutiny,
The goodness came from inside me.

Why did the whole world seem to smile?
Because I laughed with it awhile.
Why was all earth so bright with sun?
Because my light heart gave it one.

What made the future seem so bright,
The past seem dear, the future right?
What was it set the day apart?
The peace of God within my heart.
Since then, when life looks dark and grim,
My assets small, my prospects dim,
I push dark thoughts back on the shelf
And seek for heaven in myself.

The lack of wealth is easily repaired; but the poverty of the soul is irreparable.

—Montaigne

It is not growing like a tree
⠀⠀In bulk, doth make man better be;
Or standing long an oak, three hundred year,
To fall a log at last, dry, bald, and sear;
⠀⠀A lily of a day
⠀⠀Is fairer far, in May,
⠀⠀Although it fall and die that night,
⠀⠀It was a plant and flower of Light.
In small portions we just beauties see;
And in short measures life may perfect be.

—Ben Jonson

I RESOLVE

To strip the soul of all pretense,
To hold each day in reverence,
To keep the head and heart apace,
To make this world a worth-while place,
To share my bread with those in need,
To tolerate a neighbor's creed,
To keep a stride without a strut,
To make a home in manse or hut,
To have the grit to grin at loss,
To master life and be its boss!

Happiness itself is sufficient excuse. Beautiful things are right and true; so beautiful actions are those pleasing to the gods. Wise men have an inward sense of what is beautiful, and the highest wisdom is to trust this intuition and be guided by it. The answer to the last appeal of what is right lies within a man's own breast. Trust thyself.

—ARISTOTLE

ASPIRATION

Let me but live my life from year to year,
  With forward face and unreluctant soul;
  Not hurrying to, nor turning from, the
    goal;
Not mourning for the things that disappear
In the dim past, nor holding back in fear
  From what the future veils; but with a
    whole
  And happy heart, that pays its toll
To Youth and Age, and travels on with cheer.

So let the way wind up the hill or down,
  O'er rough or smooth, the journey will
    be joy:
  Still seeking what I sought when but a boy,
New friendship, high adventure, and a
    crown,
  My heart will keep the courage of the
    quest,
  And hope the road's last turn will be the
    best.

—HENRY VAN DYKE

If wrinkles must be written upon our brows, let them not be written upon the heart. The spirit should not grow old.

—JAMES A. GARFIELD

Drop Thy still dews of quietness,
  Till all our strivings cease;
Take from our souls the strain and stress,
And let our ordered lives confess
  The beauty of Thy peace.

—JOHN GREENLEAF WHITTIER

God is in every tomorrow,
  Therefore I live for today,
Certain of finding at sunrise,
  Guidance and strength for the way;
Power for each moment of weakness,
  Hope for each moment of pain,
Comfort for every sorrow,
  Sunshine and joy after rain.

Peace was the first thing the Angels sang. Peace is the mark of the sons of God. Peace is the nurse of love. Peace is the mother of unity. Peace is the rest of blessed souls. Peace is the dwelling place for eternity.

—LEO THE GREAT

THE WINDOW CALLED TODAY

Through the window of the present
  All my life must come to me!
Freedom, happiness and friendship—
  These great beauties I shall see
Only as they near my casement;
  Then my heart must bid them stay,
For God's blessings always enter
  Through the window called today.

Care my cast a fleeting shadow
  On my precious windowpane,
But I know that sunshine gathers
  Added splendor from the rain;
So, I find that each glad morning
  Life is glorious and gay,
As it greets my eager spirit
  Through the window called today.

—LAWRENCE HAWTHORNE

CALM SOUL OF ALL THINGS

Calm Soul of all things! make it mine
To feel, amid the city's jar,
That there abides a peace of thine,
Man did not make, and cannot mar.

The will to neither strive nor cry,
The power to feel with others give.
Calm, calm me more; nor let me die
Before I have begun to live.

—MATTHEW ARNOLD

Laughter, while it lasts, slackens and unbraces the mind, weakens the faculties, and causes a kind of remissness and dissolution in all the powers of the soul; and thus far it may be looked upon as a weakness in the composition of human nature. But if we consider the frequent reliefs we receive from it, and how often it breaks the gloom which is apt to depress the mind and damp our spirits, with transient, unexpected gleams of joy, one would take care not to grow too wise for so great a pleasure of life.

—JOSEPH ADDISON

Would ye learn the road to Laughtertown,
O ye who have lost the way?
Would ye have young heart though your
*   hair be gray?*
Go learn from a little child each day.
Go serve his wants and play his play,
And catch the lilt of his laughter gay,
And follow his dancing feet as they stray;
For he knows the road to Laughtertown,
O ye who have lost the way!

—KATHERINE D. BLAKE

May the outward and the inward man be as one.

—SOCRATES

PEACE

With eager heart and will on fire,
* I sought to win my great desire.*
"Peace shall be mine," I said. But life
* Grew bitter in the endless strife.*

My soul was weary, and my pride
* Was wounded deep. To heaven I cried:*
"God give me peace or I must die!"
* The dumb stars glittered no reply.*

Broken at last, I bowed my head
* Forgetting all myself and said,*
"Whatever comes, his will be done."
* And in that moment peace was won.*

—HENRY VAN DYKE

Our language has wisely sensed the two sides of man's being alone. It has created the word "loneliness" to express the pain of being alone. And it has created the word "solitude" to express the glory of being alone.

—PAUL TILLICH

INWARD PEACE

Till poverty knocked at her door
* She never knew how bare*
The uneventful days of those
* Who have but want and care.*

Till sorrow lingered at her hearth,
* She never knew the night*
Through which troubled souls might fare
* To gain the morning light.*

Till suffering had sought her house,
* She never knew what dread*
Many wrestle with, or what grim fears
* Of agony are bred.*

And yet till those unbidden guests
* Had taught her to possess*
A clearer sight, she never knew
* The height of happiness.*

—CHARLOTTE BECKER

Thou wilt keep him in perfect peace, whose mind is stayed on the . . .

—ISAIAH 26:3

WHAT MAN MAY CHOOSE

No man can choose what coming hours may
* bring*
To him of need, of joy, of suffering;
But what his soul shall bring unto each hour
To meet its challenge—this is in his power.

—PRISCILLA LEONARD

Contentment consists not in great wealth, but in few wants.

—EPICTETUS

KEEP GOING

There's no skill in easy sailing
When the skies are clear and blue.
There's no joy in merely doing
Things that anyone can do.
But there is great satisfaction,
That is mighty sweet to take
When you reach a destination
That you said you couldn't make.

It is easy in the world to live after the world's opinions; it is easy in solitude to live after our own; but the **Great Man** is he who in the midst of the crowd keeps with perfect sweetness the independence of solitude.

—RALPH WALDO EMERSON

MY PURPOSE

To awaken each morning with a smile
*   brightening my face;*
To greet the day with reverence for the
*   opportunities it contains;*
To approach my work with a clean mind;
To hold ever before me, even in the doing
*   of little things, the Ultimate Purpose toward*
*   which I am working;*
To meet men and women with laughter on
*   my lips and love in my heart;*
To be gentle, kind, and courteous through all
*   the hours;*
To approach the night with weariness that
*   ever woos sleep, and the joy that comes*
*   from work well done—*
This is how I desire to waste wisely my days.

—THOMAS DEKKER

My life is but a working-day,
*   Whose tasks are set aright:*
A while to work, a while to pray,
*   And then a quiet night.*
And then, please God, a quiet night
Where Saints and Angels walk in white.
One dreamless sleep from work and sorrow,
But reawakening on the morrow.

—CHRISTINA G. ROSSETTI

PLEASANT THOUGHTS

I want to remember lovely things:
A baby's smile, a butterfly's wings;
An evening star, the blue blue sky;
A crystal snowflake, clouds so high;
Sweet notes of birds, a sunset glow;
Refreshing showers, soft winds that blow;
To keep the storehouse of my mind
Full of thoughts that make me kind.
Lovely thoughts to live with me;
Making my life a rhapsody.
When youth's gay pleasures have passed by,
Sweet, happy thoughts must never die.

—LULA ERICK

Quiet minds can not be perplexed or frightened, but go on in fortune or misfortune at their own private pace, like a clock during a thunderstorm.

—ROBERT LOUIS STEVENSON

A WISH

Mine be a cot beside the hill;
*   A bee-hive's hum shall soothe my ear;*
A willowy brook that turns a mill
*   With many a fall shall linger near.*

The swallow, oft, beneath my thatch
*   Shall twitter from her clay-built nest;*
Oft shall the pilgrim lift the latch
*   And share my meal, a welcome guest.*

Around my ivied porch shall spring
*   Each fragrant flower that drinks the dew;*
And Lucy, at her wheel, shall sing
*   In russet gown and apron blue.*

The village church among the trees,
*   When first our marriage vows were given,*
With merry peals shall swell the breeze,
*   And point with taper spire to heaven.*

—SAMUEL ROGERS

The great essentials of life are something to do, something to love, something to hope for.

—THOMAS CHALMERS

Man is dear to man: the poorest poor
Long for some moments in a weary life
When they can know and feel that they have
 been
Themselves the fathers and the givers-out
Of some small blessings; have been kind to
 such
As need kindness, for the single cause
That we have all of us one common heart.

     —WILLIAM WORDSWORTH

The happiness of a man in this life does not consist in the absence but in the mastery of his passions.

     —ALFRED LORD TENNYSON

LOOKING FORWARD

I've shut the door on Yesterday,
 Its sorrows and mistakes;
I've locked within its gloomy walls
 Past failures and heartaches.

And now I throw the key away
 To seek another room,
And furnish it with hope and smiles,
 And every springtime bloom.

No thought shall enter this abode
 That has a hint of pain,
And every malice and distrust
 Shall never therein reign.

I've shut the door on Yesterday
 And thrown my key away—
Tomorrow holds no doubt for me,
 Since I have found Today.

TODAY

Build a little fence of trust
 Around today;
Fill each space with loving work
 And therein stay;
Look not through the sheltering bars
 Upon tomorrow,
God will help thee bear what comes,
 Of joy or sorrow.

     —MARY FRANCES BUTTS

GOSHEN!

"How can you live in Goshen?"
Said a friend from afar,
"This wretched country town
Where folks talk little things all year,
And plant their cabbage by the moon!"
Said I:
"I do not live in Goshen,—
I eat here, sleep here, work here;
I live in Greece,
Where Plato taught,
And Phidias carved,
And Epictetus wrote.
I dwell in Italy,
Where Michelangelo wrought
In color, form and mass;
Where Cicero penned immortal lines,
And Dante sang undying songs.
Think not my life is small
Because you see a puny place;
I have my books; I have my dreams;
A thousand souls have left for me
Enchantment that transcends
Both time and place.
And so I live in Paradise,
Not here."

     —EDGAR FRANK

Happiness grows at our own firesides, and is not to be picked in stranger's gardens.

HYACINTHS TO FEED THY SOUL

If of thy mortal goods thou art bereft,
And from thy slender store two loaves alone
 to thee are left,
Sell one, and with the dole
Buy hyacinths to feed thy soul.

     —GULISTAN OF MOSLIH EDDIN SAADI

Teach me to feel another's woe,
To hide the fault I see;
That mercy I to others show,
That mercy show to me.

     —ALEXANDER POPE

O, what a glory doth this world put on
For him who, with a fervent heart goes forth
Under the bright and gleaming sky, and looks
On duties well performed, and days well
    spent!
For him the wind, ay, and the yellow leaves
Shall have a voice, and give him eloquent
    teachings.
He shall so hear the solemn hymn, that Death
Has lifted up for all, that he shall go
To his long resting place without a tear.

—HENRY WADSWORTH LONGFELLOW

BARTER

Life has loveliness to sell,
    All beautiful and splendid things,
Blue waves whitened on a cliff,
    Soaring fire that sways and sings,
And children's faces looking up
Holding wonder like a cup.

Life has loveliness to sell,
    Music like a curve of gold,
Scent of pine trees in the rain,
    Eyes that love you, arms that hold,
And for your spirit's still delight,
Holy thoughts that star the night.

Spend all you have for loveliness,
    Buy it and never count the cost;
For one white singing hour of peace
Count many a year of strife well lost,
And for a breath of ectasy
Give all you have been, or could be.

—SARA TEASDALE

There is a pleasure in the pathless woods,
There is a rapture on the lonely shore,
There is society where none intrudes,
By the deep Sea, and music in its roar:
I love not Man the less, but Nature more,
From these our interviews, in which I steal
From all I may be, or have been before,
To mingle with the Universe, and feel
What I can ne'er express, yet cannot all
    conceal.

—LORD BYRON

THE SWEETEST LIVES

The sweetest lives are those to duty wed,
    Whose deeds, both great and small,
Are close-knit strands of unbroken thread
    Where love ennobles all.
The world may sound no trumpets, ring no
    bells;
The book of life the shining record tells.

The love shall chant its own beatitudes
After its own life working. A child's kiss
Set on thy sighing lips shall make thee glad;
A sick man helped by thee shall make thee
    strong;
Thou shalt be served thyself by every sense
Of service which thou renderest.

—ELIZABETH BARRETT BROWNING

A happy life must sure be his—
    The lord, not slave of things—
Who values life by what it is,
    And not by what it brings.

SEEING

They took away what should have been my
    eyes,
(But I remembered Milton's Paradise)
They took away what should have been my
    ears,
(Beethoven came and wiped away my tears)
They took away what should have been my
    tongue,
(But I had talked with God when I was
    young)
He would not let them take away my soul,
Possessing that, I still possess the whole.

—HELEN KELLER

'Mid all the traffic of the ways—
Turmoils without, within—
Make in my heart a quiet place,
And come and dwell there-in:

A little place of mystic grace,
Of self and sin swept bare,
Where I may look upon Thy face,
And talk with Thee in prayer.

Courage

Courage is armor
A blind man wears;
The calloused scar
Of outlived despairs;
Courage is Fear
That has said its prayers.

—Karle Wilson Baker

THE END OF THE ROPE

When you've lost every vestige of hope
And you think you are beaten and done,
When you've come to the end of your rope,
Tie a knot in the end and hang on.

Have courage; for here is the dope;
When you stand with your back to the wall,
Though you've come to the end of your rope
Tie a knot in the end and hang on.

Don't admit that life's getting your goat
When your friends seem to all disappear,
When you've come to the end of your rope,
Tie a knot in the end and hang on.

—Margaret Nickerson Martin

STEADFAST HEART

I've dreamed many dreams that never came
*   true*
I've seen them vanish at dawn,
But I've realized enough of my dreams,
*   Thank God,*
To make me want to dream on.

I've prayed many prayers when no answer
*   came,*
Though I waited patient and long,
But answers have come to enough of my
*   prayers*
To make me keep praying on.

I've trusted many a friend that failed,
And left me to weep alone,
But I've found enough of my friends true
*   blue,*
To make me keep trusting on.

I've sown many seed that fell by the way
For the birds to feed upon,
But I've held enough golden sheaves in my
*   hands*
To make me keep sowing on.

I've drained the cup of disappointment and
*   pain*
And gone many ways without song,
But I've sipped enough nectar from the roses
*   of life*
To make me want to live on.

Tisn't life that matters! It's the courage you bring to it.

FORTITUDE

Laugh, and the world laughs with you;
*   Weep, and you weep alone.*
For the sad old earth must borrow its mirth,
*   But has trouble enough of its own.*
Sing, and the hills will answer;
*   Sigh, it is lost on the air.*
The echoes bound to a joyful sound,
*   But shrink from voicing care.*

Rejoice, and men will seek you;
*   Grieve, and they turn and go.*
They want full measure of all your pleasure,
*   But they do not need your woe.*
Be glad, and your friends are many;
*   Be sad, and you lose them all.*
There are none to decline your nectared
*   wine,*
*   But alone you must drink life's gall.*

Feast, and your halls are crowded;
*   Fast, and the world goes by.*
Succeed and give, and it helps you live,
*   But no man can help you die.*
There is room in the halls of pleasure
*   For a long and lordly train,*
But one by one we must all file on
*   Through the narrow aisles of pain.*

—Ella Wheeler Wilcox

Man am I grown, a man's work must I do,
Follow the deer? follow the Christ, the King,
Live pure, speak true, right wrong, follow the
King—
Else, wherefore born?

—ALFRED LORD TENNYSON

One man with courage makes a majority.

—ANDREW JACKSON

Cowards die many times before their deaths; The valiant never taste of death but once.

—WILLIAM SHAKESPEARE

True courage is the result of reasoning. A brave mind is always impregnable. Resolution lies more in the head than in the veins; and a just sense of honor and of infamy, of duty and of religion, will carry us farther than all the force of mechanism.

—JEREMY COLLIER

Sound, sound the clarion, fill the fife!
*   To all the sensual world proclaim,*
One crowded hour of glorious strife
*   Is worth an age without a name.*

—SIR WALTER SCOTT

When you get into a tight place and everything goes against you, till it seems as though you could not hold on a minute longer, never give up then, for that is just the place and time that the tide will turn.

—HARRIET BEECHER STOWE

Every morning lean thine arms awhile
Upon the window-sill of heaven
And gaze upon thy Lord,
Then, with the vision in thy heart,
Turn strong to meet thy day.

DOUBTS ARE TRAITORS

A great deal of talent is lost in the world for want of a little courage. Every day sends to their graves obscure men whom timidity prevented from making a first effort; who, if they could have been induced to begin, would in all probability have gone great lengths in the career of fame. The fact is, that to do anything in the world worth doing, we must not stand back shivering and thinking of the cold and danger, but jump in and scramble through as well as we can. It will not do to be perpetually calculating risks and adjusting nice chances; it did very well before the Flood, when a man would consult his friends upon an intended publication for a hundred and fifty years, and live to see his success afterwards; but at present, a man waits, and doubts, and consults his brother, and his particular friends, till one day he finds he is sixty years old and that he has lost so much time in consulting cousins and friends that he has no more time to follow their advice.

—SIDNEY SMITH

COURAGE

Courage isn't a brilliant dash,
A daring deed in a moment's flash;
It isn't an instantaneous thing
Born of despair with a sudden spring
It isn't a creature of flickered hope
Or the final tug at a slipping rope;
But it's something deep in the soul of man
That is working always to serve some plan.
Courage isn't the last resort
In the work of life or the game of sport;
It isn't a thing that a man can call
At some future time when he's apt to fall;
If he hasn't it now, he will have it not
When the strain is great and the pace is hot.
For who would strive for a distant goal
Must always have courage within his soul.
Courage isn't a dazzling light
That flashes and passes away from sight;
It's a slow, unwavering, ingrained trait
With the patience to work and the strength
*   to wait.*

IT TAKES COURAGE

To stand for the right at all times.

To say "No!" squarely to evil when all those around you are saying "Yes."

To speak the truth when, by a little "twisting," you can gain some advantage or escape punishment.

To refuse to do a thing which you think is wrong, when it is customary and is done by many others.

To face slander and lies, and to carry yourself with cheerfulness, grace, and dignity for a long while before the lie can be corrected.

To obey your parents when other boys and girls are trying to say it's all right to "pull one over on them."

These things take courage—but boys and girls who use this courage grow up to be better men and women.

Hast thou named all the birds without a gun?
Loved the wood-rose, and left it on its stalk?
At rich men's tables eaten bread and pulse?
Unarmed, faced danger with a heart of trust?
And loved so well a high behavior,
In man or maid, that thou from speech
*   refrained*
Nobility more nobly to repay?
O, be my friend, and teach me to be thine!

—Ralph Waldo Emerson

It's part of a man when his skies are blue,
It's part of him when he has work to do.
The brave man never is freed of it.
He has it when there is no need of it.

Courage was never designed for show;
It isn't a thing that can come and go;
It's written in victory and defeat
And every trial a man may meet.
It's part of his hours, his days and his years,
Back of his smiles and behind his tears.
Courage is more than a daring deed:
'Tis the breath of life and a strong man's
*   creed.*

—Edgar A. Guest

The bravest thing—the courage we desire and prize—is not the courage to die decently, but to live manfully.

—Thomas Carlyle

Of the millions of words written about Winston Churchill, Lady Diana Cooper's are among the most revealing. She wrote, "When I said that the best thing he had done was to give the people courage," he answered, "I never gave them courage; I was able to focus theirs."

We shall steer safely through every storm,
*   so long as our heart is right,*
Our intention fervent, our courage steadfast,
*   and our trust fixed on God.*

—St. Francis de Sales

DAUNTLESS

I will not think of treasures lost,
*   Of time that's past and gone,*
As long as faith is in my heart
*   I shall go bravely on.*
And other treasures I shall find
*   To keep me and sustain;*
As long as faith is in my heart
*   Life can not be in vain.*

And though I know that I shall meet
*   Dark tempests on my way,*
As long as hope is in my heart
*   I see a shining ray; .*
And flowers shall bloom along my path
*   And birds to me shall sing;*
As long as hope is in my heart
*   My spirit high shall wing.*

And though the sweetest dreams of youth
*   In broken fragments lie,*
As long as love is in my heart
*   Those dreams can never die;*
And in those broken fragments I
*   A deeper meaning see,*
As long as love is in my heart
*   Youth will keep step with me.*

—Mary Block

Whether you be man or woman you will never do anything in this world without courage. It is the greatest quality of the mind next to honor.

—JAMES L. ALLEN

COURAGE

This is courage: to remain
Brave and patient under pain;
Cool and calm and firm to stay
In the presence of dismay;
Not to flinch when foes attack,
Even though you're beaten back;
Still to cling to what is right,
When the wrong possesses might.

This is courage: to be true
To the best men see in you;
To remember, tempest-tossed,
Not to whimper, "All is lost!"
But to battle to the end
While you still have strength to spend;
Not to cry that hope is gone
While you've life to carry on.

This is courage: to endure
Hurt and loss you cannot cure;
Patiently and undismayed,
Facing life still unafraid;
Glad to live and glad to take
Bravely for your children's sake,
Burdens they would have to bear
If you fled and ceased to care.

—EDGAR A. GUEST

He that loses wealth loses much, But he that loses courage loses all.

—CERVANTES

God give me hills to climb,
And strength for the climbing.

—ARTHUR GUITERMAN

All one's life is music, if one touched the notes rightly and in tune.

—JOHN RUSKIN

UPSTREAM

The easy roads are crowded, and
The level roads are jammed.
The pleasant little rivers
With the drifting folks are crammed.
But off yonder where it's rocky,
Where you get the better view,
You will find the ranks are thinning,
And the travelers are few.

Where the going's smooth and pleasant
You will always find the throng,
For the many—more's the pity—
Seem to like to drift along.
But the steeps that call for courage
And the task that's hard to do
In the end results in glory
For the never wavering few!

THE OLD STOIC

Riches I hold in light esteem,
And Love I laugh to scorn;
And lust of fame was but a dream
That vanished with the morn:

And if I pray, the only prayer
That moves my lips for me
Is, "Leave the heart that now I bear,
And give me liberty!"

Yes, as my swift days near their goal,
'Tis all that I implore;
Through life and death a chainless soul,
With courage to endure.

—EMILY BRONTË

DARE TO DO RIGHT

Dare to do right! Dare to be true!
You have a work that no other can do;
Do it so bravely, so kindly, so well,
Angels will hasten the story to tell.

Dare to do right! Dare to be true!
Other men's failures can never save you;
Stand by your conscience, your honor, your faith;
Stand like a hero, and battle till death.

—GEORGE L. TAYLOR

God, give me sympathy and sense,
　And help me keep my courage high;
God, give me calm and confidence,
　And—please—a twinkle in my eye.
　　Amen.

　　　　　　　　　—Margaret Bailey

SERMONS WE SEE

I'd rather see a sermon than hear one any
　day;
I'd rather one should walk with me than
　merely tell the way.
The eye's a better pupil and more willing
　than the ear,
Fine counsel is confusing, but example's al-
　ways clear;
And the best of all the preachers are the men
　who live their creeds,
For to see good put in action is what every-
　body needs.

I soon can learn to do it if you'll let me see it
　done;
I can watch your hands in action, but your
　tongue too fast may run.
And the lecture you deliver may be very wise
　and true,
But I'd rather get my lessons by observing
　what you do;
For I might misunderstand you and the high
　advice you give,
But there's no misunderstanding how you act
　and how you live.

When I see a deed of kindness, I am eager to
　be kind.
When a weaker brother stumbles and a strong
　man stays behind
Just to see if he can help him, then the wish
　grows strong in me
To become as big and thoughtful as I know
　that friend to be.
And all travelers can witness that the best of
　guides to-day
Is not the one who tells them, but the one who
　shows the way.

One good man teaches many, men believe
　what they behold;

One deed of kindness noticed is worth forty
　that are told.
Who stands with men of honor learns to hold
　his honor dear,
For right living speaks a language which to
　every one is clear.
Though an able speaker charms me with his
　eloquence, I say,
I'd rather see a sermon than to hear one, any
　day.

　　　　　　　　　—Edgar A. Guest

WILL

There is no chance, no destiny, no fate,
Can circumvent or hinder or control
The firm resolve of a determined soul.
Gifts count for nothing; will alone is great;
All things give way before it, soon or late.
What obstacle can stay the mighty force
Of the sea-seeking river in its course,
Or cause the ascending orb of day to wait?
Each wellborn soul must win what it
　deserves:
Let the fool prate of luck. The fortunate
Is he whose earnest purpose never swerves,
Whose slightest action or inaction serves
The one great aim. Why, even Death stands
　still,
And waits an hour sometimes for such a
　will.

　　　　　　　　　—Ella Wheeler Wilcox

Happy the man, and happy he alone,
He who can call to-day his own;
He who, secure within, can say,
"To-morrow, do thy worst, for I have liv'd
　to-day.
Be fair or foul, or rain or shine,
The joys I have possessed, in spite of fate,
　are mine.
Not heaven itself upon the past has power;
But what has been, has been, and I have had
　my hour."

　　　　　　　　　—John Dryden

Days

A flower unblown; a book unread;
A tree with fruit unharvested;
A path untrod; a house whose rooms
Lack yet the heart's divine perfumes;
A landscape whose wide border lies
In silent shade beneath the skies;
A wondrous fountain yet unsealed;
A casket with its gifts concealed—
This is the Year that for you waits
Beyond tomorrow's mystic gates.

—HORATIO NELSON POWERS

EASTER MORNING

Most glorious Lord of life, that on this day
Didst make thy triumph over death and sin,
And, having harrowed hell, didst bring away
Captivity thence captive, us to win;
This joyous day, dear Lord, with joy begin,
And grant that we, for whom thou didst die,
Being with thy dear blood clean washed from
* sin,*
May live forever in felicity:
And that thy love we weighing worthily,
May likewise love thee for the same again:
And for thy sake, that all like dear didst buy,
With love may one another entertain.
So let us love, dear love, like as we ought;
Love is the lesson which the Lord us taught.

—EDMUND SPENSER

A WONDERFUL MOTHER

God made a wonderful mother,
A mother who never grows old;
He made her smile of the sunshine,
And He molded her heart of pure gold;
In her eyes He placed bright shining stars,
In her cheeks, fair roses you see;
God made a wonderful mother,
And He gave that dear mother to me.

—PAT O'REILLY

And I said to the man who stood at the gate
* of the year:*
Give me a light, that I may tread safely into
* the unknown!"*
And he replied:
"Go out into the darkness and put your hand
* into the Hand of God.*
That shall be to you better than light and
* safer than a known way."*

So I went forth, and finding the Hand of
* God, trod gladly into the night.*
And He led me toward the hills and the
* breaking of day . . .*

—M. LOUISE HASKINS

LIKE MOTHER, LIKE SON

Do you know that your soul is of my soul
* such a part,*
That you seem to be fibre and core of my
* heart?*
None other can pain me as you, dear, can do,
None other can please me or praise me as you.

Remember the world will be quick with its
* blame*
If shadow or strain ever darken your name.
"Like mother, like son" is a saying so true
The world will judge largely the "mother"
* by you.*

Be yours then the task, if task it shall be,
To force the proud world to do homage to
* me.*
Be sure it will say, when its verdict you've
* won,*
"She reaped as she sowed. Lo! this is her son."

—MARGARET JOHNSTON GRAFFLIN

TIME

So the sands of Time that slowly flow
* From out my hour glass*
Will all too soon have ebbed away,
* My life will then be past.*
So I must make the most of time
* And drift not with the tide,*
For killing time's not murder,
* It's more like suicide.*

It may make a difference to all eternity whether we do right or wrong today.

—JAMES FREEMAN CLARKE

NOT IN VAIN

Hope we not in this life only.
  Christ Himself has made it plain
None who sleep in Him shall perish
  And our faith is not in vain.
Not in vain our glad hosannas;
  Since we follow where He led,
Not in vain our Easter Anthem:
  "Christ has risen from the dead."

THOUGHT FOR EASTER

O happy world to-day if we could know
The message of that morning long ago!
There is no dark despair that cannot be
Evicted from the heart's Gethsemane;
For faith is always more than unbelief,
And vibrant courage triumphs over grief.

—MARY E. McCULLOUGH

SOMEBODY'S MOTHER

The woman was old, and ragged, and gray.
And bent with the chill of the winter's day.
The street was wet with the recent snow,
And the woman's feet were aged and slow.

She stood at the crossing and waited long
Alone, uncared for, amid the throng
Of human beings who passed her by,
Nor heeded the glance of her anxious eye.

Down the street with laughter and shout,
Glad in the freedom of "school let out,"
Came the boys like a flock of sheep,
Hailing the snow piled white and deep.

Past the woman so old and gray,
Hastened the children on their way,
Nor offered a helping hand to her,
So meek, so timid, afraid to stir,
Lest the carriage wheels or the horses' feet
Should crowd her down in the slippery street.

At last came one of the merry troop,
The gayest laddie of all the group;
He paused beside her and whispered low,
"I'll help you across if you wish to go."

Her aged hand on his strong young arm
She placed, and so, without hurt or harm,

He guided her trembling feet along,
Proud that his own were firm and strong.

Then back again to his friends he went,
His young heart happy and well content.
"She's somebody's mother, boys, you know,
For all she's aged and poor and slow;

"And I hope some fellow will lend a hand
To help my mother, you understand,
If ever she's poor, and old, and gray,
When her own dear boy is far away."

And "somebody's mother" bowed low her
    head,
In her home that night, and the prayer she
    said,
Was, "God be kind to the noble boy,
Who is somebody's son and pride and joy."

A NEW YEAR PRAYER

As long as mortals have the nerve
To pray for things they don't deserve

As long as conscience has a stain,
The prayers of men will be in vain.

So, humbly, Lord, we ask of Thee
That princely gift, Sincerity,

That we may use it through life's span
To build on earth a better man;

And should we crave for gifts more royal,
Please make us, God, a bit more loyal,

That we may give to those we serve
A measure full as they deserve.

And make us rich with eager zest
To give our work our very best.

To know the wheat, reject the chaff—
To have the strength to stand the gaff.

O Lord, in mercy intervene
To keep our hearts both young and clean,

The will to give a man a lift—
Make this, O Lord, Thy New Year Gift.

What can I do? I can give myself to life
when other men refuse themselves to life.

—HORACE TRAUBEL

They talk about a woman's sphere,
　　As though it had a limit;
There's not a place in earth or heaven,
There's not a task to mankind given,
There's not a blessing or a woe,
There's not a whisper, Yes or No,
There's not a life, or death, or birth,
That has a feather's weight of worth,
　　Without a woman in it.

MOTHER'S WRINKLED HANDS

Such beautiful, beautiful hands!
Though heart were weary and sad
Those patient hands kept toiling on
That her children might be glad.
I almost weep when looking back
To childhood's distant day!
I think how these hands rested not
When mine were at their play.

Mother in gladness, Mother in sorrow,
Mother today, and Mother tomorrow,
With arms ever open to fold and caress you
O Mother of Mine, may God keep you and
　　bless you.

　　　　　　　　　—W. DAYTON WEDGEFARTH

PRAYER FOR VETERANS' DAY

Stay with me, God. The night is dark,
The night is cold: my little spark
Of courage dies. The night is long;
Be with me, God, and make me strong....
I knew that death is but a door.
I knew what we were fighting for:
Peace for the kids, our brothers freed,
A kinder world, a cleaner breed.

I'm but the son my mother bore,
A simple man, and nothing more.
But—God of strength and gentleness,
Be pleased to make me nothing less....
Help me, O God, when Death is near
To mock the haggard face of fear,
That when I fall—if fall I must—
My soul may triumph in the Dust.

　　　　　　　　　　　　—GERALD KERSH

God bless all those who labor with their
　　hands,
Who tend the loom and cultivate the sod;
Merchants and miners, cobblers, cooks, and
　　all
Whose hands, by proxy, are the hands of God.
And bless all those who labor with the mind:
Who, from the wells of beauty, have drawn
　　up
Wine for man's thirst, and at the springs of
　　life
Share with their brothers cup on brimming
　　cup.

But most of all, bless those who serve with
　　love!
No matter if the task be great or small,
A gay adventure or a dull routine,
A kindness done to one or meant for all!
Head, heart, and hands—all three are
　　instruments
Of Him who made the world and found it
　　good,
And all are blest, but doubly blest is he
Who serves with love in conscious
　　brotherhood.

　　　　　　　　　　　　—R. H. GRENVILLE

There is danger of leaving God out of our Thanksgiving Day. We are making it a holiday rather than a holy day. It is a day for the public recognition of God as the giver of all good. To leave God out of Thanksgiving Day is as absurd as leaving Christ out of Christmas.

What can I give Him
Poor as I am?
If I were a shepherd,
I would give Him a lamb,
If I were a Wise Man,
I would do my part,—
But what I can I give Him,
Give my heart.

　　　　　　　　　　—CHRISTINA G. ROSSETTI

A thankful spirit is like sunshine upon the fields.

THAT NIGHT

That night when in Judean skies
The mystic star dispensed its light,
A blind man moved in his sleep—
And dreamed that he had sight.

That night when shepherds heard the song
Of hosts angelic choiring near,
A deaf man stirred in slumber's spell—
And dreamed that he could hear.

That night when in the cattle stall
Slept child and mother cheek by jowl,
A cripple turned his twisted limbs—
And dreamed that he was whole.

That night when o'er the new born babe
The tender Mary rose to lean,
A loathsome leper smiled in sleep—
And dreamed that he was clean.

That night when to the mother's breast
The little King was held secure,
A harlot slept in happy sleep
And dreamed that she was pure.

That night when in the manger lay
The sanctified who came to save
A man moved in the sleep of death—
And dreamed there was no grave.

When troubles come, go at them with songs. When griefs arise, sing them down. Lift the voice of praise against cares.

—Henry Ward Beecher

THE COMING CHILD

Welcome! all Wonders in one sight!
  Eternity shut in a span.
Summer in winter, day in night,
  Heaven in earth, and God in man.
Great little one! whose all-embracing birth
  Lifts earth to heaven, stoops heav'n to
    earth!

—Richard Crashaw

Work is the grand cure for all the maladies that ever beset mankind—honest work which you intend getting done.

—Thomas Carlyle

THE NOBLEST MEN

The noblest men that live on earth.
  Are men whose hands are brown with toil.
Who backed by no ancestral graves
  Hew down the woods and till the soil;
And win thereby a prouder name
  Than follows kings or warrior's fame.

The working men, what'er their task,
  Who carve the stone, or bear the hod,
They wear upon their honest brows
  The royal stamp and seal of God;
And worthier are their drops of sweat
  Than diamonds in a coronet.

God bless the noble working men.
  Who rear the cities of the plain!
Who dig the mines, who build the ships,
  And drive the commerce of the main!
God bless them! For their toiling hands
  Have wrought the glory of all lands.

Once more the liberal year laughs out
  O'er richer stores than gems of gold;
Once more with harvest-song and shout
  Is Nature's bloodless triumph told.

—John Greenleaf Whittier

Ingratitude is not only the basest and meanest of sins, but it is the most frequent.

—Wilton Merle Smith

God taught mankind on that first Christmas
  day
What 'twas to be a man; to give, not take;
To serve, not rule; to nourish, not devour;
To help, not crush; if need, to die, not live.

—Charles Kingsley

Remember the week day, and keep it holy too.

AT CHRISTMAS

*A man is at his finest towards the finish of
  the year;
  He is almost what he should be when the
  Christmas season's here;
Then he's thinking more of others than he's
  thought the months before,
  And the laughter of his children is a joy
  worth toiling for.
He is less a selfish creature than at any other
  time;
  When the Christmas spirit rules him he
  comes close to the sublime.*

*When it's Christmas man is bigger and is
  better in his part;
  He is keener for the service that is
  prompted by the heart.
All the petty thoughts and narrow seem to
  vanish for awhile
  And the true reward he's seeking is the
  glory of a smile.
Then for others he is toiling and somehow
  it seems to me
That at Christmas he is almost what God
  wanted him to be.*

*If I had to paint a picture of a man I
  think I'd wait
  Till he'd fought his selfish battles and
  had put aside his hate.
I'd not catch him at his labors when his
  thoughts are all of self,
  On the long days and the dreary when
  he's striving for himself.
I'd not take him when he's sneering, when
  he's scornful or depressed,
  But I'd look for him at Christmas when
  he's shining at his best.
Man is ever in a struggle and he's oft
  misunderstood;
  There are days the worst that's in him is
  the master of the good,
But at Christmas kindness rules him and he
  puts himself aside
  And his petty hates are vanquished and his
  heart is opened wide.*

*Oh, I don't know how to say it, but it seems
  to me
  That at Christmas man is almost what God
  sent him here to be.*

—EDGAR A. GUEST

THANKSGIVING

*O precious Father, as we bow
  Before Thy throne today—
We count the many blessings
  Thou hast shower'd upon our way.
The comfort of our humble homes,
  Our health and happiness,
The strength provided for each day
  To meet the strain and stress.*

*We thank Thee for Thy precious Son
  Who brought salvation free,
And for this mighty land of ours—
  A land of liberty!*

*So, Lord, help us to give Thee thanks
  For all that we hold dear—
Not only on Thanksgiving Day
  But each day of the year!*

WHAT MAKES CHRISTMAS?

*"What is Christmas?"
I asked my soul,
And this answer
Came back to me:
"It is the
Glory of heaven come down
In the hearts of humanity—
Come in the spirit and heart of a Child,
And it matters not what we share
At Christmas; it is not Christmas at all
Unless the Christ Child be there."*

HOW TROUBLESOME IS DAY

*How troublesome is day!
It calls us from our sleep away;
It bids us from our pleasant dreams awake,
It sends us forth to keep or break
Our promises to pay.*

—THOMAS LOVE PEACOCK

A GOOD THANKSGIVING

Said Old Gentleman Gay, "On a Thanks-
giving Day,
If you want a good time, then give some-
thing away."
So he sent a fat turkey to Shoemaker Price,
And the shoemaker said, "What a big bird!
How nice!
And, since such a good dinner's before me,
I ought
To give poor Widow Lee the small chicken
I bought."

"This fine chicken, O see!" said the pleased
Widow Lee,
"And the kindness that sent it, how precious
to me!
I would like to make someone as happy as I—
I'll give Washerwoman Biddy my big
pumpkin pie."

"And, O sure!" Biddy said, " 'tis the queen
of all pies!
Just to look at its yellow face gladdens my
eyes!
Now it's my turn, I think; and a sweet
ginger-cake
For the motherless Finigan children I'll bake."

"A sweet-cake all our own! 'Tis too good to
be true!"
Said the Finigan children, Rose, Denny and
Hugh;
"It smells sweet of spice, and we'll carry a
slice
To poor little lame Jake—who has nothing
that's nice."

"O, I thank you, and thank you!" said little
lame Jake:
"O what a bootiful, bootiful, bootiful cake!
And O, such a big slice! I will save all the
crumbs,
And will give 'em to each little Sparrow that
comes!"

And the sparrows, they twittered, as if they
would say,
Like Old Gentleman Gay, "On a Thanks-
giving Day,
If you want a good time, then give something
away!"

—Annie Douglas Green Robinson

It is assumed that labor is available only in connection with capital; that nobody labors unless somebody else, owning capital, somehow by the use of it, induces him to labor. This assumed, it is next considered whether it is best that capital shall hire laborers, and thus induce them to work by their own consent, or buy them and drive them to do it without their consent. Having proceeded so far, it is naturally concluded that all laborers are either hired laborers or what we call slaves.

Now, there is no such relation between capital and labor as here assumed. . . . Labor is prior to and independent of capital. Capital is only the fruit of labor, could never have existed if labor had not first existed. Labor is the superior of capital, and deserves much the higher consideration.

—Abraham Lincoln

A WEDDING HYMN

Jesus, stand beside them
On this day of days,
That in happy wedlock
They may live always.

Join their hands together,
And their hearts make one;
Guard the troth now plighted
And the life begun.

On their pleasant homestead
Let Thy radiance rest;
Making joy and sorrow
By Thy presence blest.

Gild their common duties
With a light divine,
As, in Cana, water
Thou didst change to wine.

Leave them nor forsake them;
Ever be their Friend;
Guarding, guiding, blessing
To their journey's end.

—Thomas Tiplady

SEPTEMBER

The golden-rod is yellow;
　　The corn is turning brown;
The trees in apple orchards
　　With fruit are bending down.

The gentian's bluest fringes
　　Are curling in the sun;
In dusty pods the milkweed
　　Its hidden silk has spun.

The sedges flaunt their harvest,
　　In every meadow nook;
And asters by the brook-side
　　Make asters in the brook,

From dewy lanes at morning
　　The grapes' sweet odors rise;
At noon the roads all flutter
　　With yellow butterflies.

By all these lovely tokens
　　September days are here,
With summer's best of weather,
　　And autumn's best of cheer.

But none of all this beauty
　　Which floods the earth and air
Is unto me the secret
　　Which makes September fair.

'Tis a thing which I remember;
　　To name it thrills me yet:
One day of one September
　　I never can forget.

　　　　　　—Helen Hunt Jackson

HOW OLD ARE YOU?

Age is a quality of mind.
If you have left your dreams behind,
If hope is cold,
If you no longer look ahead,
If your ambitions' fires are dead—
Then you are old.

But if from life you take the best,
And if in life you keep the jest,
If love you hold;
No matter how the years go by,
No matter how the birthdays fly—
You are not old.

　　　　　　—H. S. Fritsch

THE GOSPEL OF LABOR

But I think the king of that country comes
　　out from his tireless host
And walks in the world of the weary, as if
　　he loved it the most:
For here in the dusty confusion, with eyes
　　that are heavy and dim
He meets again the laboring men who are
　　looking and longing for Him.

He cancels the curse of Eden, and brings
　　them a blessing instead,
Blessed are they that labor for Jesus partakes
　　of their bread,
He puts His hand to their burdens, He
　　enters their homes at night:
Who does his best shall have as his guest
　　the Master of life and light.

And courage will come with His presence,
　　and patience return at His touch,
And manifold sins be forgiven to those who
　　love Him much;
And the cries of envy and anger will change
　　to the songs of cheer,
For the toiling age will forget its rage when
　　the Prince of Peace draws near.

This is the gospel of labor, ring it, ye bells
　　of the kirk,—
The Lord of Love comes down from above
　　to live with the men who work,
This is the rose that He planted, here in
　　the thorn cursed soil—
Heaven is blessed with perfect rest, but the
　　blessing of earth is toil.

　　　　　　—Henry Van Dyke

TURN AGAIN TO LIFE

If I should die and leave you here a while,
Be not like others, sore undone, who keep
Long vigil by the silent dust and weep.
For my sake turn again to life and smile,
Nerving thy heart and trembling hand to do
That which will comfort other souls than
　　thine;
Complete these dear unfinished tasks of mine,
And I, perchance, may therein comfort you.

　　　　　　—Mary Lee Hall

Death

Life! I know not what thou art,
But know that thou and I must part;
And when, or how, or where we met
I own to me's a secret yet.

Life! We've been long together,
Through pleasant and through cloudy
    weather;
'Tis hard to part when friends are dear—
Perhaps 'twill cost a sigh, a tear;
    Then steal away, give little warning,
Choose thine own time;
Say not Good Night,—but in some clime
    Bid me Good Morning.

—ANNA LETITIA BARBAULD

ON DEATH

As a fond mother, when the day is o'er
  Leads by the hand her little child to bed,
  Half willing, half reluctant to be led,
  And leave his broken playthings on the
    floor,
Still gazing at them through the open door,
  Nor wholly reassured and comforted
  By promises of others in their stead,
Which, though more splendid, may not please
    him more;
So Nature deals with us, and takes away
  Our playthings one by one, and by the
    hand
  Leads us to rest so gently, that we go
  Scarce knowing if we wish to go or stay,
  Being too full of sleep to understand
  How far the unknown transcends the what
    we know.

—HENRY WADSWORTH LONGFELLOW

HEAVEN

I never saw a moor,
  I never saw the sea;
Yet know I how the heather looks,
  And what a wave must be.

I never spake with God,
  Nor visited in Heaven;
Yet certain am I of the spot
  As if the chart were given.

—EMILY DICKINSON

Death is the golden key that opens the palace of eternity.

—JOHN MILTON

From "THANATOPSIS"

So live that when thy summons comes to join
The innumerable caravan which moves
To that mysterious realm where each shall
  take
His chamber in the silent halls of death,
Thou go not, like the quarry-slave at night,
Scourged to his dungeon, but, sustained and
  soothed
By an unfaltering trust, approach thy grave
Like one who wraps the drapery of his couch
About him, and lies down to pleasant dreams.

—WILLIAM CULLEN BRYANT

Fear not that thy life shall come to an end, but rather fear that it shall never have a beginning.

—CARDINAL NEWMAN

Because I could not stop for Death
He kindly stopped for me.
The carriage held but just ourselves—
And Immortality.
We slowly drove, He knew no haste
And I had put away
My labor and my leisure too,
For his civility.
We passed the school where children strove
At recess in the ring—
We passed the fields of gazing grain
We passed the setting sun
We paused before a house that seemed
A swelling of the ground
The roof was scarcely visible,
The cornice in the ground
Since then 'tis centuries—and yet
Feels shorter than the day
I first surmised the horses' heads
Were toward Eternity.

—EMILY DICKINSON

From "L'ENVOI"

When Earth's last picture is painted,
*   and the tubes are twisted and dried,*
When the oldest colors have faded, and
*   the youngest critic has died,*
We shall rest, and, faith, we shall need
*   it—lie down for an eon or two,*
Till the Master of All Good Workmen
*   shall set us to work anew!*

And those that were good shall be happy:
*   they shall sit in a golden chair;*
They shall splash at a ten-league canvas
*   with brushes of comet's hair;*
They shall find real saints to draw from—
*   Magdalene, Peter, and Paul;*
They shall work for an age at a sitting
*   and never be tired at all!*

And only the Master shall praise us, and
*   only the Master shall blame;*
And no one shall work for money, and
*   and no one shall work for fame;*
But each for the joy of the working, and
*   each, in his separate star*
Shall draw the Thing as he sees It for
*   the God of Things as They Are!*

—Rudyard Kipling

Winter is on my head, but eternal spring is in my heart; I breathe at this hour the fragrance of the lilacs, the violets, and the roses, as at twenty years ago. The nearer I approach to the end, the plainer I hear around me the immortal symphonies of the worlds which invite me.

—Victor Hugo

The consciousness of being loved softens the keenest pang, even at the moment of parting; yea, even the eternal farewell is robbed of half its bitterness when uttered in accents that breathe love to the last sigh.

—Joseph Addison

LIFE

"Tell me, thou strangest and unfathomed
*   mystery—*
*   Tell me, I pray—*
*   Whence thy beginning? What is thy history?*
*   Where dost thou stay?*
What of the pilgrims through thy domain
*   trav'ling?*
*   Tell me I pray thee this mystery unrav'ling.*
*   Body and spirit held fast in thy keeping,*
*   And end but in sleeping*
'Mid sorrow and weeping—
*   Why such an ending of the mystic day?*
*   Tell me the secret of thy short abiding,*
*   In body with breath*
*   And then, in a moment so swiftly divided*
*   Thy portion with death—*
*   Where shall I be in the time intervening?*
*   Tell me, I pray thee, this mystery explaining;*
*   Tell me the secret—Oh! tell me the meaning*
*   Of Life and her twin sister Death."*

We often sing of the "sweet mystery of life," and, indeed, life is a mystery if we do not read it through the focus of faith.

It is as natural to die, as to be born; and to a little infant, perhaps, the one is as painful as the other. He that dies in an earnest pursuit is like one that is wounded in hot blood; who, for the time, scarce feels the hurt; and, therefore, a mind fixed, and bent upon somewhat that is good, doth avert the dolours of death: but, above all, believe it, the sweetest canticle is, *Nunc dimittis;* when a man hath obtained worthy ends, and expectations: Death hath this also; that it openeth the gate to good fane, and extinguisheth envy.

—Francis Bacon

The angels from their thrones on high
Look down on us with wondering eye,
That when we are but passing guests
We build such strong and solid nests,
But where we think to dwell for aye
We scarce take heed a stone to lay.

To believe in immortality is one thing, but it is first needful to believe in life.

—ROBERT LOUIS STEVENSON

Let us endeavor so to live that, when we come to die, even the undertaker will be sorry.

—MARK TWAIN

TELL ME, YE WINGED WINDS

"Tell me, ye winged winds,
  That round my pathway roar,
Do ye not know some spot
  Where mortals weep no more?
Some lone and pleasant dell,
  Some valley in the west,
Where, free from toil and pain,
  The weary soul may rest?

The loud wind dwindled to a whisper low,
And sigh'd for pity as it answer'd 'No.'

"Tell me, my secret soul,
  Oh! tell me, Hope and Faith,
Is there no resting-place
  From sorrow, sin, and death?
Is there no happy spot
  Where mortals may be blessed,
Where grief may find a balm,
  And weariness a rest?

Faith, Hope, and Love, best boons to mortals
    given,
  Wav'd their bright wings, and whisper'd,
  'Yes, in heaven!' "

—CHARLES MACKAY

WALK SLOWLY

If you should go before me, dear, walk slowly
Down the ways of death, well-worn and wide,
For I would want to overtake you quickly
And seek the journey's ending by your side.

I would be so forlorn not to descry you
Down some shining highroad when I came;
Walk slowly, dear, and often look behind you
And pause to hear if someone calls your name.

—ADELAIDE LOVE

POEM FOR THE LIVING

When I am dead,
Cry for me a little.
Think of me sometimes,
But not too much.
It is not good for you
Or your wife or your husband
Or your children
To allow your thoughts to dwell
Too long on the dead.
Think of me now and again
As I was in life
At some moment which it is pleasant to recall.
But not for long.
Leave me in peace
As I shall leave you, too, in peace.
While you live,
Let your thoughts be with the living.

—THEODORA KROEBER

THE LOVE THAT
WILT NOT LET ME GO

O Love that wilt not let me go,
  I rest my weary soul in Thee;
I give Thee back the life I owe,
That in Thine ocean depths its flow
  May richer, fuller be.

O Light that followest all my way,
  I yield my flickering torch to Thee;
My heart restores its borrowed ray,
That in Thy sunshine's blaze its day
  May brighter, fairer be.

O Joy that seekest me through pain,
  I cannot close my heart to Thee;
I trace the rainbow through the rain,
And feel the promise is not vain
  That morn shall tearless be.

O Cross that liftest up my head,
  I dare not ask to fly from Thee;
I lay in dust life's glory dead,
And from the ground there blossoms red
  Life that shall endless be.

—GEORGE MATHESON

THE BUSTLE IN A HOUSE

The bustle in a house
The morning after death
Is solemnest of industries
Enacted upon earth,—

The sweeping up the heart,
And putting love away
We shall not want to use again
Until eternity.

—EMILY DICKINSON

A SOUL'S SOLILOQUY

Today the journey is ended,
I have worked out the mandates of fate;
Naked, alone, undefended,
I knock at the Uttermost Gate.
Behind is life and its longing,
Its trial, its trouble, its sorrow;
Beyond is the Infinite Morning
Of a day without a tomorrow.

Go back to dust and decay,
Body, grown weary and old;
You are worthless to me from today—
No longer my soul can you hold.
I lay you down gladly forever
For a life that is better than this;
I go where partings ne'er sever
You into oblivion's abyss.

Lo, the gate swings wide at my knocking,
Across endless reaches I see
Lost friends with laughter come flocking
To give a glad welcome to me.
Farewell, the maze has been threaded,
This is the ending of strife;
Say not that death should be dreaded—
'Tis but the beginning of life.

—WENONAH STEVENS ABBOTT

This is not the whole sad story of creation,
Told by toiling millions o'er and o'er!
One day, then black annihilation,
A sun-lit passage to a sunless shore!

—RALPH WALDO EMERSON

PROSPICE

Fear death?—to feel the fog in my throat,
The mist in my face,
When the snows begin, and the blasts denote
I am nearing the place,
The power of the night, the press of the
storm,
The post of the foe;
Where he stands, the Arch Fear in a visible
form,
Yet the strong man must go;
For the journey is done and the summit
attained,
And the barriers fall,
Though a battle's to fight ere the guerdon
be gained,
The reward of it all.
I was ever a fighter, so—one fight more,
The best and the last!
I would hate that death bandaged my eyes,
and forebore,
And bade me creep past.
No! let me taste the whole of it, fare like
my peers
The heroes of old,
Bear the brunt, in a minute pay glad life's
arrears
Of pain, darkness and cold.
For sudden the worst turns the best to the
brave,
The black minute's at end,
And the elements' rage, the fiend-voices that
rave,
Shall dwindle, shall blend,
Shall change, shall become first a peace out
of pain,
Then a light, then thy breast,
O thou soul of my soul! I shall clasp thee
again,
And with God be the rest!

—ROBERT BROWNING

LIFE BEYOND

Would it be like God to create such beautiful unselfish loves, most like the love of heaven of any type we know—just for our three-score years and ten? Would it be like Him to let two souls grow together here, so that the separating of the day is pain, and then wrench them apart for eternity? What is meant by such expressions as "risen together, sitting together in heavenly places?" If they mean anything, they mean recognition, friendship, enjoyment. Our friends are not dead, nor asleep; they go on living; they are near us alway, and God has said, "We should know each other there."

—Elizabeth Stuart Phelps

So be my passing!
My task accomplish'd and the long day done,
My wages taken, and in my heart
Some late lark singing,
Let me be gather'd to the quiet west,
The sundown splendid and serene,
Death.

—William Ernest Henley

AFTER WORK

Lord, when Thou seest that my work is done,
Let me not linger on,
With failing powers,
Adown the weary hours,—
A workless worker in a world of work.
But, with a word,
Just bid me home,
And I will come
Right gladly,—
Yea, right gladly
Will I come.

—John Oxenham

From "THE BHAGAVAD-GITA"

As when one layeth
His worn-out robes away,
And, taking new ones, sayeth,
"These will I wear to-day!"
So putteth by the spirit
Lightly its garb of flesh,
And passeth to inherit
A residence afresh.

LAST LINES

No coward soul is mine,
No trembler in the world's storm-troubled
    sphere:
I see Heaven's glories shine,
And faith shines equal, arming me from fear.

O God within my breast,
Almighty, ever-present Deity!
Life—that in me has rest,
As I—undying Life—have power in Thee!

Vain are the thousand creeds
That move men's hearts: unutterably vain;
Worthless as wither'd weeds,
Or idlest froth amid the boundless main,

To waken doubt in one
Holding so fast by Thine infinity;
So surely anchor'd on
The steadfast rock of immortality.

With wide-embracing love
Thy Spirit animates eternal years,
Pervades and broods above,
Changes, sustains, dissolves, creates and rears.

Though earth and man were gone,
And suns and universes cease to be,
And Thou were left alone,
Every existence would exist in Thee.

There is not room for Death,
Nor atom that his might could render void:
Thou—Thou art Being and Breath,
And what Thou art may never be destroyed.

—Emily Brontë

Be comforted; . . .
The face of Death is toward the Sun of Life,
His shadow darkens earth: his truer name
Is "Onward," no discordance in the roll
And march of that Eternal Harmony
Whereto the worlds beat time, tho' faintly
    heard
Until the great Hereafter. Mourn in hope!

—Alfred Lord Tennyson

A DIEU! AND AU REVOIR

As you love me, let there be
No mourning when I go,—
No tearful eyes,
No hopeless sighs,
No woe,—nor even sadness!
Indeed I would not have you sad,
For I myself shall be full glad,
With the high triumphant gladness
Of a soul made free
Of God's sweet liberty.
—No windows darkened;
For my own
Will be flung wide, as ne'er before,
To catch the radiant inpour
Of Love that shall in full atone
For all the ills that I have done;
And the good things left undone;
—No voices hushed;
My own, full-flushed
With an immortal hope, will rise
In ecstasies of new-born bliss
And joyful melodies.
Rather, of your sweet courtesy,
Rejoice with me
At my soul's loosing from captivity.
Wish me "Bon Voyage!"
As you do a friend
Whose joyous visit finds its happy end.
And bid me both "à Dieu!"
And "au revoir!"
Since, though I come no more,
I shall be waiting there to greet you,
At His Door.
And, as the feet of The Bearers tread
The ways I trod,
Think not of me as dead,
But rather—
"Happy, thrice happy, he whose course is
* sped!*
He has gone home—to God,
His Father!"

—JOHN OXENHAM

Death takes our loved ones—
We are bowed in grief. For whom?
Are we not selfish?
A mourner weeps for himself,
The dead know nought of sorrow.
              —MARGARET E. BRUNER

DEATH BE NOT PROUD

Death, be not proud, though some have
* called thee*
Mighty and dreadful, for thou art not so:
For those whom thou think'st thou dost
* overthrow*
Die not, poor Death; nor yet canst thou kill
* me.*
From rest and sleep, which but thy picture
* be,*
Much pleasure; then from thee much more
* must flow;*
And soonest our best men with thee do go—
Rest of their bones and souls' delivery!
Thou'rt slave to fate, chance, kings, and
* desperate men,*
And dost with poison, war, and sickness
* dwell;*
And poppy or charms can make us sleep
* as well*
And better than thy stroke. Why swell'st
* thou then?*
* One short sleep past, we wake eternally,*
* And Death shall be not more: Death, thou*
* shalt die!*

—JOHN DONNE

CROSSING THE BAR

Sunset and evening star,
* And one clear call for me,*
And may there be no moaning of the bar,
* When I put out to sea.*

But such a tide as moving seems asleep,
* Too full for sound and foam,*
When that which drew from out the
* boundless deep*
* Turns again home.*

Twilight and evening bell,
* And after that the dark!*
And may there be no sadness of farewell,
* When I embark;*

For tho' from out our bourne of time and
* place*
* The flood may bear me far,*
I hope to see my Pilot face to face
* When I have crossed the bar.*

—ALFRED LORD TENNYSON

JUST THINK

Just think! some night the stars will gleam
*   Upon a cold, grey stone,*
And trace a name with silver beam
*   And lo! 'twill be your own.*

That night is speeding on to greet
*   Your epitaphic rhyme.*
Your life is but a little beat
*   Within the heart of Time.*

A little gain, a little pain,
*   A laugh, lest you may moan;*
A little blame, a little fame,
*   A star-gleam on a stone.*

*   —*Robert Service

THE HILLS OF REST

Beyond the last horizon's rim,
*   Beyond adventure's farthest quest,*
Somewhere they rise, serene and dim,
*   The happy, happy Hills of Rest.*

Upon their sunlit slopes uplift
*   The castles we have built in Spain—*
While fair amid the summer drift
*   Our faded gardens flower again.*

Sweet hours we did not live go by
*   To soothing note, on scented wing;*
In golden-lettered volumes lie
*   The songs we tried in vain to sing.*

They all are there: the days of dream
*   That build the inner lives of men;*
The silent, sacred years we deem
*   The might be, and the might have been.*

Some evening when the sky is gold
*   I'll follow day into the west;*
Nor pause, nor heed, till I behold
*   The happy, happy Hills of Rest.*

*   —*Albert Bigelow Paine

WHEN LIFE'S DAY CLOSES

When on my day the evening shadows fall,
*   I will go down to where a quiet river flows*
Into a sea from whence no man returns;
*   And there embark for lands where life*
*   immortal grows.*

*   —*Thomas Tiplady

IMMORTALITY

There is no death! What seems so is transition.
*   This life of mortal breath*
Is but a suburb of the life elysian,
*   Whose portal we call Death.*
She is not dead,—the child of our affection,
*   But gone unto that school*
Where she no longer needs our poor
*   protection,*
*   And Christ himself doth rule.*
In that great cloister's stillness and seclusion,
*   By guardian angels led,*
Safe from temptation, safe from sin's
*   pollution,*
*   She lives, whom we call dead.*
Day after Day we think what she is doing
*   In those bright realms of air;*
Year after year her tender steps pursuing,
*   Behold her grown more fair.*
Thus do we walk with her, and keep
*   unbroken*
*   The bond which nature gives,*
Thinking that our remembrance, though
*   unspoken,*
*   May reach her where she lives.*
Not as a child shall we again behold her;
*   For when with raptures wild*
In our embraces we again enfold her,
*   She will not be a child;*
But a fair maiden, in her Father's mansion,
*   Clothed with celestial grace;*
And beautiful with all the soul's expansion
*   Shall we behold her face.*

*   —*Henry Wadsworth Longfellow

They that love beyond the world can not be separated by it.

Death can not kill what never dies.

Nor can spirits ever be divided, that love and live in the same divine principle, the root and record, of their friendship ❧ ❧ Death is but crossing the world, as friends do the seas; they live in one another still.

. . .

This is the comfort of friends, that though they may be said to die, yet their friendship and society are, in the best sense, ever present because immortal.

                   —William Penn

HE IS NOT DEAD

I cannot say, and I will not say
That he is dead. He is just away.
With a cherry smile, and a wave of the hand,
He has wandered into an unknown land
And left us dreaming how very fair
It needs must be, since he lingers there.
And you—oh, you, who the wildest yearn
For an old-time step, and the glad return,
Think of him faring on, as dear
In the love of There as the love of Here
Think of him still as the same. I say,
He is not dead—he is just away.

—JAMES WHITCOMB RILEY

EASTER

I will repudiate the lie
Men tell of life:
How it will pass
As fragile flower, or butterfly,
Whose dust shall nourish
April grass.

Since One, for love, died on a tree
And in the stony
Tomb was lain,
Behold I show a mystery:
All sepulchres
Are sealed in vain!

—JOHN RICHARD MORELAND

THE BUTTERFLY

I hold you at last in my hand,
*   Exquisite child of the air.*
Can I ever understand
*   How you grew to be so fair?*

You came to my linden tree
*   To taste its delicious sweet,*
I sitting here in the shadow and shine
*   Playing around its feet.*

Now I hold you fast in my hand,
*   You marvelous butterfly,*
Till you help me to understand
*   The eternal mystery.*

From that creeping thing in the dust
*   To this shining bliss in the blue!*
God give me courage to trust
*   I can break my chrysalis too!*

—ALICE FREEMAN PALMER

From "THE PILGRIM'S PROGRESS"

Now I saw in my dream, that these two men (Christian and Hopeful) went in at the Gate; and lo, as they entered, they were transfigured: and they had raiment put on that shone like Gold. . . . Then I heard in my dream, that all the bells in the city rang again for joy; and that it was said unto them, Enter ye into the Joy of our Lord. . . .

"Now, just as the Gates were opened to let in the men, I looked in after them; and behold the City shone like the Sun, the streets also were paved with Gold, and in them walked many men with crowns on their heads, Palms in their hands, and Golden Harps to sing praises withal.

". . . And after that, they shut up the Gates: which when I had seen, I wished myself among them."

—JOHN BUNYAN

REQUIEM

Under the wide and starry sky,
Dig the grave and let me lie.
Glad did I live and gladly die,
*   And I laid me down with a will.*

This be the verse you grave for me:
Here he lies where he longed to be,
Home is the sailor, home from sea,
*   And the hunter home from the hill.*

—ROBERT LOUIS STEVENSON

NO FUNERAL GLOOM

No funeral gloom, my dears, when I am gone,
Corpse-gazings, tears, black raiment, grave-
*   yard grimness.*
Think of me as withdrawn into the dimness,
Yours still, you mine.
Remember all the best of our past moments
*   and forget the rest,*
And so to where I wait come gently on.

—ELLEN TERRY

From "VANITY OF VANITIES"

Vain, frail, short-liv'd, and miserable Man,
Learn what thou art when thy estate is best:
A restless Wave o' th' troubled Ocean,
A Dream, a lifeless Picture finely drest.

A Wind, a Flower, a Vapour and a Bubble,
A Wheel that stands not still, a trembling
    Reed,
A trolling Stone, dry Dust, light Chaff and
    Stuff,
A shadow of something but truly nought
    indeed.

Learn what deceitful Toyes, and empty
    things,
This World, and all its best Enjoyments be:
Out of the Earth no true Contentment
    springs,
But all things here are vexing Vanitie.

For what is Beauty, but a fading Flower?
Or what is Pleasure, but the Devil's bait,
Whereby he catcheth whom he would devour,
And multitudes of Souls doth ruinate?

And what are Friends, but mortal men, as we,
Whom Death from us may quickly separate;
Or else their hearts may quite estrangéd be,
And all their love be turnéd into hate.

And what are Riches to be doted on?
Uncertain, fickle, and ensnaring things;
They draw Men's Souls into Perdition,
And when most needed, take them to their
    wings.

Ah foolish man! that sets his heart upon
Such empty shadows, such wild Fowl as these,
That being gotten will be quickly gone,
And whilst they stay increase but his disease.

—MICHAEL WIGGLESWORTH

DEATH STANDS ABOVE ME

Death stands above me, whispering low
    I know not what into my ear:
Of his strange language all I know
    Is, there is not a word of fear.

—WALTER SAVAGE LANDOR

LET ME DIE WORKING

Let me die, working.
Still tackling plans unfinished, tasks undone!
Clean to its end, swift may my race be run.
No laggard steps, no faltering, no shirking;
    Let me die, working!
Let me die, thinking.
Let me fare forth still with an open mind,
Fresh secrets to unfold, new truths to find,
My soul undimmed, alert, no question
    blinking;
    Let me die, thinking!

Let me die, laughing.
No sighing o'er past sins; they are forgiven.
Spilled on this earth are all the joys of
    Heaven;
The wine of life, the cup of mirth quaffing.
    Let me die, laughing!

—S. HALL YOUNG

LEAD, KINDLY LIGHT

Lead, kindly Light, amid the encircling
    gloom,
        Lead thou me on.
The night is dark, and I am far from home—
        Lead thou me on.
Keep thou my feet; I do not ask to see
The distant scene—one step enough for me.

I was not ever thus, nor prayed that thou
        Shouldst lead me on;
I loved to choose and see my path; but now
        Lead thou me on.
I loved the garish day, and, spite of fears,
Pride ruled my will; remember not past years.

So long thy power hath blest me, sure it still
        Will lead me on,
O'er moor and fen, o'er crag and torrent, till
        The night is gone;
And with the morn those angel faces smile
Which I have loved long since, and lost
    awhile.

—JOHN HENRY NEWMAN

Defeat

Defeat may serve as well as victory
To shake the soul and let the glory out.
When the great oak is straining in the wind,
The boughs drink in new beauty, and the
    trunk
Sends down a deeper root on the windward
    side.
Only the soul that knows the mighty grief
Can know the mighty rapture. Sorrows come
To stretch our spaces in the heart for joy.

—Edwin Markham

DON'T GIVE UP

'Twixt failure and success the point's so fine
Men sometimes know not when they touch
   the line,
Just when the pearl was waiting one more
   plunge,
How many a struggler has thrown in the
   sponge!
Then take this honey from the bitterest cup:
"There is no failure save in giving up!"

Before God's footstool to confess
A poor soul knelt, and bowed his head;
"I failed," he cried. The Master said,
"Thou didst thy best—that is success!"

There is always another chance. . . . This
thing that we call "failure" is not the
falling down, but the *staying* down.

—MARY PICKFORD

SUCCESS IS COUNTED SWEETEST

Success is counted sweetest
By those who ne'er succeed.
To comprehend a nectar
Requires sorest need.

Not one of all the purple host
Who took the flag today
Can tell the definition,
So clear, of victory,

As he, defeated, dying,
On whose forbidden ear
The distant strains of triumph
Break, agonized and clear.

—EMILY DICKINSON

Stoop, angels, hither from the skies!
   There is no holier spot of ground
Than where defeated valor lies,
   By mourning beauty crowned!

THE REAL TEST

The test of a man is the fight he makes,
   The grit that he daily shows;
The way he stands on his feet and takes
   Fate's numerous bumps and blows,
A coward can smile when there's naught to
    fear,
   When nothing his progress bars;
But it takes a man to stand up and cheer
   While some other fellow stars.

It isn't the victory, after all,
   But the fight that a brother makes;
The man who, driven against the wall,
   Still stands up erect and takes
The blows of fate with his head held high:
   Bleeding, and bruised, and pale,
Is the man who'll win in the by and by,
   For he isn't afraid to fail.

It's the bumps you get, and the jolts you get,
   And the shocks that your courage stands,
The hours of sorrow and vain regret,
   The prize that escapes your hands,
That test your mettle and prove your worth;
   It isn't the blows you deal,
But the blows you take on the good old earth,
   That show if your stuff is real.

Defeat isn't bitter if you don't swallow it.

The men who try to do something and fail are infinitely better than those who try to do nothing and succeed.

—LLOYD JONES

"A man must live!" We justify
Low shift and trick to treason high,
   A little vote for a little gold
   To a whole senate bought and sold,
With this self-evident reply.

But is it so? Pray tell me why
Life at such cost you have to buy?
   In what religion were you told
   "A man must live?"
There are times when a man must die.

Imagine for a battle cry
   From soldiers with a sword to hold,
   From soldiers with the flag unrolled,
The coward's whine, this liar's lie,
   "A man must live!"

Success is never final and failure never fatal.

—GEORGE F. TILTON

SUCCESS

They said he was a failure since
   He won no eminence nor fame,
And no one but his friends were stirred
   At any mention of his name.

Ah, foolish ones, they could not gauge
   The measurement of his success—
He left his friends glad memories,
   And gave one woman happiness.

—CHARLOTTE BECKER

And he alone is great who turns the voice of the wind into a song made sweeter by his own loving.

—KAHLIL GIBRAN

IO VICTIS

I sing the hymn of the conquered, who fell
   in the Battle of Life,—
The hymn of the wounded, the beaten, who
   died overwhelmed in the strife;
Not the jubilant song of the victors, for
   whom the resounding acclaim
Of nations was lifted in chorus, whose brows
   wear the chaplet of fame,
But the hymn of the low and the humble,
   the weary, the broken in heart,
Who strove and who failed, acting bravely
   a silent and desperate part;

Whose youth bore no flower in its branches,
   whose hopes burned in ashes away,
From whose hands slipped the prize they had
   grasped at, who stood at the dying of day
With the wreck of their life all around them,
   unpitied, unheeded, alone,
With Death swooping down o'er their failure,
   and all but their faith overthrown,
While the voice of the world shouts its
   chorus,—its paean for those who have won;
While the trumpet is sounding triumphant,
   and high to the breeze and the sun

Glad banners are waving, hands clapping, and
   hurrying feet
Thronging after the laurel-crowned victors,
   I stand on the field of defeat,
In the shadow, with those who are fallen,
   and wounded, and dying, and there
Chant a requiem low, place my hand on their
   pain-knotted brows, breathe a prayer,
Hold the hand that is helpless, and whisper,
   "They only the victory win,
Who have fought the good fight, and have
   vanquished the demon that tempts us
   within;

Who have held to their faith unseduced by
   the prize that the world holds on high;
Who have dared for a high cause to suffer,
   resist, fight—if need be, to die."
Speak, History! Who are Life's victors?
   Unroll thy long annals and say;
Are they those whom the world called the

victors, who won the success of a day?
The martyrs, or Nero? The Spartans, who
    fell at Thermopylae's tryst,
Or the Persians and Xeres? His judges or
Socrates, Pilate or Christ?

—WILLIAM WETMORE STORY

I will go forth 'mong men
Not mailed in scorn
But in the armor of a pure intent.
Great duties are before me and great songs
And whether crowned or crownless when
    I fall
It matters not so as God's work is done.
I've learned to prize the quiet lightning deed,
Not the applauding thunder at its heels
Which men call Fame.

—ALEXANDER SMITH

FOR THOSE WHO FAIL

"All honor to him who shall win the prize,"
    The world has cried for a thousand years;
But to him who tries and who fails and dies,
    I give great honor and glory and tears.

O great is the hero who wins a name
    But greater many and many a time,
Some pale-faced fellow who dies in shame,
    And lets God finish the thought sublime.

And great is the man with the sword
        undrawn,
    And good is the man who refrains from
        wine;
But the man who fails and yet fights on,
    Lo! he is the twin-born brother of mine!

—JOAQUIN MILLER

A SMILE

Let others cheer the winning man,
There's one I hold worth while;
'Tis he who does the best he can,
Then loses with a smile.
Beaten he is, but not to stay
Down with the rank and file;
That man will win some other day,
Who loses with a smile.

WE MET THEM ON THE COMMON WAY

We met them on the common way,
They passed and gave no sign,—
The heroes that had lost the day,
The failures half divine.

Ranged in a quiet place we see
Their mighty ranks contain
Figures too great for victory,
Hearts too unspoiled for gain.

Here are earth's splendid failures, come
From glorious foughten fields;
Some bear the wounds of combat, some
Are prone upon their shields.

To us that will do battle here,
If we in aught prevail,
Grant, God, the triumph not too dear,
Or strength, like theirs, to fail!

—ELIZABETH C. CARDOZO

From "A MINOR PROPHET"

The earth yields nothing more Divine
Than high prophetic vision—than the Seer
Who fasting from man's meaner joy beholds
The paths of beauteous order, and constructs
A fairer type, to shame our low content . . .

The faith that life on earth is being shaped
To glorious ends, that order, justice, love,
Mean man's completeness, mean effect as sure
As roundness in the dew-drop—that great
    faith
Is but the rushing and expanding stream
Of thought, of feeling, fed by all the past.
Our finest hope is finest memory. . . .

Even our failures are a prophecy,
Even our yearnings and our bitter tears
After that fair and true we cannot grasp;
As patriots who seem to die in vain
Make liberty more sacred by their pangs.

—GEORGE ELIOT

THE INEVITABLE

I like the man who faces what he must,
  With step triumphant and a heart of cheer;
  Who fights the daily battle without fear;
Sees his hopes fail, yet keeps unfaltering
    trust
That God is God,—that somehow, true and
    just
  His plans work out for mortals; not a tear
  Is shed when fortune, which the world
    holds dear,
Falls from his grasp—better, with love, a crust
  Than living in dishonor: envies not,
Nor loses faith in man; but does his best,
  Nor ever murmurs at his humblest lot;
But, with a smile and words of hope, gives
    zest
  To every toiler: he alone is great
  Who by a life heroic conquers fate.

—SARAH KNOWLES BOLTON

VICTORY

I sheath my sword. In mercy go.
  Turn back from me your hopeless eyes,
  For in them all my anger dies:
I cannot face a beaten foe.

My cause was just, the fight was sweet.
  Go from me, O mine enemy,
  Before, in shame of victory,
You find me kneeling at your feet.

—ALINE KILMER

If I am right, Thy grace impart
  Still in the right to stay;
If I am wrong, oh, teach my heart
  To find the better way!

We don't always win but we don't have
to be conquered.

He jests at scars that never felt a wound.

—WILLIAM SHAKESPEARE

UNDEFEATED

He sang of joy; whate'er he knew of sadness
  He kept for his own heart's peculiar share;
So well he sang, the world imagined gladness
  To be sole tenant there.

For dreams were his, and in the dawn's fair
    shining,
  His spirit soared beyond the mounting lark;
But from his lips no accent of repining
  Fell when the days grew dark;
And though contending long dread Fate to
    master,
  He failed at last her enmity to cheat,
He turned with such a smile to face disaster
That he sublimed defeat.

—FLORENCE EARLE COATES

TRIUMPH OF THE DEFEATED

They never fail who die
In a great cause. The block may soak their
    gore;
Their heads may sodden in the sun; their
    limbs
Be strung to city gates and castle walls;
But still their spirit walks abroad.
    Though years
Elapse and others share as dark a doom,
They but augment the deep and sweeping
    thoughts
Which overpower all others and conduct
The world, at last, to freedom.

—LORD BYRON

UNSUBDUED

I have hoped, I have planned, I have striven,
  To the will I have added the deed;
The best that was in me I've given,
  I have prayed, but the gods would not heed.

I have dared and reached only disaster,
  I have battled and broken my lance;
I am bruised by a pitiless master
  That the weak and the timid call chance.

I am old, I am bent, I am cheated
  Of all that Youth urged me to win;
But name me not with the defeated,
  Tomorrow again, I begin.

—S. E. KISER

HOW DID YOU DIE?

Did you tackle that trouble that came your
    way
    With a resolute heart and cheerful?
Or hide your face from the light of day
    With a craven soul and fearful?
Oh, a trouble's a ton, or a trouble's an ounce,
    Or a trouble is what you make it.
And it isn't the fact that you're hurt that
    counts,
    But only how did you take it?

You are beaten to earth? Well, well, what's
    that?
    Come up with a smiling face,
It's nothing against you to fall down flat,
    But to lie there—that's disgrace.
The harder you're thrown, why the higher
    you bounce;
    Be proud of your blackened eye!
It isn't the fact that you're licked that counts;
    It's how did you fight and why?

And though you be done to death, what then?
    If you battled the best you could;
If you played your part in the world of men,
    Why, the Critic will call it good.
Death comes with a crawl, or comes with
    a pounce,
    And whether he's slow or spry,
It isn't the fact that you're dead that counts,
    But only, how did you die?

—EDMUND VANCE COOKE

THE BEYOND

It seemeth such a little way to me,
Across to that strange country, the Beyond;
And yet, not strange, for it has grown to be
The home of those of whom I am so fond;
They make it seem familiar and most dear,
As journeying friends bring distant countries
    near.

And so for me there is no sting to death,
And so the grave has lost its victory;
It is but crossing with abated breath
And white, set face, a little strip of sea,
To find the loved ones waiting on the shore,
More beautiful, more precious than before.

—ELLA WHEELER WILCOX

Many a time I have been stricken to the
    earth,
But the earth is full of strength which I take
    to my heart;
I have been defeated again and again,
But there is something within me which is
    never defeated,
    For I am full of new beginnings.

—DON MARQUIS

THE JOURNEY

When Death, the angel of our higher dreams,
Shall come, far ranging from the hills of light
He will not catch me unaware; for I
Shall be as now communing with the dawn.
For I shall make all haste to follow him
Along the valley, up the misty slope
Where life lets go and Life at last is born.
There I shall find the dreams that I have lost
On toilsome earth, and they will guide me on,
Beyond the mists unto the farthest height.
I shall not grieve except to pity those
Who cannot hear the songs that I shall hear!

—THOMAS CURTIS CLARK

One prayed in vain to paint the vision blest,
Which shone upon his heart by night and day.
But homely duties in his dwelling pressed,
And hungry hearts that would not turn away,
And cares that still his eager hands bade stay.
The canvas never knew the pictured Face,
But year by year, while yet the vision shone,
An angel near him, wondering, bent to trace
On his own life the Master's image grown
And unto men made known.

YOU'LL NEVER KNOW

It's easy to sit in the shine
    And talk to the man in the shade,
It's easy to sit in a well-made boat
    And tell others where to wade.

It's easy to tell the toiler
    How best to carry his pack.
But you'll never know the weight of the load
    Till the pack is on your back!

Faith

So I go on, not knowing,
—I would not, if I might—
I would rather walk in the dark with God
Than go alone in the light;
I would rather walk with Him by faith
Than walk alone by sight.

—Mary Gardner Brainard

Without faith a man can do nothing; with it all things are possible.

—WILLIAM OSLER

Only he who can see the invisible can do the impossible.

CLOSING THE DOORS

I have closed the door on Doubt.
    I will go by what light I can find,
    And hold up my hands and reach them out
To the glimmer of God in the dark, and call,
"I am Thine, though I grope and stumble
        and fall.
    I serve, and Thy service is kind."

I have closed the door on Fear.
    He has lived with me far too long.
    If he were to break forth and reappear,
I would lift my eyes and look at the sky,
And sing aloud and run lightly by;
    He will never follow a song.

I have closed the door on Gloom.
    His house has too narrow a view.
    I must seek for my soul a wider room,
With windows to open and let in the sun,
And radiant lamps when the day is done,
    And the breeze of the world blowing
        through.

—IRENE PETTIT McKEEHAN

SOME FAITH AT ANY COST

No vision and you perish;
    No ideal, and you're lost;
Your heart must ever cherish
    Some faith at any cost.

Some hope, some dream to cling to,
    Some rainbow in the sky,
Some melody to sing to,
    Some service that is high.

—HARRIETT DU AUTERMONT

I WILL NOT DOUBT

I will not doubt, though all my ships at sea
    Come drifting home with broken masts
        and sails;
    I shall believe the Hand which never fails,
From seeming evil worketh good to me;
    And, though I weep because those sails
        are battered,
    Still will I cry, while my best hopes lie
        shattered,
        "I trust in Thee."

I will not doubt, though all my prayers
        return
    Unanswered from the still, white realm
        above;
    I shall believe it is an all-wise Love
Which has refused those things for which I
        yearn;
    And though, at times, I cannot keep from
        grieving,
    Yet the pure ardor of my fixed believing
        Undimmed shall burn.

I will not doubt, though sorrows fall like rain,
    And troubles swarm like bees about a hive;
    I shall believe the heights for which I strive,
Are only reached by anguish and by pain;
    And, though I groan and tremble with my
        crosses,
    I yet shall see, through my severest losses,
        The greater gain.

I will not doubt; well anchored in the faith,
    Like some stanch ship, my soul braves
        every gale,
    So strong its courage that it will not fail
To breast the mighty, unknown sea of death.
    Oh, may I cry when body parts with spirit,
    "I do not doubt," so listening worlds may
        hear it
        With my last breath.

—ELLA WHEELER WILCOX

MY PRAYER

If there be some weaker one,
Give me strength to help him on;
If a blinder soul there be,
Let me guide him nearer Thee.
Make my mortal dreams come true
With the work I fain would do;
Clothe with life the weak intent,
Let me be the thing I meant;
Let me find in Thy employ
Peace that dearer is than joy;
Out of self to love be led
And to heaven acclimated,
Until all things sweet and good
Seem my natural habitude.

—JOHN GREENLEAF WHITTIER

Stanzas from "IN MEMORIAM"

Strong Son of God, immortal Love,
Whom we, that have not seen thy face,
By faith, and faith alone, embrace,
Believing where we cannot prove;

Thine are these orbs of light and shade;
Thou madest Life in man and brute;
Thou madest Death; and lo, thy foot
Is on the skull which thou hast made.

Thou wilt not leave us in the dust:
Thou madest man, he knows not why;
He thinks he was not made to die;
And thou hast made him: thou art just.

Thou seemest human and divine,
The highest, holiest manhood, thou:
Our wills are ours, we know not how;
Our wills are ours, to make them thine.

Our little systems have their day;
They have their day and cease to be:
They are but broken lights of thee,
And thou, O Lord, art more than they.

—ALFRED LORD TENNYSON

I know not what the future hath
Of marvel or surprise,
Assured alone that life and death
His mercy underlies.

Trust and obey,
For there's no other way
To be happy in Jesus,
But to trust and obey.

I BELIEVE

I BELIEVE in boys and girls, the men and women of a great tomorrow; that whatsoever the boy soweth, the man shall reap. I BELIEVE in the curse of ignorance, in the efficacy of schools, in the dignity of teaching, and in joy of serving another. I BELIEVE in wisdom as revealed in human lives as well as in the pages of a printed book; in lessons taught not so much by percept as by example; in ability to work with the hands as well as to think with the head; in everything that makes life large and lovely. I BELIEVE in beauty in the schoolroom, in the daily life and out-of-doors. I BELIEVE in laughing, in all ideals and distant hopes that lure us on. I BELIEVE that every hour of every day we receive a just reward for all we do. I BELIEVE in the present and its opportunities, in the future and its promises, and in the divine joy of living.

—EDWIN OSGOOD GROVER

An atheist's most embarrassing moment is when he feels profoundly thankful for something, and can't think of anybody to thank for it.

OVERHEARD IN AN ORCHARD

Said the Robin to the Sparrow:
"I should really like to know
Why these anxious human beings
Rush about and worry so."

Said the Sparrow to the Robin:
"Friend, I think that it must be
That they have no heavenly Father
Such as cares for you and me."

—ELIZABETH CHENEY

From "MORTE D'ARTHUR"

More things are wrought by prayer
Than this world dreams of. Wherefore, let
*   thy voice*
Rise like a fountain for me night and day.
For what are men better than sheep or goats
That nourish a blind life within the brain,
If, knowing God, they lift not hands of
*   prayer*
Both for themselves and those who call them
*   friend?*
For so the whole round earth is every way
Bound by gold chains about the feet of God.

—ALFRED LORD TENNYSON

PRAYER

If radio's slim fingers
Can pluck a melody
From night and toss it over
A continent or sea;

If the petaled notes
Of a violin
Are blown across a mountain
Or a city's din;

If songs like crimson roses
Are culled from thin, blue air,
Why should mortals wonder
If God hears prayer?

—ETHEL ROMIG FULLER

The man who has not anything to boast of but his illustrious ancestors is like a potato—the only good belonging to him is underground.

Then to side with Truth is noble when we
*   share her wretched crust,*
Ere her cause bring fame and profit, and 'tis
*   prosperous to be just;*
Then it is the brave man chooses, while the
*   coward stands aside,*
Doubting in his abject spirit, till his Lord is
*   crucified,*
And the multitude make virtue of the faith
*   they had denied.*

—JAMES RUSSELL LOWELL

EACH IN HIS OWN TONGUE

A fire mist and a planet—
*   A crystal and a cell,—*
A jellyfish and a saurian,
*   And caves where the cavemen dwell;*
Then a sense of law and beauty,
*   And a face turned from the clod—*
Some call it Evolution,
*   And others call it God.*

A haze on the far horizon,
*   The infinite, tender sky,*
The ripe, rich tint of the cornfields,
*   And the wild geese sailing high;*
And all over upland and lowland
*   The charm of the goldenrod—*
Some of us call it Autumn,
*   And others call it God.*

Like tides on a crescent sea beach,
*   When the moon is new and thin,*
Into our hearts high yearning
*   Come welling and surging in—*
Come from the mystic ocean,
*   Whose rim no foot has trod—*
Some of us call it Longing,
*   And others call it God.*

A picket frozen on duty,
*   A mother starved for her brood,*
Socrates drinking the hemlock,
*   And Jesus on the rood;*
And millions who, humble and nameless,
*   The straight, hard pathway plod—*
Some call it Consecration,
*   And others call it God.*

—WILLIAM HERBERT CARRUTH

The ablest men in all walks of modern life are men of faith. Most of them have much more faith than they themselves realize.

—BRUCE BARTON

Build on, and make thy castles high and fair,
*   Rising and reaching upward to the skies;*
Listen to voices in the upper air,
*   Nor lose thy simple faith in mysteries.*

—HENRY WADSWORTH LONGFELLOW

Other refuge have I none;
   Hangs my helpless soul on Thee;
Leave, ah! leave me not alone,
   Still support and comfort me!
All my trust on Thee is stay'd,
   All my help from Thee I bring:
Cover my defenceless head
   With the shadow of Thy wing!

                —CHARLES WESLEY

THIS YEAR IS YOURS

God built and launched this year for you;
Upon the bridge you stand;
It's your ship, aye, your own ship
And you are in command.
Just what the twelve months' trip will do
Rest wholly, solely, friend with you!

Your log book, kept from day to day
My friend what will it show?
Have you on your appointed way
Made progress . . . yes or no?
The log will tell, like guiding star,
The sort of Captain that you are.

Contrary winds may oft beset,
Mountainous seas may press,
Fierce storms prevail and false light lure,
You even may know real stress.
Yet, does God's hand hold fast the helm,
There's naught can e'er your ship o'erwhelm.

For weal or woe, this year is yours;
For ship is on life's sea;
Your acts, as captain, must decide
Whichever it shall be;
So now, in starting on your trip,
Ask God to help you sail your ship.

Flower in the crannied wall,
I pluck you out of the crannies,
I hold you here, root and all, in my hand,
Little flower—but if I could understand
What you are, root and all, and all in all,
I should know what God and man is.

           —ALFRED LORD TENNYSON

Thou wilt keep him in perfect peace, whose mind is stayed on Thee: because he trusteth in Thee.

RISKY BUSINESS

It's a risk to have a husband, a risk to have
   a son:
A risk to pour your confidences out to
   anyone;
A risk to pick a daisy, for there's sure to
   be a cop;
A risk to go on living, but a greater risk
   to stop.

           —RUTH MASON RICE

The winds blow from a thousand ways and
   waft their balms abroad,
The winds blow toward a million goals—but
   all winds blow from God.

           —SIR WALTER FOSS

THE DREAM THAT COMES TRUE

Once upon a time a scientist said of Thomas A. Edison, "This poor fellow is wasting his time. Two fundamental laws of physics prove that he is attempting the impossible. The first is that there can be no light without combustion; the second is that no combustion can take place in a vacuum. Therefore, no light can be made in a vacuum." But even in the face of these "impossibilities," Edison went right ahead and perfected the incandescent electric lamp.

When Harvey insisted that blood flowed through the body, he was scoffed at. Pasteur's theories of germ life were scorned. Langley's plans for a machine which would fly without the help of a balloon were ridiculed. Even today, the man who is five years ahead of his time is looked upon as being a trifle balmy.

The progress of the world depends upon men with vision and the courage to make their dreams come true.

PRAYER

Lord, make me an instrument of Thy peace.
Where there is hate, may I bring love;
Where offense, may I bring pardon;
May I bring union in place of discord;
Truth, replacing error;
Faith, where once there was doubt;
Hope, for despair;
Light, where was darkness;
Joy to replace sadness.
Make me not to so crave to be loved as to love.
Help me to learn that in giving I may receive;
In forgetting self, I may find life eternal.

—St. Francis of Assisi

A PRESCRIPTION FOR YOU

If you are impatient, sit down quietly and
  talk with Job.
If you are just strong-headed, go and see
  Moses.
If you are getting weak-kneed, take a good
  look at Elijah.
If there is no song in your heart, listen to
  David.
If you are a policy man, read Daniel.
If you are getting sordid, spend awhile with
  Isaiah.
If you are chilly, get the beloved disciple
  to put his arms around you.
If your faith is below par, read Paul.
If you are getting lazy, watch James.
If you are losing sight of the future, climb
  up the stairs of Revelation and get a glimpse
  of the promised land.

Be like the bird
That, pausing in her flight
Awhile on boughs too slight,
  Feels them give way
Beneath her and yet sings,
Knowing that she hath wings.

—Victor Hugo

Faith draws the poison from every grief;
takes the sting from every loss; and
quenches the fire of every pain; and only
faith can do it.

—J. G. Holland

GOOD IMPULSES

It isn't the thing you do;
It's the thing you leave undone,
Which gives you a bit of heartache
At the setting of the sun.
The tender word forgotten,
The letter you did not write,
The flower you might have sent,
Are your haunting ghosts at night.

—Margaret E. Sangster

Faith is to believe what we do not see,
and the reward of this faith is to see
what we believe.

—St. Augustine

The road winds up the hill to meet the height,
Beyond the locust hedge it curves from sight—
  And yet no man would foolishly contend
  That where he sees it not, it makes an end.

—Emma Carleton

WHAT I NEED

I need a strength to keep me true
And straight in everything I do;
I need power to keep me strong
When I am tempted to do wrong;
I need a grace to keep me pure
When passion tries its deadly lure;
I need a love to keep me sweet
When hardness and mistrust I meet;
I need an arm to be my stay
When dark with trouble grows my day:
And naught on earth can these afford,
But all is found in Christ my Lord.

—Theodore Horton

Optimism is the faith that leads to achievement. Nothing can be done without
hope.

—Helen Keller

Friendship

'Tis the human touch in this world that
    counts,
    The touch of your hand and mine,
Which means far more to the fainting heart
    Than shelter and bread and wine;
For shelter is gone when the night is o'er,
    And bread lasts only a day,
But the touch of the hand and the sound of
    the voice
    Sing on in the soul alway.

—SPENCER MICHAEL FREE

From "THE VISION OF SIR LAUNFAL"

And the voice that was calmer than silence
said,
"Lo, it is I be not afraid!
In many climes, without avail,
Thou hast spent thy life for the Holy Grail;
Behold, it is here,—this cup which thou
Didst fill at the streamlet for me but now;
This crust is my body broken for thee,
This water his blood that died on the tree;
The Holy Supper is kept, indeed,
In whatso we share with another's need;
Not what we give, but what we share—
For the gift without the giver is bare;
Who gives himself with his alms feeds three—
Himself, his hungering neighbor, and me."

—JAMES RUSSELL LOWELL

FELLOWSHIP

When a feller hasn't got a cent
And is feelin' kind of blue,
And the clouds hang thick and dark
And won't let the sunshine thro',
It's a great thing, oh my brethren,
For a feller just to lay
His hand upon your shoulder
In a friendly sort o' way.

It makes a man feel queerish,
It makes the tear-drops start.
And you kind o' feel a flutter
In the region of your heart.
You can't look up and meet his eye,
You don't know what to say
When a hand is on your shoulder
In a friendly sort o' way.

Oh this world's a curious compound
With its honey and its gall;
Its cares and bitter crosses,
But a good world after all.
And a good God must have made it,
Leastwise that is what I say,
When a hand is on your shoulder
In a friendly sort o' way.

'Tis something to be willing to commend;
But my best praise is that I am your friend.

—THOMAS SOUTHERNE

TELL HIM NOW

If with pleasure you are viewing any work a
man is doing,
If you like him or you love him, tell him
now;
Don't withhold your approbation till the
parson makes oration
And he lies with snowy lilies on his brow;
No matter how you shout it he won't really
care about it;
He won't know how many teardrops you
have shed;
If you think some praise is due him now's
the time to slip it to him,
For he cannot read this tombstone when
he's dead.

More than fame and more than money is the
comment kind and sunny
And the hearty, warm approval of a friend.
For it gives to life a savor, and it makes you
stronger, braver,
And it gives you heart and spirit to the end;
If he earns your praise—bestow it; if you like
him let him know it;
Let the words of true encouragement be
said;

Do not wait till life is over and he's under-
neath the clover,
   For he cannot read his tombstone when
he's dead.

                    —BERTON BRALEY

TO A FRIEND

You entered my life in a casual way,
   And saw at a glance what I needed;
There were others who passed me or met
   me each day,
   But never a one of them heeded.
Perhaps you were thinking of other folks
   more,
   Or chance simply seemed to decree it;
I know there were many such chances before,
   But the others—well, they didn't see it.

You said just the thing that I wished you
   would say,
   And you made me believe that you meant
   it;
I held up my head in the old gallant way,
   And resolved you should never repent it.
There are time when encouragement means
   such a lot,
   And a word is enough to convey it;
There were others who could have, as easy
   as not—
   But, just the same, they didn't say it.

There may have been someone who could
   have done more
   To help me along, though I doubt it;
What I needed was cheering, and always
   before
   They had let me plod onward without it.
You have helped to refashion the dream of
   my heart,
   And made me turn eagerly to it;
There were others who might have (I
   question that part)—
   But, after all, they didn't do it!

                —GRACE STRICKER DAWSON

Friendship is a plant that we must water often.

I LOVE YOU

I love you not only for what you are
but for what I am when I'm with you;

I love you not only for what you have
made of yourself but what you are making
of me;

I love you for putting your hand into my
heaped up heart and passing over all the
foolish weak things you can't help dimly
seeing there, and drawing out in the light
all the beautiful belongings that no one
else had looked quite far enough to find;

I love you because you are helping me to
make of the lumber of my life not a tavern
but a temple, out of the work of my every
   day
life not a reproach but a song;

I love you because you have done more than
any creed could have done to make me good
and more than any fate could have done to
make me happy;

You have done it without a touch, without
a word, without a sigh;

You have done it by being yourself.

Perhaps that is what being a friend means,
after all.

Make new friends, but keep the old;
   Those are silver, these are gold.
New-made friendships, like new wine,
   Age will mellow and refine.
Friendships that have stood the test—
   Time and change—are surely best.
Brow may wrinkle, hair grow gray;
   Friendship never knows decay.
For 'mid old friends, tried and true,
   Once more we our youth renew.
But old friends, alas! may die;
   New friends must their place supply.
Cherish friendship in your breast—
   New is good, but old is best;
Make new friends, but keep the old;
   Those are silver, these are gold.

                —JOSEPH PARRY

Friend! How sacred the word. Born in the heart of God, and given to man as a treasure from the eternities—no word in the languages so heavily freighted with meaning.

Mother! That dearest name is lost in the sphere of Friendship for I have seen a mother cast off her child, but a friend does not know how to cast off or turn from.

I am a crank on the subject of Friendship. With one friend I would count myself rich; to possess more than one, I were rich beyond comparison. A friend is a priceless gem for the crown of life here and a cherished star in memory forever.

—CYRUS S. NUSBAUM

FRIEND

I would empty thy chalice of heart-ache and
   pain,
Would freshen thy desert with flowers and
   rain,
Would draw out the bitter and pour in the
   sweet,
And remove every thorn from the way of
   thy feet;
Would sing in the gladness of summer and
   bloom,
And sing out the sadness of winter and
   gloom,
Would lessen thy load by enlarging thy life,
I would sing back repose, and would sing
   away strife.

—CHARLES COKE WOODS

I made courtiers; I never pretended to make friends, said Napoleon. . . . On a rocky little island he fretted away the last years of his life—alone.

—BRUCE BARTON

LETTERS

Letters are a silken thread
That runs from heart to heart,
Weaving a web of things unsaid
When we must be apart.

In the hours of distress and misery, the eyes of every mortal turn to friendship; in the hour of gladness and conviviality, what is our want? It is friendship. When the heart overflows with gratitude, or with any other sweet and sacred sentiment, what is the word to which it would give utterance?

—WALTER SAVAGE LANDOR

FRIENDSHIP

Friendship is in loving rather than in being lov'd, which is its mutual benediction and recompense; and tho' this be, and tho' love is from lovers learn'd, it springeth none the less from the old essence of self. No friendless man ('twas well said) can be truly himself; what a man looketh for in his friend and findeth, and loving self best, loveth better than himself, is his own better self, his live lovable idea, flowering by expansion in the loves of his life.

—ROBERT BRIDGES

FRIENDSHIP

The daylight is gone—but before we depart,
One cup shall go 'round to the friend of my
   heart,
The kindest, the dearest—oh, judge by the
   tear
I now shed while I name him, how kind and
   how dear.

Oh, say, is it thus in the mirth bringing hour,
When friends are assembled, when wit, in
   full flower
Shoots forth from the lip under Bacchus's
   dew,
In blossoms of thought ever springing and
   new—

Do you sometimes remember, and hallow the
   brim
Of your cup with a sigh, as you crown it to
   him
Who is lonely and sad in these valleys so
   fair,
And would pine in Elysium, if friends were
   not there.

—THOMAS MOORE

FRIENDSHIP

Dear friend, I pray thee, if thou wouldst be
    proving
   Thy strong regard for me,
Make me no vows. Lip service is not loving;
   Let thy faith speak for thee.

Swear not to me that nothing can divide us,
   So little such oaths mean,
But when distrust and envy creep beside us,
   Let them not come between.

Say not to me the depths of thy devotion
   Are deeper than the sea;
But watch, lest doubt of some unkind emotion
   Embittered them for me.

Vow not to love me ever and forever,
   Words are such idle things,
But when we differ in opinions, never
   Hurt me by little stings.

I'm sick of words, they are so lightly spoken
   And spoken as but air.
I'd rather feel thy trust in me unbroken
   Than list to thy words so fair.

If all the little proofs of trust are heeded,
   If thou art always kind,
No sacrifice, no promise will be needed
   To satisfy my mind.

          —ELLA WHEELER WILCOX

FRIENDS

I think that God will never send
A gift so precious as a friend,
A friend who always understands
And fills each need as it demands
Whose loyalty will stand the test,
When skies are bright or overcast.

Who sees the faults that merit blame.
But keeps on loving just the same;
Who does far more than creeds could do
To make us good, to make us true,
Earth's gifts a sweet enjoyment lend
But only God can give a friend.

          —DR. ROSALIE CARTER

PASS IT ON

Have you had a kindness shown?
   Pass it on.
'Twas not given for thee alone,
   Pass it on.
Let it travel down the years,
Let it wipe another's tears,
'Till in heav'n the deed appears—
   Pass it on.

Did you hear the loving word?
   Pass it on—
Like the singing of a bird?
   Pass it on.
Let its music live and grow,
Let it cheer another's woe;
You have reaped what others sow—
   Pass it on.

'Twas the sunshine of a smile—
   Pass it on.
Staying but a little while!
   Pass it on.
April beam's a little thing,
Still it wakes the flowers of spring,
Makes the silent birds to sing—
   Pass it on.

Have you found the heavenly light?
   Pass it on.
Souls are groping in the night,
   Daylight gone-
Hold thy lighted lamp on high,
Be a star in someone's sky,
He may live who else would die—
   Pass it on.

Be not selfish in thy greed,
   Pass it on.
Look upon thy brother's need,
   Pass it on.
Live for self, you live in vain;
Live for Christ, you live again;
Live for Him, with Him you reign—
   Pass it on.

          —HENRY BURTON

TELL HIM SO

If you hear a kind word spoken
  Of some worthy soul you know,
It may fill his heart with sunshine
  If you only tell him so.

If a deed, however humble,
  Helps you on your way to go,
Find the one whose hand helped you,
  Seek him out and tell him so.

TOUCHING SHOULDERS

There's a comforting thought at the close
  of the day,
When I'm weary and lonely and sad
That sort of grips hold of this crusty old
  heart
And bids it be merry and glad.
It gets in my soul, and drives out the blues
And finally thrills through and through.
It is just a sweet memory that chants the
  refrain
I'm glad I touched shoulders with you.

Or you know you were brave, did you
  know you were strong?
Did you know there was one leaning hard?
Did you know that I waited and listened
  and prayed?
And was cheered by your simplest word?
Did you know that I longed for that smile
  on your face?
For the sound of your voice ringing true?
Did you know I grew stronger, and better
  because,
I had merely rubbed shoulders with you?

THE BOOMERANG

When a bit of sunshine hits ye,
  After passing of a cloud,
When a fit of laughter gits ye
  And ye'r spine is feelin' proud,
Don't forget to up and fling it
  At a soul that's feelin' blue,
For the minit that ye sling it
  It's a boomerang to you.

—Capt. Jack Crawford

LET SOMETHING GOOD BE SAID

When over the fair fame of friend or foe
  The shadow of disgrace shall fall instead
Of words of blame, or proof of thus and so,
  Let something good be said.

Forget not that no fellow-being yet
  May fall so low but love may lift his head;
Even the cheek of shame with tears is wet,
  If something good be said.

No generous heart may vainly turn aside,
  In ways of sympathy; no soul so dead
But may awaken strong and glorified,
  If something good be said.

And so I charge ye, by the thorny crown,
  And by the cross on which the Savior bled,
And by our own soul's hope of fair renown,
  Let something good be said!

—James Whitcomb Riley

IF I HAD KNOWN

If I had known what trouble you were
  bearing;
What griefs were in the silence of your face;
I would have been more gentle, and more
  caring,
And tried to give you gladness for a space.
I would have brought more warmth into the
  place,
  If I had known.

If I had known what thoughts despairing
  drew you;
(Why do we never try to understand?)
I would have lent a little friendship to you,
And slipped my hand within your hand,
And made your stay more pleasant in the land,
  If I had known.

—Mary Carolyn Davies

Life would be a perpetual flea hunt if a man were obliged to run down all the innuendoes, inveracities, insinuations and misrepresentations which are uttered against him.

—Henry Ward Beecher

A FUNNY THING

It is a funny thing, but true,
That folks you don't like, don't like you;
I don't know why this should be so,
But just the same I always know
If I am "sour," friends are few;
If I am friendly, folks are, too.
Sometimes I get up in the morn
A-wishing' I was never born;
I make of cross remarks a few,
And then my family wishes, too,
That I had gone some other place
Instead of showing them my face.
But let me change my little "tune,"
And sing and smile, then pretty soon
The folks around me sing and smile;
I guess 'twas catching all the while.
Yes, 'tis a funny thing, but true,
The folks you like will sure like you.

LOYALTY

He may be six kinds of a liar,
    He may be ten kinds of a fool,
He may be a wicked highflyer
    Beyond any reason or rule;
There may be a shadow above him
    Of ruin and woes to impend,
And I may not respect, but I love him,
    Because—well, because he's my friend.

I know he has faults by the billion,
    But his faults are a portion of him;
I know that his record's vermilion,
    And he's far from the sweet Seraphim;
But he's always been square with yours truly,
    Ready to give or to lend,
And if he is wild and unruly,
    I like him—because he's my friend.

I criticize him but I do it
    In just a frank, comradely key,
And back-biting gossips will rue it
    If ever they knock him to me!
I never make diagrams of him,
    No maps of his soul have I penned;
I don't analyze—I Just love him,
    Because—well, because he's my friend.

—BERTON BRALEY

THE FRIEND WHO STANDS BY

When trouble comes your soul to try,
You love the friend who just stands by.
Perhaps there's nothing he can do;
The thing is strictly up to you,
For there are troubles all your own,
And paths the soul must tread alone;
Times when love can't smooth the road,
Nor friendship lift the heavy load.

But just to feel you have a friend,
Who will stand by until the end;
Whose sympathy through all endures,
Whose warm handclasp is always yours.
It helps somehow to pull you through,
Although there's nothing he can do;
And so with fervent heart we cry,
"God bless the friend who just stands by."

Let me not shut myself within myself
    Nor dedicate my days to petty things,
Let there be many windows in my life,
    The entrance to my heart a door that
        swings.

Save me from self-preferment that would gain
    Its cloistered place, safe sheltered from the
        strife.
But purposeful and calm and sweet and sane,
    Lord, keep me in the Living Room of life.

Do not keep the alabaster boxes of your love and tenderness sealed up until your friends are dead. Fill their lives with sweetness. Speak approving, cheering words while their ears can hear them and while their hearts can be thrilled by them.

—HENRY WARD BEECHER

I've often wished that I had clear,
For life, six-hundred pounds a year,
A handsome house to lodge a friend,
A river at my garden's end.

—JONATHAN SWIFT

I am no friend to purely psychological attachments. In some unknown future they may be satisfying, but in the present I want your words and your voice, with your thoughts, your looks, and your gestures to interpret your feelings. The warm strong grasp of Great Heart's hand is as dear to me as the steadfast fashion of his friendships.

—Henry Van Dyke

WE LIVE IN DEEDS

We live in deeds, not years; in thoughts, not
* breaths;*
In feelings, not in figures on a dial.
We should count time by heart-throbs. He
* most lives*
Who thinks most, feels the noblest, acts the
* best.*
And he whose heart beats quickest lives the
* longest:*
Lives in one hour more than in years do some
Whose fat blood sleeps as it slips along their
* veins.*

—Philip James Bailey

Art thou lonely, O my brother?
Share thy little with another!
Stretch a hand to one unfriended,
And thy loneliness is ended.

—John Oxenham

They parted ne'er to meet again,
But never either found another
To free the hollow heart from paining;
They stood aloof, the scars remaining,
Like cliffs which have been rent asunder,
A dreary sea now rolls between;
And neither heat, nor frost, nor thunder,
Shall wholly do away, I ween,
The marks of that which once hath been.

Flowers are lovely; love is flower-like;
* Friendship is a sheltering tree;*
Oh, the joys that came down shower-like,
* Of friendship, love and liberty,*
*   Ere I was old!*

—Samuel Taylor Coleridge

IF YOU'RE EVER GOING TO LOVE ME

If you're ever going to love me love me now,
* while I can know*
All the sweet and tender feelings which from
* real affection flow.*
Love me now, while I am living; do not wait
* till I am gone*
And then chisel it in marble—warm love words
* on ice-cold stone.*

If you've dear, sweet thoughts about me, why
*   not whisper them to me?*
Don't you know 'twould make me happy and
* as glad as glad could be?*
If you wait till I am sleeping, ne'er to waken
* here again,*
There'll be walls of earth between us and I
* couldn't hear you then.*

If you knew someone was thirsting for a drop
* of water sweet*
Would you be so slow to bring it? Would
* you step with laggard feet?*
There are tender hearts all round us who are
* thirsting for our love;*
Why withhold from them what nature makes
* them crave all else above?*

I won't need your kind caresses when the
* grass grows o'er my face;*
I won't crave your love or kisses in my last
* resting place.*
So, then, if you love me any, if it's but a little
* bit,*
Let me know it now while living; I can own
* and treasure it.*

He who has a thousand friends has not a
* friend to spare,*
And he who has one enemy shall meet him
* everywhere.*

—Ali Ben Abu Taleb

A true friend is distinguished in the crisis of hazard and necessity; when the gallantry of his aid may show the worth of his soul and the loyalty of his heart.

—Ennius

Love

Because you love me all my life
  Is circled with unquestioned rest;
Yes, even Life and even Death
  Is all unquestioned and all blest.

I hold it true, what'er befall;
  I feel it, when I sorrow most;
  'Tis better to have loved and lost
Than never to have loved at all.

—ALFRED LORD TENNYSON

To love is the great Amulet that makes this world a garden.

—ROBERT LOUIS STEVENSON

Love is friendship set to music.

—POLLOCK

HOW DO I LOVE THEE

How do I love thee? Let me count the ways.
I love thee to the depth and breadth and height
My soul can reach, when feeling out of sight
For the ends of Being and ideal Grace.
I love thee to the level of everyday's
Most quiet need, by sun and candle-light.
I love thee freely, as men strive for Right;
I love thee purely, as they turn from Praise.
I love thee with the passion put to use
In my old griefs, and with my childhood's
* faith.*
I love thee with a love I seemed to lose
With my lost saints,—I love thee with the
* breath,*
Smiles, tears of all my life!—and, if God
* choose,*
I shall but love thee better after death.

—ELIZABETH BARRETT BROWNING

Love comes unseen; we only see it go.

—AUSTIN DOBSON

LOVE'S STRENGTH

Measure thy life by loss instead of gain,
Not by the wine drunk, but the wine poured
* forth;*
For love's strength standeth in love's sacrifice,
And whoso suffers most hath most to give.
For labor, the common lot of man,
Is part of the kind Creator's plan;
And he is a king whose brow is wet
With the pearl-gemmed crown of honest
* sweat.*
Some glorious day, this understood,
All toilers will be a brotherhood,
With brain or hand the purpose is one,
And the Master-workman, God's own Son.

Come, let us make love deathless, thou and I, Seeing that our footing on earth is brief. . . .

—HERBERT TRENCH

A life without love in it is like a heap of ashes upon a deserted hearth—with the fire dead, the laughter stilled, and the light extinguished. It is like a winter landscape—with the sun hidden, the flowers frozen, and the wind whispering through the withered leaves ❧ God knows we need all the unselfish love that can come to us. For love is seldom unselfish. There is usually the motive and the price. Do you remember William Morris, and how his life was lived, his fortune spent, his hands busied—in the service of others? He was the father of the settlement movement, of co-operative homes for working people, and of the arts and crafts revival, in our day. He was a "soldier of the common good." After he was gone—his life began to grow in radiance and power, like a beacon set high upon a dangerous shore. In the twilight of his days he wrote what I like to think was his creed—and mine: "I'm going your way, so let us go hand in hand. You help me and I'll help you. We shall not be here very long, for soon death, the kind old nurse, will come back and rock us all to sleep. Let us help one another while we may."

—FRANK P. TEBBETTS

Riches take wings, comforts vanish, hope withers away, but love stays with us. God is love.

—LEW WALLACE

LOVE

There is beauty in the forest
When the trees are green and fair,
There is beauty in the meadow
When wild flowers scent the air.
There is beauty in the sunlight
And the soft blue beams above.
Oh, the world is full of beauty
When the heart is full of love.

TRUE LOVE
Sonnet XVI

Let me not to the marriage of true minds
Admit impediments. Love is not love
Which alters when it alteration finds,
Or bends with the remover to remove.
O, no! it is an ever-fixed mark,
That looks on tempests and is never shaken;
It is the star to every wandering bark,
Whose worth's unknown, although his height
    be taken.
Love's not Time's fool, though rosy lips and
    cheeks
Within his bending sickle's compass come;
Love alters not with his brief hours and weeks,
But bears it out even to the edge of doom.
    If this be error and upon me proved,
    I never writ, nor no man ever loved.

—WILLIAM SHAKESPEARE

COMPANIONSHIP

It isn't that we talk so much!
Sometimes the evening through
You do not say a word to me;
I do not talk to you.
I sit beside the reading lamp,
You like your easy chair,
And it is joy enough for me
To know that you are there!

It isn't that we go so much!
Sometimes we like to roam
To concert or to theater,
But best of all is home.
I sew a bit or read aloud
A book we want to share,
And it is joy enough for me
To know that you are there!

It isn't that you tell to me
The thing I've come to know.
It goes too deep for words, I think,
The fact you love me so.
You only have to touch my hand
To learn how much I care,
And it is joy enough for me
To know that you are there!

—ANNE CAMPBELL

RETALIATION

How often, for some trivial wrong,
    In anger, we retaliate,
We learn, although it takes us long,
    That life is far too brief for hate.

—MARGARET E. BRUNER

YOU AND I

My hand is lonely for your clasping, dear;
    My ear is tired waiting for your call.
I want your strength to help, your laugh to
        cheer;
    Heart, soul and senses need you, one and all.

I droop without your full, frank sympathy;
    We ought to be together—you and I;
We want each other so, to comprehend
    The dream, the hope, things planned, or
        seen, or wrought.

Companion, comforter and guide and friend,
    As much as love asks love, does thought
        ask thought.
Life is so short, so fast the lone hours fly,
    We ought to be together, you and I.

—HENRY ALFORD

I WANT YOU

I want you when the shades of eve are falling
 And purpling shadows drift across the land;
When sleepy birds to loving mates are calling—
 I want the soothing softness of your hand.
I want you when the stars shine up above me,
 And Heaven's flooded with the bright
  moonlight;
I want you with your arms and lips to love me
 Throughout the wonder watches of the
  night.

I want you when in dreams I still remember
 The ling'ring of your kiss—for old times'
  sake—
With all your gentle ways, so sweetly tender,
 I want you in the morning when I wake.
I want you when the day is at its noontime,
 Sun-steeped and quiet, or drenched with
  sheets of rain;
I want you when the roses bloom in June-
  time;
 I want you when the violets come again.

I want you when my soul is thrilled with
  passion;
 I want you when I'm weary and depressed;
I want you when in lazy, slumbrous fashion
 My senses need the haven of your breast.
I want you when through field and wood I'm
  roaming;
 I want you when I'm standing on the shore;
I want you when the summer birds are
  homing—
 And when they've flown—I want you
  more and more.

I want you, dear, through every changing
  season;
 I want you with a tear or with a smile;
I want you more than any rhyme or reason—
 I want you, want you, want you—all the
  while.

 —Arthur L. Gillom

O Love, that wilt not let me go,
 I rest my weary soul in Thee;
I give Thee back the life I owe,
That in Thine ocean depth its flow
 May richer, fuller be.

L ove knows no limit to its endurance, no end to its trust, no fading of its hope: it can outlast anything. It is, in fact, the one thing that still stands when all else has fallen.

 —I Corinthians 13:7-8
 (J. B. Phillips, *Letters to Young Churches*)

WHAT IS LOVE?

It's silence when your words would hurt,
It's patience when your neighbor's curt.
It's deafness when the scandal flows,
It's thoughtfulness for another's woes.
It's promptness when stern duty calls,
It's courage when misfortune falls.

MISS YOU

Miss you, miss you, miss you;
Everything I do
Echoes with the laughter
And the voice of You.
You're on every corner
Every turn and twist,
Every old familiar spot
Whispers how you're missed.

Miss you, miss you, miss you!
Everywhere I go
There are poignant memories
Dancing in a row.
Silhouette and shadow
Of your form and face
Substance and reality
Everywhere displace.

Oh, I miss you, miss you!
God! I miss you, Girl!
There's a strange silence
'Mid the busy whirl
Just as tho' the ordinary
Daily things I do
Wait with me, expectant
For a word from You.

Miss you, miss you, miss you!
Nothing now seems true
Only that 'twas heaven
Just to be with You.

 —David Cory

THE PENALTY OF LOVE

If Love should count you worthy, and
    should deign
    One day to seek your door and be your
    guest,
    Pause! ere you draw the bolt and bid him
    rest,
If in your old content you would remain,
For not alone he enters; in his train
    Are angels of the mist the lonely guest,
    Dreams of the unfulfilled and unpossessed,
And sorrow and Life's immemorial pain.

He wakes desires you never may forget,
    He shows you stars you never saw before.
    He makes you share with him, for
    evermore,
The burden of the world's divine regret.
How wise you were to open not! and yet,
    How poor if you should turn him from
    the door!

    —SIDNEY ROYSE LYSAGHT

NOTHING SHALL PART US

Distance nor death shall part us, dear,
Nor yet the traitor word;
And love shall live within our home
As blithe as any bird.

The sight of you is in my eyes,
Your touch is in my hand;
They cannot part us now, my love,
With miles of weary land.

Man with his sword and Death his scythe,
Are but the tricks of time,
To tease me with empty years
Before we shared one name.

    —HENRY TREECE

Loving means to love that which is un-
lovable, or it is no virtue at all; forgiving means to pardon the unpardonable,
or it is no virtue at all; faith means believing
the unbelievable, or it is no virtue at all.
And to hope means hoping when things are
hopeless, or it is no virtue at all.

    —GILBERT K. CHESTERTON

GOD KEEP YOU

God keep you, dearest, all this lonely night:
    The winds are still,
    The moon drops down behind the western
    hill;
God keep you safely, dearest, till the light.

God keep you then when slumber melts away,
    And care and strife
    Take up new arms to fret our waking life,
God keep you through the battle of the day.

God keep you. Nay, beloved soul, how vain,
    How poor is prayer!
I can but say again, and yet again,
    God keep you every time and everywhere.

    —MADELINE BRIDGES

Intreat me not to leave thee,
    And to return from following after thee:
For whither thou goest, I will go;
    And where thou lodgest, I will lodge;
Thy people shall be my people,
    And thy God my God;
Where thou diest, will I die,
    And there will I be buried:
The Lord do so to me,
And more also,
    If aught but death part thee and me.

    —RUTH 1:16-17

LOVE AND HATE

The sole thing I hate is Hate;
For Hate is death; and Love is life,
A peace, a splendor from above;
And Hate, a never ending strife,
A smoke, a blackness from the abyss
Where unclean serpents coil and hiss!
Love is the Holy Ghost within;
Hate the unpardonable sin!
Who preaches otherwise than this
Betrays his Master with a kiss!

    —HENRY WADSWORTH LONGFELLOW

A new commandment I give unto you,
That ye love one another; as I have
loved you, that ye also love one another.

    —JOHN 13:34

IF YOU BUT KNEW

If you but knew
How all my days seemed filled with dreams
    of you,
How sometimes in the silent night
Your eyes thrill through me with their tender
    light,
How oft I hear your voice when others speak,
How you 'mid other forms I seek—
Oh, love more real than though such dreams
    were true
If you but knew.

Could you but guess
How you alone make all my happiness,
How I am more than willing for your sake
To stand alone, give all and nothing take,
Nor chafe to think you bound while I am
    free,
Quite free, till death, to love you silently,
Could you but guess.

Could you but learn
How when you doubt my truth I sadly yearn
To tell you all, to stand for one brief space
Unfettered, soul to soul, as face to face,
To crown you king, my king, till life shall
    end,
My lover and likewise my truest friend,
Would you love me, dearest, as fondly in
    return,
Could you but learn?

From "SONNETS FROM THE PORTUGUESE"

If thou must love me, let it be for naught
Except for love's sake only. Do not say,
"I love her for her smile—her look—her way
Of speaking gently,—for a trick of thought
That falls in well with mine, and certes
    brought
A sense of pleasant ease on such a day"—
For these things in themselves, Beloved, may
Be changed, or change for thee,—and love,
    so wrought,

May be unwrought so. Neither love me for
Thine own dear pity's wiping my cheeks
    dry,—

A creature might forget to weep, who bore
Thy comfort long, and lose thy love thereby!
But love me for love's sake, that evermore
Thou mayst love on, through love's eternity.

Go from me. Yet I feel that I shall stand
Henceforward in thy shadow. Nevermore
Alone upon the threshold of my door
Of individual life I shall command
The uses of my soul, nor lift my hand
Serenely, in the sunshine as before,
Without the sense of that which I forebore—
Thy touch upon the palm. The widest land
Doom takes to part us, leaves thy heart in
    mine
With pulses that beat double. What I do
And what I dream include thee, as the wine
Must taste of its own grapes. And when I sue
Go for myself, He hears that name of thine,
And sees within my eyes the tears of two.

—Elizabeth Barrett Browning

MAKE IT UP

Life is too short for grievances—
For quarrels and for tears,
What's the use of wasting
Precious days and precious tears.

If there's something to forgive—
Forgive without delay—
Maybe you too, were part to blame,
So make it up today.

Be generous—forget the past
And take the broader view,
Cast away all bitterness and
Let the sunshine through.

If it's within your power
A broken heart to mend,
Remember—Love is all that
Really matters—in the end.

EMPHASIS

We flatter those we scarcely know,
    We please the fleeting guest,
And deal full many a thoughtless blow
    To those we love the best.

—Ella Wheeler Wilcox

FIDELIS

You have taken back the promise
That you spoke so long ago;
Taken back the heart you gave me—
I must even let it go.
Where Love once has breathed, Pride dieth;
So I struggled, but in vain,
First to keep the links together,
Then to piece the broken chain.

But it might not be—so freely
All your friendship I restore,
And the heart that I had taken
As my own forevermore.
No shade of reproach shall touch you,
Dread no more a claim from me—
But I will not have you fancy
That I count myself as free.

I am bound by the old promise;
What can break that golden chain?
Not even the words that you have spoken,
Or the sharpness of my pain:
Do you think, because you fail me
And draw back your hand today,
That from out the heart I gave you
My strong love can fade away?

I will live. No eyes may see it;
In my soul it will lie deep,
Hidden from all; but I shall feel it
Often stirring in its sleep.
So remember that the friendship
Which you now think poor and vain,
Will endure in hope and patience,
Till you ask for it again.

Perhaps in some long twilight hour,
Like those we have known of old,
When past shadows gather round you,
And your present friends grow cold,
You may stretch your hands out towards me—
Ah! You will—I know not when—
I shall nurse my love and keep it
Faithfully, for you, till then.

—ADELAIDE ANNE PROCTER

The kindest and the happiest pair
Will find occasion to forbear;
And something, every day they live,
To pity, and perhaps forgive.

—WILLIAM COWPER

We may give without loving, but we cannot love without giving.

Self is the only prison that can ever bind the
soul;
Love is the only angel who can bid the
gates unroll;
And when he comes to thee, arise and
follow fast;
His way may lie through darkness, but it
leads to light at last.

LOVE THAT GIVES

Love that asketh love again
Finds the barter naught but pain;
Love that giveth in full store
Aye receives as much and more.
Love exacting nothing back
Never knoweth any lack;
Love, compelling love to pay,
Sees him bankrupt every day.

Believe me, if all those endearing young
charms,
Which I gaze on so fondly to-day,
Were to change by to-morrow, and fleet in
my arms,
Like fairy-gifts fading away,
Thou wouldst still be adored, as this
moment thou art,
Let thy loveliness fade as it will,
And around the dear ruin each wish of my
heart
Would entwine itself verdantly still.

It is not while beauty and youth are thine
own,
And thy cheeks unprofaned by a tear,
That the fervor and faith of a soul may be
known,
To which time will but make thee more
dear!
No, the heart that has truly loved never
forgets,
But as truly loves on to the close,
As the sunflower turns to her god when he
sets
The same look which she turned when he
rose!

—THOMAS MOORE

CHOOSE CAREFULLY

A careless word may kindle strife;
*   A cruel word may wreck a life.*
*   A bitter word may hate instill;*
*   A brutal word may smite and kill.*

A gracious word may smooth the way;
*   A joyous word may light the day.*
*   A timely word may lessen stress;*
*   A loving word may heal and bless.*

LET MY LIFE SING

Make me too brave to lie or be unkind.
Make me too understanding, too, to mind
The little hurts companions give, and friends,
The careless hurts that no one quite intends.
May I forget
What ought to be forgotten, and recall,
Unfailing, all
That ought to be recalled, each kindly thing,
Forgetting what might sting.
To all upon my way,
Day after day,
Let me be joy, be hope! Let my life sing!

—DAVIES

What shall I do, my friend,
*   When you are gone forever?*
My heart its eager need will send
*   Through the years to find you never.*
And how will it be with you,
*   In the weary world, I wonder,*
Will you love me with a love as true,
*   When our paths lie far asunder?*

The way is short, O friend,
*   That reaches out before us;*
God's tender heavens above us bend,
*   His love is smiling o'er us;*
A little while is ours
*   For sorrow or for laughter;*
I'll lay the hand you love in yours
*   On the shore of the Hereafter.*

—MARY CLEMMER

Where true love bestows its sweetness,
Where true friendship lays its hand,
Dwells all greatness, all completeness,
All the wealth of every land.

—J. G. HOLLAND

Love is the river of life in this world. Think not that ye know it who stand at the little tinkling rill, the first small fountain.

Not until you have gone through the rocky gorges, and not lost the stream; not until you have gone through the meadow, and the stream has widened and deepened until fleets could ride on its bosom; not until beyond the meadow you have come to the unfathomable ocean, and poured your treasures into its depths—not until then can you know what love is.

—HENRY WARD BEECHER

OUT OF THE PAST

Out of the past what now I would reclaim
*   And know once more if such a joy could*
*   be?*
The brilliant deed which brought the touch
*   of fame?*
*   The smart investments from which profits*
*   came?*
What is it that is gone I long to see?
*   What is it that still haunts the soul of me?*

What torches through the night of memory
*   flame?*
I would turn back not once again to know
The victories that were, nor to amend
The failures, but to meet the friend
Who shared the struggles of the long ago;
To live the joys which had so swift an end;
The charms which only friendships can
*   bestow.*

Gratitude

The greatest saint in the world is not he who prays most or fasts most; it is not he who gives most alms, or is most eminent for temperance, chastity or justice. It is he who is most thankful to God, and who has a heart always ready to praise God. This is the perfection of all virtues. Joy in God and thankfulness to God is the highest perfection of a divine and holy life.

—WILLIAM LAW

ADORATION, PRAISE, AND THANKSGIVING

I thank thee, God, that I have lived
In this great world and known its many joys;
The song of birds, the strong, sweet scent
*   of hay*
And the cooling breezes in the secret dusk,
The flaming sunsets at the close of day,
Hills, and the lonely, heather-covered moors,
Music at night, and moonlight on the sea,
The heat of waves upon the rocky shore
And wild, white spray, flung high in ecstasy:
The faithful eyes of dogs, and treasured
*   books,*
The love of kin and fellowship of friends,
And all that makes life dear and beautiful.

I thank Thee, too, that there has come to me
A little heartache and the loneliness
That comes with parting, and the word,
*   "Goodbye,"*
Dawn breaking after dreary hours of pain,
When I discovered that night's gloom must
*   yield*
And morning light break through to me
*   again.*
Because of these and other blessings poured
Unasked upon my wondering head,
Because I know that there is yet to come
An even richer and more glorious life,
And most of all, because Thine only Son
Once sacrificed life's loveliness for me—
I thank Thee, God, that I have lived.

—Elizabeth Craven

The world is too much with us; late and soon,
Getting and spending, we lay waste our
*   powers:*
Little we see in Nature that is ours;
We have given our hearts away, a sordid
*   boon!*
This sea that bares her bosom to the moon,
The winds that will be howling at all hours,
And are up-gathered now like sleeping
*   flowers;*
For this, for everything, we are out of tune;
It moves us not.—Great God! I'd rather be
A pagan suckled in a creed outworn;
So might I, standing on this pleasant lea,
Have glimpses that would make me less
*   forlorn;*
Have sight of Proteus rising from the sea;
Or hear old Triton blow his wreathed horn.

—William Wordsworth

Gratitude is the heart's memory.

—J. B. Massieu

Blow, blow, thou winter wind!
*   Thou art not so unkind*
*   As man's ingratitude;*
*   Thy tooth is not so keen*
*   Because thou art not seer*
*   Although thy breath be rude.*

—William Shakespeare

THE SELKIRK GRACE

Some hae meat, and canna eat,
And some wad eat that want it;
But we hae meat and we can eat,
And sae the Lord be thankit.

—Robert Burns

Poor soul! God's goodness hath been great to
*   thee:*
Let never day nor night unhallow'd pass,
But still remember what the Lord hath done.

—William Shakespeare

A THANKSGIVING

For summer rain, and winter's sun,
For autumn breezes crisp and sweet;
For labors doing, to be done,
    And labors all complete;
For April, May, and lovely June,
For bud, and bird, and berried vine;
For joys of morning, night, and noon,
    My thanks, dear Lord, are Thine!

For loving friends on every side;
For children full of joyous glee;
For all the blessed Heavens wide,
    And for the sounding sea;
For mountains, valleys, forests deep;
For maple, oak, and lofty pine;
For rivers on their seaward sweep,
    My thanks, dear Lord, are Thine!

For light and air, for sun and shade,
For merry laughter and for cheer;
For music and the glad parade
    Of blessings through the year;
For all the fruitful earth's increase,
For home, and life, and love divine,
For hope, and faith, and perfect peace,
    My thanks, dear Lord, are Thine!

—JOHN KENDRICK BANGS

If a man does not keep pace with his companions, perhaps it is because he hears a different drummer. Let him step to the music which he hears, however measured or far away.

—HENRY DAVID THOREAU

From "ROOFS"

They say that life is a highway and its mile-
    stones are the years,
And now and then there's a toll-gate where
    you buy your way with tears.
It's a rough road and a steep road, and it
    stretches broad and far,
But at last it leads to a golden Town where
    golden Houses are.

—JOYCE KILMER

Gratitude is the fairest blossom which springs from the soul.

—BALLOU

THANKFULNESS

My God, I thank Thee who has made
    The earth so bright;
So full of splendor and of joy,
    Beauty and light;
So many glorious things are here,
    Noble and right!

I thank Thee, too, that Thou has made
    Joy to abound;
So many gentle thoughts and deeds
    Circling us round,
That in the darkest spot of earth
    Some love is found.

I thank Thee more that all our joy
    Is touched with pain;
That shadows fall on brightest hours;
    That thorns remain;
So that earth's bliss may be our guide,
    And not our chain.

I thank Thee, Lord, that Thou hast kept
    The best in store;
We have enough, yet not too much
    To long for more:
A yearning for a deeper peace,
    Not known before.

I thank Thee, Lord, that here our souls,
    Though amply blest,
Can never find, although they seek,
    A perfect rest,—
Nor ever shall, until they lean
    On Jesus' breast!

—ADELAIDE ANNE PROCTER

OUR PRAYER

Thou that hast given so much to me,
Give one thing more—a grateful heart;
Not thankful when it pleaseth me,
As if Thy blessings had spare days;
But such a heart, whose pulse may be
Thy praise.

—GEORGE HERBERT

I NEVER THOUGHT
TO OFFER THANKS

*I've always said my daily prayers
For I thought that I should pray.
And so I learned the routine ones
And said them every day.*

*They were the ones that someone else
Had written long ago
So they were never quite my own;
But how was I to know*

*Just what to say to God that would
Explain to Him my needs
When I had everything I wanted?
I never thought of it as greed*

*To ask for more and more of life;
For fortune and for great success
With all about me friends to make
And share my happiness.*

*And so for all the wealth of life—
The kind not stored in banks—
For just the breath I drew each day,
I never thought to offer thanks.*

*But now it seems that I grow wiser
With the coming of each day
And I am substituting "Thanks" for "Please"
When it's time for me to pray.*

—ELIZABETH SMITH

GRATITUDE

*I thank You for these gifts, dear God,
    Upon Thanksgiving Day—
For love and laughter and the faith
    That makes me kneel to pray.*

*For life that lends me happiness,
    And sleep that gives me rest,
These are the gifts that keep my heart
    Serene within my breast.*

*Love, laughter, faith and life and sleep,
    We own them, every one—
They carry us along the road
    That leads from sun to sun.*

—MARGARET E. SANGSTER

We all belong to each other, but friendship is the especial accord of one life with a kindred life. We tremble at the threshold of any new friendship with awe and wonder and fear lest it should not be real or, believing that it is, lest we should prove ourselves unworthy of the solemn and holy contact of life with life, of soul with soul. We cannot live unworthy lives in the constant presence of noble beings to whom we belong and who believe that we are at least endeavoring after nobleness.

—RALPH WALDO EMERSON

WE ARE THANKFUL FOR THESE

*These to be thankful for: a friend,
A work to do, a way to wend,
And these in which to take delight;
The wind that turns the poplars white,*

*Wonder and gleam of common things,
Sunlight upon a sea-gull's wings,
Odors of earth and dew-drenched lawns,
The pageantry of darks and dawns;*

*Blue vistas of a city street
At twilight, music, passing feet,
The thrill of Spring, half joy, half pain,
The deep voice of the Autumn rain.*

*Shall we not be content with these
Imperishable mysteries?
And jocund-hearted take our share
Of joy and pain and find life fair?——*

*Wayfarers on a road where we
Set forth each day right valiantly,
Expectant, dauntless, blithe, content,
To make the great experiment.*

MY LIFE CLOSED TWICE
BEFORE ITS CLOSE

*My life closed twice before its close;
It yet remains to see
If Immortality unveil
A third event to me,
So huge, so hopeless to conceive,
As these that twice befell.
Parting is all we know of heaven,
And all we need of hell.*

—EMILY DICKINSON

Happiness

Happiness is a sunbeam which may pass through a thousand bosoms without losing a particle of its original ray; nay, when it strikes a kindred heart, like the converged light upon a mirror, it reflects itself with redoubled brightness. It is not perfected till it is shared.

—JANE PORTER

The longer I live the more I am convinced that the one thing worth living for and dying for is the privilege of making someone more happy and more useful. No man who ever does anything to lift his fellows ever makes a sacrifice.

—Booker T. Washington

THINKING HAPPINESS

Think of the things that make you happy,
  Not the things that make you sad;
Think of the fine and true in mankind,
  Not its sordid side and bad;
Think of the blessings that surround you,
  Not the ones that are denied;
Think of the virtues of your friendships,
  Not the weak and faulty side;

Think of the gains you've made in business,
  Not the losses you've incurred;
Think of the good of you that's spoken,
  Not some cruel, hostile word;
Think of the days of health and pleasure,
  Not the days of woe and pain;
Think of the days alive with sunshine,
  Not the dismal days of rain;

Think of the hopes that lie before you,
  Not the waste that lies behind;
Think of the treasures you have gathered,
  Not the ones you've failed to find;
Think of the service you may render,
  Not of serving self alone;
Think of the happiness of others,
  And in this you'll find your own!

—Robert E. Farley

What right have I to make every one in the house miserable because I am miserable? Troubles must come to all, but troubles need not be wicked, and it is wicked to be a destroyer of happiness.

—Amelia E. Barr

CHARACTER OF A HAPPY LIFE

How happy is he born and taught
That serveth not another's will;
Whose armour is his honest thought
And simple truth his utmost skill!

Whose passions not his masters are,
Whose soul is still prepared for death,
Not tied unto the world with care
Of public fame, or private breath;

Who envies none that chance doth raise
Or vice; who never understood
How deepest wounds are given by praise;
Nor rules of state, but rules of good:

Who hath his life from rumours freed,
Whose conscience is his strong retreat;
Whose state can neither flatterers feed,
Nor ruin make accusers great;

Who God doth late and early pray
More of his grace than gifts to lend;
And entertains the harmless day
With a well-chosen book or friend;

—This man is freed from servile bands
Of hope to rise, or fear to fall;
Lord of himself, though not of lands;
And having nothing, yet hath all.

—Sir Henry Wotton

People are lonely because they build walls instead of bridges.

Happiness is a perfume you cannot pour on others without getting a few drops on yourself.

May you have enough happiness to keep you sweet, enough trials to keep you strong—enough sorrows to keep you human, enough hope to keep you happy—enough failure to keep you humble, enough success to keep you eager—enough friends to give you comfort, enough wealth to meet your needs—enough enthusiasm to look forward, enough faith to banish depression, enough determination to make each day a better day than yesterday!

HAPPINESS

Happiness is like a crystal,
Fair and equisite and clear,
Broken in a million pieces,
Shattered, scattered far and near.
Now and then along life's pathway,
Lo! some shining fragments fall;
But there are so many pieces
No one ever finds them all.

You may find a bit of beauty,
Or an honest share of wealth,
While another just beside you
Gathers honor, love or health.
Vain to choose or grasp unduly,
Broken is the perfect ball;
And there are so many pieces
No one ever finds them all.

Yet the wise as on they journey
Treasure every fragment clear,
Fit them as they may together,
Imaging the shattered sphere,
Learning ever to be thankful,
Though their share of it is small;
For it has so many pieces
No one ever finds them all.

—PRISCILLA LEONARD

Instead of trying so hard, as some of us do, to be happy, as if that were the sole purpose of life, I would, if I were a boy again, try still harder to deserve happiness.

—JAMES T. FIELDS

The Golden Rule never tarnishes.

There is a wonderful, mystical law of nature that the three things we crave most in life—happiness, freedom, and peace of mind—are always attained by giving them to someone else.

Hail the small, sweet courtesies of life, for smooth do they make the road of it!

—LAURENCE STERNE

To look fearlessly upon life; to accept the laws of nature, not with meek resignation, but as her sons, who dare to search and question; to have peace and confidence within our souls—these are the beliefs that make for happiness.

—MAETERLINCK

DIVINE LAW

If you would keep young and happy, be good; live a high moral life; practice the principles of the brotherhood of man; send out good thoughts to all, and think evil of no man. This is in obedience to the great natural law; to live otherwise is to break this great Divine law. Other things being equal, it is the cleanest, purest minds that live long and are happy. The man who is growing and developing intellectually does not grow old like the man who has stopped advancing, but when ambition, aspirations and ideals halt, old age begins.

Happiness is as a butterfly, which, when pursued, is always beyond our grasp, but which, if you will sit down quietly, may alight upon you.

—NATHANIEL HAWTHORNE

The grand essentials to happiness in this life are something to do, something to love; and something to hope for.

—JOSEPH ADDISON

HAPPY THE MAN

Happy the man, whose wish and care
A few paternal acres bound,
Content to breathe his native air
In his own ground.

Whose herds with milk, whose fields with
bread,
Whose flocks supply him with attire;
Whose trees in summer yield him shade,
In winter fire.

Blest who can unconcernedly find
House, days, and years, slide soft away
In health of body, peace of mind;
Quiet by day.

Sound sleep by night; study and ease
Together mixed, sweet recreation,
And innocence, which most does please
With meditation.

Thus let me live, unseen, unknown;
Thus unlamented let me die;
Steal from the world, and not a stone
Tell where I lie.

—ALEXANDER POPE

UPLIFTING

It was 9 a.m. on a gloomy Monday and the elevator was filled with grumpy office workers. As the car started up, the elevator man began humming a tune and dancing a little jig. "You seem to be happy today," said one passenger glumly. "Yes Sir," was the reply, "I ain't never lived this day before."

Happiness in this world, when it comes, comes incidentally. Make it the object of pursuit, and it leads us a wild-goose chase, and is never attained.

—NATHANIEL HAWTHORNE

HAPPINESS

Happy is he who by love's sweet song,
Is cheered today as he goes along.
Happier is he who believes that tomorrow
Will ease all pain and take away all sorrow,
Happiest he who on earthly sod
Has faith in himself, his friends, and God.

TALK HAPPINESS

Talk happiness. *The world is sad enough*
Without your woe. No path is wholly
rough;
Look for the places that are smooth and clear,
And speak of those, to rest the weary ear
Of Earth, so hurt by one continuous strain
Of human discontent and grief and pain.

Talk faith. *The world is better off without*
Your uttered ignorance and morbid doubt.
If you have faith in God, or man, or self,
Say so. If not, push back upon the shelf
Of silence, all your thoughts, till faith shall
come;
No one will grieve because your lips are
dumb.

Talk health. *The dreary, never-ending tale*
Of mortal maladies is more than stale.
One cannot charm, or interest, or please
By harping on that minor chord, disease.
Say you are well, or all is well with you,
And God shall hear your words and make
them true.

—ELLA WHEELER WILCOX

VACATION BLESSING

Friend, may you keep your luggage light
And yours be all fair weather!
Your purse be full, your cares be slight,
Your shoes be sturdy leather!

And may some places that you find
Be nowhere mapped or charted:
The country of the carefree mind,
The hills of the high-hearted.

Happy surprises crowd your days
And nights, and bring sound sleeping;
And may you have a sense always
That you have God's safekeeping.

—JAMES DILLET FREEMAN

Peace is happiness digesting.

—VICTOR HUGO

BED-ROCK

I have been tried,
Tried in the fire,
And I say this,
As the result of dire distress,
And tribulation sore—
That a man's happiness doth not consist
Of that he hath, but of the faith
And trust in God's great love
These bring him to.
Nought else is worth consideration.
For the peace a man may find
In perfect trust in God
Outweighs all else, and is
The only possible foundation
For true happiness.

—JOHN OXENHAM

THE THINGS THAT COUNT

Not what we have, but what we use;
Not what we see, but what we choose—
These are the things that mar or bless
The sum of human happiness.

The things near by, not things afar;
Not what we seem, but what we are—
These are things that make or break,
That give the heart its joy or ache.

Not what seems fair, but what is true;
Not what we dream, but good we do—
These are the things that shine like gems,
Like stars, in Fortune's diadems.

Not as we take, but as we give;
Not as we pray, but as we live—
These are the things that make for peace,
Both now and after Time shall cease.

—CLARENCE URMY

REVELATION

Till Poverty knocked at her door
She never knew how bare
The uneventful days of those
Who have but want and care.

Till Sorrow lingered at her hearth
She never knew the night
Through which troubled souls might fare
To gain the morning's light.

Till Suffering had sought her house
She never knew what dread
May wrestle with, nor what grim fears
Of agony are bred.

And yet these unbidden guests
Had taught her to possess
A clear sight she never knew—
The height of happiness!

—CHARLOTTE BECKER

Happiness, I have discovered, is nearly always a rebound from hard work. It is one of the follies of men to imagine that they can enjoy mere thought, or emotion, or sentiment! As well try to eat beauty! For happiness must be tricked! She loves to see men at work. She loves sweat, weariness, self-sacrifice. She will be found not in palaces but lurking in cornfields and factories and hovering over littered desks: she crowns the unconscious head of the busy child. If you look up suddenly from hard work, you will see her,—but if you look too long she fades sorrowfully away.

—DAVID GRAYSON

BAD TIMES

Why slander we the times?
    What crimes
    Have days and years, that we
Thus charge them with iniquity?
    If we would rightly scan,
It's not the times are bad, but man.
    If thy desire it be
        To see
    The times prove good, be thou
But such thyself, and surely know
    That all thy days to thee
Shall spite of mischief happy be.

—JOSEPH BEAUMONT

THE MEANS TO ATTAIN HAPPY LIFE

Martial, the things that do attain
  The happy life be these, I find:—
The richesse left, not got with pain;
  The fruitful ground, the quiet mind;

The equal friend; no grudge, no strife;
  No charge of rule, nor governance;
Without disease, the healthful life;
  The household of continuance;

The mean diet, no delicate fare;
  True wisdom join'd with simpleness;
The night dischargèd of all care,
  Where wine the wit may not oppress.

The faithful wife, without debate;
  Such sleeps as may beguile the night;
Contented with thine own estate
  Ne wish for death, ne fear his might.

—HENRY HOWARD

A PLEA

Give me one friend, just one, who meets
  The needs of all my varying moods;
Be we in noisy city streets,
  Or in dear Nature's solitudes.

One who can let the World go by,
  And suffer not a minute's pang;
Who'd dare to shock propriety
  With me, and never care a hang.

Who, in my rarely righteous streaks,
  Should love me,—love me not the less
When I am given to outbreaks
  Of pure, besotted selfishness.

One who, when I am sick and glum,
  Can lay conventions on the shelf,
And just for my dear sake become
  A blooming heathen, like myself.

One who can share my grief or mirth,
  And know my days to praise or curse;
And rate me just for what I'm worth,
  And find me still,—Oh, not so worse!

Give me one friend, for peace or war,
  And I shall hold myself well-blest,
And richly compensated for
  The cussedness of all the rest.

—ESTHER M. CLARK

Make yourself an honest man, and then you may be sure that there is one rascal less in the world.

—THOMAS CARLYLE

When a fellow pleases you,
  Let him know it;
It's a simple thing to do—
  Let him know it.
Can't you give the scheme a trial?
It is sure to bring a smile
And that makes it worth the while—
  Let him know it!

You are pleased when anyone
  Lets you know it.
When the man who thinks "Well done!"
  Lets you know it.
For it gives you added zest
To bring out your very best—
Just because some mortal blest
  Lets you know it.

GOD BLESS YOU

I seek in prayerful words, dear friend,
  My heart's true wish to send you,
That you may know that, far or near,
  My loving thoughts attend you.

I cannot find a truer word,
  Nor better to address you;
Nor song, nor poem have I heard
  Is sweeter than God bless you!

God bless you! So I've wished you all
  Of brightness life possesses;
For can there any joy at all
  Be yours unless God blesses?

God bless you! So I breathe a charm
  Lest grief's dark night oppress you,
For how can sorrow bring you harm
  If 'tis God's way to bless you?

And so, "through all thy days
  May shadows touch thee never—"
But this alone—God bless thee—
  Then art thou safe forever.

Home

O happy home, where thou art loved the
    dearest,
Thou loving friend, and Savior of our race,
And where among the guests there never
    cometh
One who can hold such high and honored
    place!
O happy home, where each one serves thee,
    lowly,
Whatever his appointed work may be,
Till every common task seems great and
    holy,
When it is done, O Lord, as unto thee!

—Carl J. P. Spitta

HOME

It takes a heap o' livin' in a house t' make
 it home,
A heap o' sun an' shadder, an' ye sometimes
 have t' roam
Afore ye really 'preciate the things ye lef'
 behind,
An' hunger fer 'em somehow, with 'em allus
 on yer mind.
It don't make any difference how rich ye
 get t' be,
How much yer chairs an' tables cost, how
 great yer luxury;
It ain't home t' ye, though it be the palace
 of a king,
Until somehow yer soul is sort o' wrapped
 round everything.

Home ain't a place that gold can buy or get
 up in a minute;
Afore it's home there's got t' be a heap
 o' livin' in it;
Within the walls there's got t' be some babies
 born, and then
Right there ye've got t' bring em' up t'
 women good, an' men;
And gradjerly, as time goes on, ye find ye
 wouldn't part
With anything they ever used—they've
 grown into yer heart:
The old high chairs, the playthings, too, the
 little shoes they wore
Ye hoard; an' if ye could ye'd keep the
 thumb-marks on the door.

Ye've got t' weep t' make it home, ye've
 got t' sit an' sigh
An' watch beside a loved one's bed, an'
 know that Death is nigh;
An' in the stillness o' the night t' see Death's
 angel come,
An' close the eyes o' her that smiled, an'
 leave her sweet voice dumb.
For these are scenes that grip the heart,
 an' when yer tears are dried,
Ye find the home is dearer than it was, an'
 sanctified;
An' tuggin' at ye always are the pleasant
 memories
O' her that was an' is no more—ye can't
 escape from these.

Ye've got to sing an' dance fer years, ye've
 got t' romp an' play,
An' learn t' love the things ye have by usin'
 'em each day;
Even the roses round the porch must blossom
 year by year
Afore they 'come a part o' ye, suggestin'
 someone dear
Who used t' love 'em long ago, and trained
 'em just t' run
The way they do, so's they would get the
 early mornin' sun;
Ye've got to love each brick an' stone from
 cellar up t' dome:
It takes a heap o' livin' in a house t' make
 it home.

—EDGAR A. GUEST

Home is where the heart is.

—PLINY

He is the happiest, be he king or peasant,
who finds peace in his home.

—GOETHE

A house is built of logs and stone,
 Of tiles and posts and piers;
A home is built of loving deeds
 That stand a thousand years.

—VICTOR HUGO

WHERE THERE IS
ONE TO LOVE US

Home's not merely four square walls,
Though with pictures hung and gilded;
Home is where Affection calls—
Filled with shrines the Heart had builded!
Home! God watch the faithful dove,
Sailing 'neath the heaven above us.
Home is where there's one to love!
Home is where there's one to love us.
Home's not merely roof and room,
It needs something to endear it;
Home is where the heart can bloom,
Where there's some kind lip to cheer it!
What is home with none to meet,
None to welcome, none to greet us?
Home is sweet, and only sweet,
Where there's one we love to meet us!

—Charles Swain

You painted no Madonnas
On chapel walls in Rome
But with a touch diviner
You lived one in your home.

PRAYER OF A HUSBAND

Lord, may there be no moment in her life
When she regrets that she became my wife,
And keep her dear eyes just a trifle blind
To my defects, and to my failings kind!
Help me to do the utmost that I can
To prove myself her measure of a man,
But, if I often fail as mortals may,
Grant that she never sees my feet of clay!
And let her make allowance—now and then—
That we are only grown-up boys, we men,
So, loving all our children, she will see,
Sometimes, a remnant of the child in me!
Since years must bring to all their load of
*   care,*
Let us together every burden bear,
And when Death beckons one its path along,
May not the two of us be parted very long!

—Mazie V. Caruthers

HOW TO BUILD A HOUSE

The walls of a house are not built of wood, brick or stone, but of truth and loyalty.

Unpleasant sounds, the friction of living, the clash of personalities, are not deadened by Persian rugs or polished floors, but by conciliation, concession, and self-control. . . .

The house is not a structure where bodies meet, but a hearthstone upon which flames mingle, separate flames of souls, which, the more perfectly they unite, the more clearly they shine and the straighter they rise toward heaven.

Your house is your fortress in a warring world, where a woman's hand buckles on your armour in the morning and soothes your fatigue and wounds at night.

The beauty of a house is harmony.

The security of a house is loyalty.

The joy of a house is love.

The plenty of a house is in children.

The rule of a house is service.

The comfort of a house is in contented spirits. . . .

The maker of a house, of a real human house, is God himself, the same who made the stars and built the world.

—Frank Crane

Where does the family start? It starts with a young man falling in love with a girl—no superior alternative has yet been found.

—Winston Churchill

Train up a child in the way he should go and walk there yourself once in awhile.

—Josh Billings

If you are going to train children at home, it's necessary for both parents and children to spend some time there.

—Wes Izzard

THE HOMEMAKER'S PRAYER

Lord of all pots and pans and things; since
I've no time to be
A saint by doing lovely things, or watching
late with Thee,
Or dreaming in the dawn light, or storming
heaven's gate,
Make me a saint by getting meals, and
washing up the plates.
Altho I must have Martha's hands, I have a
Mary mind;
And when I black the boots and shoes, Thy
sandals, Lord, I find,
I think of how they trod the earth, what
time I scrub the floor;
Accept this meditation, Lord, I haven't time
for more.
Warm all the kitchen with Thy love, and
light it with Thy peace;
Forgive me all my worrying, and make my
grumbling cease,
Thou who didst love to give men food, in
room or by the sea,
Accept this service that I do—I do it unto
Thee.
Little muddy footprints
Tracking up the floor,
Sticky finger marks upon
The newly painted door,
Toys and books and cowboy guns
Seldom put away,
Laughter ringing loud and clear
Through each shining day,
Barkings of a happy dog
Joining in the fun,
Whispered prayers at Mother's knee
When the day is done—
Any little house can hold
Happiness within
If it boasts the telltale marks
Where a child has been.

—MARGUERITE GODE

Sophisticated, worldly-wise,
I searched for God and found Him not,
Until one day, the world forgot,
I found Him in my baby's eyes.

—MARY AFTON THACKER

A BRIDE'S PRAYER

Oh, Father, my heart is filled with a happiness so wonderful that I am almost afraid. This is my wedding day, and I pray Thee that the beautiful joy of this morning may never grow dim with years of regret for the step which I am about to take. Rather, may its memories become more sweet and tender with each passing anniversary.

Thou has sent to me one who seems all worth of my deepest regard. Grant unto me the power to keep him ever true and loving as now. May I prove indeed a helpmate, a sweetheart, a friend, a steadfast guiding star among the temptations that beset the impulsive hearts of men. Give me skill to make the home the best loved place of all. Help me to make its lights shine farther than any glow that would dim its radiance. Let me, I pray Thee, meet the little misunderstandings and cares of my new life bravely. Be with me as I start on my mission of womanhood and stay Thou my path from failure. Walk Thou with us even to the end of our journey, hand in hand down the highway to the Valley of Final Shadow, which we will be able to lighten with sunshine of good and happy lives. Amen.

WE KISS'D AGAIN WITH TEARS

As through the land at eve we went,
And pluck'd the ripen'd ears,
We fell out, my wife and I,
O we fell out I know not why,
And kiss'd again with tears.
And blessings on the falling out
That all the more endears,
When we fall out with those we love,
And kiss again with tears!
For when we came where lies the child
We lost in other years,
There above the little grave,
O there above the little grave,
We kiss'd again with tears.

—ALFRED LORD TENNYSON

TELL HER SO

Amid the cares of married strife,
In spite of toil and business life,
If you value your sweet wife
    Tell her so!

When days are dark and deeply blue
She has her troubles, same as you.
Show her that your love is true—
    Tell her so!

There was a time you thought it bliss
To get the favor of one kiss;
A dozen now won't come amiss—
    Tell her so!

Don't act, if she has passed her prime
As tho' to please her were a crime;
If ever you loved her, now's the time—
    Tell her so.

She'll return, for each caress,
An hundredfold of tenderness!
Hearts like hers were made to bless!
    Tell her so.

You are hers and hers alone;
Well you know she's all your own;
Don't wait to carve it on a stone—
    Tell her so.

Never let her heart grow cold—
Richer beauties will unfold;
She is worth her weight in gold!
    Tell her so.

A WOMAN'S QUESTION

Do you know you have asked for the costliest
    thing
    Ever made by the Hand above?
A woman's heart, and a woman's life—
    And a woman's wonderful love.

Do you know you have asked for this
    priceless thing
    As a child might ask for a toy?
Demanding what others have died to win,
    With the reckless dash of a boy.

You have written my lesson of duty out;
    Manlike, you have questioned me.
Now stand at the bar of my woman's soul
    Until I shall question thee.

You require your mutton shall be always hot,
    Your socks and your shirt be whole;
I require your heart to be true as God's stars
    And as pure as His heaven your soul.

You require a cook for your mutton and beef;
    I require a far greater thing;
A seamstress you're wanting for socks and
    shirts—
    I look for a man and a king.

A king for the beautiful realm called Home,
    And a man that his Maker, God,
Shall look upon as He did on the first
    And say: "It is very good."

I am fair and young, but the rose may fade
    From my soft young cheek one day;
Will you love me then 'mid the falling leaves,
    As you did 'mong the blossoms of May?

Is your heart an ocean so strong and deep,
    I may launch my all on its tide?
A loving woman finds heaven or hell
    On the day she is made a bride.

I require all things that are grand and true,
    All things that a man should be;
If you give this all, I would stake my life
    To be all you demand of me.

If you cannot be this, a laundress and cook
    You can hire and little to pay;
But a woman's heart and a woman's life
    Are not to be won that way.

—LENA LATHROP

I believe that marriage should be a perfect partnership; that a woman should have all the rights that man has, and one more—the right to be protected. I do not like the man who thinks he is boss. The fellow in the dugout was always talking about being boss. I do not like a man who thinks he has got authority and that the woman belongs to him—that wants his wife for a slave. I would not want the love of a woman that is not great enough, grand enough, and splendid enough to be free. I will never give to any woman my heart upon whom I afterwards put chains.

—ROBERT G. INGERSOLL

HIS FAULTS

There never was a man who had more faults
Than he. Her mother used to tell her so.
But living with him for a little while,
She turned upon his foibles the warm glow
Of her affection. If you look for weeds,
She thought, you'll find them sure; but a man
needs
The comfort of an uncomplaining wife
To cultivate the garden of his life.
As the years passed, and understanding came,
With time she learned to value and revere
The man she married, and his many faults
Seemed to her mind to make him doubly dear.
And when at last the tie that bound them
parted,
And she was left to mourn him, broken-
hearted,
Never through her last years could she recall
That he had ever had a fault at all!

—ANNE CAMPBELL

AN ANGRY WORD

An angry word is like a boomerang;
Its force returns upon the one who sent it,
And yet unlike it, for it has a fang
Whose poison doubles after one has spent it.

—MARGARET E. BRUNER

BECAUSE YOU CARE

Because you care, each task will be much
lighter,
Each burden so much easier to bear;
And each new morning's outlook better,
brighter,
And each new day more blest, because you
care.
Because you care, each joy will seem com-
pleter,
Each treasure doubly dear and true and
rare;
And in my heart I'll always find it sweeter
To want the higher things, because you
care.

—FRANK CRANE

Tho' world on world in myriad myriads roll
Round us, each with different powers,
And other forms of life than ours,
What know we greater than the soul?
On God and Godlike men we build our trust.

—ALFRED LORD TENNYSON

A man is a great thing upon the earth and through eternity; but every jot of the greatness of man is unfolded out of woman.

—WALT WHITMAN

TO A CHILD THAT ENQUIRES

How did you come to me, my sweet?
From the land that no one knows
Did Mr. Stork bring you here on his wings?
Or were you born in the heart of a rose?

Did an angel fly with you down from the sky?
Were you found in a gooseberry patch?
Did a fairy bring you from fairyland
To my door that was left on the latch?

No, my darling was born of a wonderful love,
A love that was Daddy's and mine,
A love that was human, but deep and pro-
found
A love that was almost divine.

Do you remember, sweetheart, when we
went to the Zoo
And we saw the big bear with the grouch,
And the tigers and lions and that tall kangaroo,
That carried her babes in a pouch?

Do you remember I told you she kept them
there safe
From the cold and the wind 'till they grew
Big enough to take care of themselves?
And, dear heart, that's just how I first cared
for you.

I carried you under my heart, my sweet,
And I sheltered you safe from alarms,
'Till one wonderful day, the dear God looked
down
And my darling lay safe in my arms.

—OLGA PETROVA

The highest happiness on earth is in marriage. Every man who is happily married is a successful man even if he has failed in everything else. And every man whose marriage is a failure is not a successful man even if he has succeeded in everything else.

—WILLIAM LYON PHELPS

The happy married man dies in good stile at home, surrounded by his weeping wife and children. The old bachelor don't die at all—he sort of rots away, like a pollywog's tail.

—ARTEMUS WARD

LOVE FINDS A WAY

A bright portent of future marital happiness was recently revealed in the tender thoughtfulness of a young bride in a small English village.

The young woman had just been married, and at the conclusion of the ceremony the bridegroom, a bit reluctant and hesitant, signed the parish register with an **X** mark. His charming young bride followed him, and likewise made her "**X**".

"Why, Mary," whispered the minister's wife, "you can write your name. You were one of the best scholars in the parish school."

"Yes," the young woman replied, "but John cannot write, and I would not shame him for the world. I will teach him to write, and then I can join with him in the pleasure of writing our names."

—ANDREW MEREDITH

However dull a woman may be, she will understand all there is in love; however intelligent a man may be, he will never know but half of it.

—MADAME FEE

Something else every couple should save for their old age is their marriage.

—IMOGENE FEY

THOSE WE LOVE THE BEST

They say the world is round, and yet
   I often think it square,
So many little hurts we get
   From corners here and there.
But one great truth in life I've found,
   While journeying to the West—
The only folks we really wound
   Are those we love the best.

The man you thoroughly despise
   Can rouse your wrath, 'tis true;
Annoyance in your heart will rise
   At things mere strangers do;
But those are only passing ills;
   This rule all lives will prove;
The rankling wound which aches and thrills
   Is dealt by hands we love.

The choicest garb, the sweetest grace,
   Are oft to strangers shown;
The careless mien, the frowning face,
   Are given to our own.
We flatter those we scarcely know,
   We please the fleeting guest,
And deal full many a thoughtless blow
   To those who love us best.

Love does not grow on every tree,
   Nor true hearts yearly bloom.
Alas for those who only see
   This cut across a tomb!
But, soon or late, the fact grows plain
   To all through sorrow's test:
The only folks who give us pain
   Are those we love the best.

—ELLA WHEELER WILCOX

Children have more need of models than of critics.

Love is a hammer that will break the hardest heart.

Man can not degrade woman without himself falling into degradation; he can not elevate her without at the same time elevating himself.

—ALEXANDER WALKER

THE SOUL OF A CHILD

The soul of a child is the loveliest flower
That grows in the garden of God.
Its climb is from weakness to knowledge and
*   power,*
To the sky from the clay and the clod.
To beauty and sweetness it grows under care,
Neglected, 'tis ragged and wild;
'Tis a plant that is tender, but wondrously
*   rare—*
The sweet wistful soul of a child!
Be tender, A gardener, and give it it's share
Of moisture, of warmth, and of light,
And let it not lack for they painstaking care
To protect it from frost and blight.
A glad day will come when its bloom shall
*   unfold,*
In the sensitive soul of a child.

VACATION AT HOME

You don't have to go on a journey,
You really need not travel far,
You can have a delightful vacation
At home, or wherever you are.

Have you tried taking life a bit easy
Have you tried making everything fun,
Have you gone for a walk in the moonlight
Or rested awhile in the sun?

Have you ever sought peace in a garden
Looking up to the blue arc of sky
Watching the bright panorama
Of clouds drifting lazily by?

Have you taken time out just to wander,
To go fishing perhaps, or just dream
Where the willows are trailing their branches
In a pool, or a gurgling stream?

No you don't have to go on a journey,
You really need not travel far
There are all sorts of vacation treasures
Right at home or wherever you are.

—Mrs. Roy L. Peifer

Nobody knows what a boy is worth, and the world must wait and see; for every man in an honored place, is a boy that used to be.

Are you willing to stoop down and consider the needs and the desires of little children; to remember the weakness and loneliness of people who are growing old; to stop asking how much your friends love you, and ask yourself whether you love them enough; to bear in mind the things that those who live in the same house with you really want, without waiting for them to tell you; to trim your lamp so that it will give more light and less smoke, and to carry it in front so that your shadow will fall behind you; to make a grave for your ugly thoughts, and a garden for your kindly feelings, with the gate open?

—Henry Van Dyke

ANY WIFE OR HUSBAND

Let us be guests in one another's house
With deferential "No" and courteous "Yes";
Let us take care to hide our foolish moods
Behind a certain show of cheerfulness.

Let us avoid all sullen silences;
We should find fresh and sprightly things to
*   say;*
I must be fearful lest you find me dull,
And you must dread to bore me any way.

Let us knock gently at each other's heart,
Glad of a chance to look within—and yet
Let us remember that to force one's way
Is the unpardoned breach of etiquette.

So shall I be hostess—you, the host—
Until all need for entertainment ends;
We shall be lovers when the last door shuts,
But what is better still—we shall be friends.

—Carol Haynes

However important sex instruction may be to marriage, there is one thing more important—*character*. Two people unselfish and considerate, tactful and warmhearted, and salted with humor, who are in love, have the most essential of all qualifications for a successful marriage—they have character.

—William Lyon Phelps

Hope

Keep a brave spirit, and never despair;
Hope brings you messages through the keen
  air—
Good is victorious—God everywhere.

Grand are the battles which you have to fight,
Be not downhearted, but valiant for right;
Hope, and press forward, your face to the
  light.

I steer my bark with Hope ahead and Fear astern.

—THOMAS JEFFERSON

BEYOND THE FARTHEST HORIZON

We have dreamed dreams beyond our com-
    prehending,
Visions too beautiful to be untrue;
We have seen mysteries that yield no clue,
And sought our goals on ways that have no
    ending.

. . .

We have seen loveliness that shall not pass;
We have beheld immortal destinies;

. . .

Ay, we whose flesh shall perish as the grass
Have flung the passion of the heart that dies
Into the hope of everlasting life.

. . .

But lo! remains the miracle supreme,
That we, whom death and change have shown
    our fate,
We, the chance progeny of earth and time,
Should ask for more than earth and time
    create,
And, goalless and without the strength to
    climb,
Should dare to climb where we were born to
    grope;
That we the lowly could conceive the great,
Dream in our dust of destinies sublime,
And link our moments to immortal hope.
So, let us turn to the unfinished task
That earth demands, strive for one hour to
    keep
A watch with God, nor watching fall asleep,
Before immortal destinies we ask.
Before we seek to share

A larger purpose, a sublimer care,
Let us o'ercome the bondage of our fears,
And fit ourselves to bear
The burden of our few and sinful years.
Ere we would claim a right to comprehend
The meaning of the life that has no end
Let us be faithful to our passing hours,
And read their beauty, and that light pursue
Which gives the dawn its rose, the noon its
    blue,
And tells its secret to the wayside flowers.

—SIDNEY ROYCE LYSACHT

Hope is like the sun, which, as we journey toward it, casts the shadow of our burden behind us.

THE STAR OF HOPE

No, it is not for the rude breath of man to blow out the lamp of hope.
Instead, let us hold it high, a guide by day, a pillar of fire by night, to cheer each pilgrim on his way.
For have there not been times, O God, when we peered into the gloom, and the heavens were hung with black, and then when life was well-nigh gone, we saw a light. It was the Star of Hope!

—ELBERT HUBBARD

The men whom I have seen succeed best in life have always been cheerful and hopeful men, who went about their business with a smile on their faces, and took the changes and chances of this mortal life like men, facing rough and smooth alike as it came.

—CHARLES KINGSLEY

HOPE

Hope springs eternal in the human breast:
Man never is, but always to be blest.

—ALEXANDER POPE

HOPE

Hope, like a gleaming taper's light,
  Adorns and cheers our way;
And still, as darker grows the night,
  Emits a brighter ray.

—OLIVER GOLDSMITH

Live each day to the fullest. Get the most from each hour, each day, and each age of your life. Then you can look forward with confidence, and back without regrets.

Be yourself—but be your best self. Dare to be different and to follow your own star.

And don't be afraid to be happy. Enjoy what is beautiful. Love with all your heart and soul. Believe that those you love, love you.

Forget what you have done for your friends, and remember what they have done for you. Disregard what the world owes you, and concentrate on what you owe the world.

When you are faced with a decision, make that decision as wisely as possible—then forget it. The moment of absolute certainty never arrives.

And above all, remember that God helps those who help themselves. Act as if everything depended upon you, and pray as if everything depended upon God.

—S. H. PAYER

HOPE

I shall wear laughter on my lips
Though in my heart is pain—
God's sun is always brightest after rain.

I shall go singing down my little way
Though in my breast the dull ache grows—
The song birds come again after the snows.

I shall walk eager still for what Life holds
Although it seems the hard road will not
  end—
One never knows the beauty round the bend!

—ANNA BLAKE MEZQUIDA

That God, which ever lives and loves,
  One God, one law, one element,
  And one far-off divine event,
To which the whole creation moves.

—ALFRED LORD TENNYSON

Friends and lovers we have none, nor wealth
  nor blest abode,
But the hope of the City of God at the other
  end of the road.

EAST LONDON

'Twas August, and the fierce sun overhead
Smote on the squalid streets of Bethnal Green,
And the pale weaver, through his windows
  seen
In Spitalfields, look'd thrice dispirited,

I met a preacher there I knew, and said:
"Ill and o'er-worked, how fare you in this
  scene?"
"Bravely!" said he; "for I of late have been
Much cheer'd by thoughts of Christ, the liv-
  ing bread."

BE HOPEFUL

Be hopeful, friend, when clouds are dark and
  days are gloomy, dreary,
Be hopeful even when the heart is sick and
  sad and weary.
Be hopeful when it seems your plans are all
  opposed and thwarted;
Go not upon life's battlefield despondent and
  fainthearted.
And, friends, be hopeful of yourself. Do by-
  gone follies haunt you?
Forget them and begin afresh. And let no
  hindrance daunt you.
Though unimportant your career may seem
  as you begin it,
Press on, for victory's ahead. Be hopeful,
  friend, and win it.

—STRICKLAND GILLILAN

HOPE

'Tis better to hope, though clouds hang low,
    And keep the eyes uplifted,
For the sweet blue sky will soon peep
        through,
    When the ominous clouds are rifted.

There was never a night without a day
    Or an evening without a morning,
And the darkest hour, as the proverb goes,
    Is the hour before the dawning.

ETERNAL HOPE

Eternal Hope! When yonder spheres, sublime,
Pealed their first notes to sound the march of
        Time,
Thy joyous youth began,—but not to fade.
When all the sister planets have decayed;
When, wrapped in fire, the realms of ether
        glow,
And Heaven's last thunder shakes the world
        below,
Thou, undismayed, shalt o'er the ruins smile,
And light thy torch at Nature's funeral pile.

HOPE

Never go gloomy, man with a mind,
    Hope is a better companion than fear;
Providence, ever benignant and kind,
    Gives with a smile what you take with a
        tear;
        All will be right,
        Look to the light.
Morning was ever the daughter of night;
All that was black will be all that is bright,
    Cheerily, cheerily, then cheer up.

Many a foe is a friend in disguise,
    Many a trouble a blessing most true,
Helping the heart to be happy and wise,
    With love ever precious and joys ever new.
        Stand in the van,
        Strike like a man!
This is the bravest and cleverest plan;
Trusting in God while you do what you can.
    Cheerily, cheerily, then cheer up.

The poor man is not he who is without
a cent, but he who is without a dream.

—HARRY KEMP

BE STRONG

Be strong to hope, O Heart!
    Though day is bright,
The stars can only shine
    In the dark night.
Be strong, O Heart of mine,
    Look toward the light!

Be strong to bear, O Heart!
    Nothing is vain:
Strive not, for life is care,
    And God sends pain;
Heaven is above, and there
    Rest will remain!

Be strong to love, O Heart!
    Love knows not wrong;
Didst thou love—creatures even,
    Life were not long;
Didst thou love God in heaven,
    Thou wouldst be strong!

—ADELAIDE ANNE PROCTER

It is currently said that hope goes with youth, and lends to youth its wings of a butterfly; but I fancy that hope is the last gift given to man, and the only gift not given to youth. Youth is preeminently the period in which a man can be lyric, fantastical, poetic; but youth is the period in which a man can be hopeless. The end of every episode is the end of the world. But the power of hoping through everything, the knowledge that the soul survives its adventures, that great inspiration comes to the middle-aged; God has kept that good wine until now. . . . There is nothing that so much mystifies the young as the consistent frivolity of the old. They have discovered their indestructibility. They are in their second and clearer childhood, and there is a meaning in the merriment of their eyes. They have seen the end of the End of the World.

—G. K. CHESTERTON

Humility

Though Heaven be high, the gate is low,
And he that comes in there must bow:
   The lofty looks shall ne'er
     Have entrance there.

O God! since Thou delight'st to rest
In the humble contrite breast,
   First make me so to be,
     Then dwell with me.

                 —Thomas Washbourne

No man is wise who is not good. No man is wise who is not humble.

So long as we love, we serve. So long as we are loved by others I would almost say we are indispensable; and no man is useless while he has a friend.

—ROBERT LOUIS STEVENSON

Talk not of strength, till your heart has
    known
And fought with weakness through long hours
    alone.

Talk not of virtue, till your conquering soul
Has met temptation and gained full control.

Boast not of garments, all unscorched by sin,
Till you have passed unscathed through fires
    within.

THE UNDERSTANDING HEART

May sorrow pass you by, yet as she passes,
    May her garments light brush you—
    That you may be kind.

May failure pass you by, yet as she passes,
    May her shadow lightly touch you—
    That you may be humble.

May loneliness pass you by, yet as she passes,
    May her coldness slightly chill you—
    That you may be friendly.

May enmity pass you by, yet as she passes,
    May her arrow lightly sting you—
    That you may be tolerant.

And lo, my friend, as down the year you
    journey,
    You will find the way to happiness—
    An understanding heart.

—BONNIE WHITE BAKER

I'm careful of the words I say
    To keep them soft and sweet;
I never know from day to day
    Which ones I'll have to eat.

THE INDISPENSABLE MAN

Sometime when you're feeling important,
Sometime when your ego's in bloom,
Sometime when you take it for granted
You're the best qualified in the room,

Sometime when you feel that your going
Would leave an unfillable hole,
Just follow these simple instructions
And see how they humble your soul.

Take a bucket and fill it with water,
Put your hand in it up to your wrist,
Pull it out and the hole that's remaining
Is a measure of how you'll be missed.

You can splash all you wish when you enter,
You may stir up the water galore,
But stop, and you'll find that in no time
It looks quiet the same as before.

The moral in this quaint example
Is do just the best that you can.
Be proud of yourself, but remember . . .
There's no indispensable man.

WISDOM

Knowledge and wisdom, far from being one,
Have oft times no connection. Knowledge
    dwells
In heads replete with thoughts of other men:
Wisdom in minds attentive to their own.
Knowledge is proud that he has learn'd so
    much;
Wisdom is humble that he knows no more.

—WILLIAM COWPER

OH! WHY SHOULD THE SPIRIT OF MORTAL BE PROUD?

Oh! why should the spirit of mortal be proud?
Like a swift-fleeting meteor, a fast-flying
  cloud,
A flash of the lightning, a break of the wave,
Man passeth from life to his rest in the grave.

The leaves of the oak and the willow shall
  fade,
Be scattered around, and together be laid;
And the young and the old, and the low and
  the high
Shall molder to dust and together shall die.

The infant a mother attended and loved;
The mother that infant's affection who
  proved;
The husband that mother and infant have
  blessed—
Each, all, are away to their dwellings of rest.

The maid on whose cheek, on whose brow,
  in whose eye,
Shone beauty and pleasure—her triumphs are
  by:
And the memory of those who loved her
  and praised
Are alike from the minds of the living erased.

The hand of the king that the scepter hath
  borne;
The brow of the priest that the miter hath
  worn;
The eye of the sage, and the heart of the
  brave,
Are hidden and lost in the depth of the grave.

The peasant whose lot was to sow and to
  reap;
The heardsman who climbed with his goats
  up the steep;
The beggar who wandered in search of his
  bread,
Have faded away like the grass that we tread.

The saint who enjoyed the communion of
  heaven;
The sinner who dared to remain unforgiven;
The wise and the foolish, the guilty and just,
Have quietly mingled their bones in the dust.

So the multitude goes, like the flowers or the
  weed
That withers away to let others succeed;
So the multitude comes, even those we behold,
To repeat every tale that has often been told.

For we are the same our fathers have been;
We see the same sights our fathers have seen;
We drink the same stream, and view the same
  sun,
And run the same course our fathers have
  run.

The thoughts we are thinking our fathers
  would think;
From the death we are shrinking our fathers
  would shrink;
To the life we are clinging they also would
  cling;
But it speeds for us all, like a bird on the wing.

They loved, but the story we cannot unfold;
They scorned, but the heart of the haughty is
  cold;
They grieved, but no wail from their slumbers will come:
They joyed, but the tongue of their gladness
  is dumb.

They died, aye! they died; and we things that
  are now,
Who walk on the turf that lies over their
  brow,
Who make in their welling a transient abode,
Meet the things that they met on their pilgrimage road.

Yea! hope and despondency, pleasure and pain,
We mingle together in sunshine and rain;
And the smiles and the tears, the song and the
  dirge,
Still follow each other, like surge upon surge.

'Tis the wink of an eye, 'tis the draught of a
  breath,
From the blossom of health to the paleness
  of death,
From the gilded saloon to the bier and the
  shroud—
Oh! why should the spirit of mortal be proud?

—WILLIAM KNOX

THE HAPPIEST HEART

Who drives the horses of the sun
* Shall lord it but a day.*
Better the lowly deed were done
* And kept the humble way.*

The rust will find the sword of fame;
* The dust will hide the crowd,*
Aye, none shall nail so high his name
* Time will not tear it down.*

The happiest heart that ever beat
* Was in some quiet breast*
That found the common daylight sweet
* And left the heaven the rest.*

—John Vance Cheney

O wad some Power the giftie gie us
To see oursels as ithers see us!
It wad frae monie a blunder free us,
* An' foolish notion.*
What airs in dress an' gait wad lea'e us,
An' ev'n devotion!

—Robert Burns

NO GREAT, NO SMALL

There is no great and no small
* To that Soul that maketh all:*
And where it cometh, all things are;
* And it cometh everywhere.*

I am owner of the sphere,
* Of the seven stars and the solar year,*
Of Caesar's hand, and Plato's brain,
* Of Lord Christ's heart, and Shakespeare's*
*   strain.*

—Ralph Waldo Emerson

I will tell you, scholar, I have heard a grave divine say, that God has two dwellings, one in heaven, and the other in a meek and thankful heart.

—Izaak Walton

THE SHEPHERD BOY'S SONG

He that is down needs fear no fall,
* He that is low, no pride;*
He that is humble ever shall
* Have God to be his guide.*

I am content with what I have,
* Little be it or much:*
And, Lord, contentment still I crave
* Because Thou savest such.*

Fullness to such a burden is
* That go on pilgrimage:*
Here little, and hereafter bliss,
* Is best from age to age.*

—John Bunyan

And whosoever will be chief among you, let him be your servant.

—Matthew 20:27

When the oak is felled the whole forest echoes with its fall, but a hundred acorns are sown in silence by an unnoticed breeze.

—Thomas Carlyle

Great men never feel great; small men never feel small.

That man is great, and he alone,
Who serves a greatness not his own,
* For neither praise nor pelf:*
Content to know and be unknown:
* Whole in himself.*

—Owen Meredith

Dwight L. Moody gave this discerning and memorable summary of Moses' life: "In the first forty years, in Egypt, Moses learned to be a Somebody. In the second forty years, in the wilderness, Moses learned to be a Nobody. In the third forty years, he learned what God can do with a Somebody who is willing to be a Nobody."

THE TEACHER

Lord, who am I to teach the way
To other people day by day,
So prone myself to go astray.
I teach them knowledge, but I know
How faint the flicker and how low
The candles of my knowledge glow.
I teach them power to will and do.
But only now to learn anew
My own great weakness through and
    through.
I teach them love for all mankind
And all God's creatures, but I find
My love comes lagging far behind.
Lord, if their guide I still must be,
Oh, let the other people see
The teacher leaning hard on Thee.

—LESLIE HILL

We can do little things for God: I turn
the cake that is frying on the pan, for
love of him; and that done, if there is
nothing else to call me, I prostrate myself
in worship before him who has given me
Grace to work; afterwards I rise happier
than a king.

—BROTHER LAWRENCE

MY WORLD

God gave my world to me,
And I rebelliously cried out
"How small, and is this all?"
His voice was sad, yet mild:
"All that you love, my child."
Myself that moment died,
And born anew, I cried,
"Love take control and lead my soul
To serve my small estate."
And lo, my world is great!

—CHAUNCEY R. PIETY

LOVE THYSELF LAST

Love thyself last; look near, behold thy duty
    To those who walk beside thee down life's
    road;
Make glad their days by little acts of beauty,
    And help them bear the burden of earth's
    load.

Love thyself last; look far and find the
    stranger
    Who staggers 'neath his sin and his despair;
Go, lend a hand and lead him out of danger
    To heights where he may see the world is
    fair.

Love thyself last; the vastnesses above thee
    Are filled with spirit forces, strong and
    pure;
And fervently these faithful friends shall love
    thee,
    Keep thy watch over others and endure.

Love thyself last; and thou shalt grow in
    spirit
    To see, to hear, to know and understand;
The message of the stars, lo, thou shalt hear it,
    And all God's joys shall be at thy command.

—ELLA WHEELER WILCOX

He leads the humble in what is right,
    And teaches the humble his way.

—PSALM 25:9

I believe the first test of a truly great man
is his humility.

—JOHN RUSKIN

Humility is perfect quietness of heart. It
is for me to have no trouble: never
to be fretted or vexed or irritated or sore or
disappointed. It is to expect nothing, to wonder at nothing that is done to me, to feel nothing done against me. It is to be at rest when
nobody praises me, and when I am blamed
or despised. It is to have a blessed home in
the Lord, where I can go in and shut the
door, and kneel to my Father in secret, and
am at peace as in a deep sea of calmness
when all around and above is trouble. It is
the fruit of the Lord Jesus Christ's redemp-
tive work on Calvary's Cross, manifest in
those of His own who are definitely subjected
to the Holy Spirit.

—ANDREW MURRAY

HUMILITY

Humility, the fairest, loveliest flower
That grew in Paradise, and the first that died,
Has rarely flourished since on mortal soil.
It is so frail, so delicate a thing,
'Tis gone, if it but look upon itself;
And they who venture to believe it theirs
Prove by that single thought they have it not.

—TRYON EDWARDS

O MASTER, LET ME WALK WITH THEE

O Master, let me walk with Thee
In lowly paths of service free;
Tell me Thy secret; help me bear
The strain of toil, the fret of care.

Help me the slow of heart to move
By some clear, winning word of love;
Teach me the wayward feet to stay,
And guide them in the homeward way.

Teach me Thy patience; still with Thee
In closer, dearer company,
In work that keeps faith sweet and strong,
In trust that triumphs over wrong.

In hope that sends a shining ray
Far down the future's broadening way;
In peace that only Thou canst give,
With Thee, O Master, let me live.

—WASHINGTON GLADDEN

HOPE

Hope, like a gleaming taper's light,
Adorns and cheers our way;
And still, as darker grows the night,
Emits a brighter ray.

—OLIVER GOLDSMITH

There's a blessing on the hearth,
A special providence for fatherhood.

—ROBERT BROWNING

All human wisdom is summed up in two words,—wait and hope.

—ALEXANDRE DUMAS

TO AN ADOPTED CHILD

Dear, do not weep. By every act of mine
I am your mother . . . by my sleepless nights,
By every step in the long day's design
That I have taken; by the sweet delights
Of your blessed companionship; by the clear
* gaze,*
By all my care in your beginning days;
Your warm, soft body held against my breast
Warmed me and dried my disappointed tears.
You made a real home of our lonely nest.
Now we look forward to the fruitful years
With you beside us bearing in your hands
The love that every mother heart demands.
I am your mother, though you may not be
Flesh of my flesh. Our love goes deeper still.
You are my heart's adopted part of me.
I am your mother by the power of will.
Because I did not want to walk alone . . .
From the whole world, I chose you for my
* own.*

—ANNE CAMPBELL

RESOLVE

Build on resolve, and not upon regret,
* The structure of thy future. Do not grope*
Among the shadows of old sins, but let
* Thine own soul's light shine on the path of*
*   hope*
And dissipate the darkness. Waste no tears
Upon the blotted record of lost years,
But turn the leaf and smile, oh, smile, to see
The fair white pages that remain for thee.
Prate not of thy repentance. But believe
* The spark divine dwells in thee: let it grow.*
That which the upreaching spirit can achieve
* The grand and all-creative forces know;*
They will assist and strengthen as the light
Lifts up the acorn to the oak tree's height.
Thou hast but to resolve, and lo! God's whole
Great universe shall fortify thy soul.

—ELLA WHEELER WILCOX

Life

I do not like the phrase: Never cross a bridge till you come to it. The world is owned by men who cross bridges on their imaginations miles and miles in advance of the procession.

—BRUCE BARTON

MY TASK

To be honest, to be kind;
To earn a little and to spend less;
To make upon the whole a family happier for
his presence;
To renounce when that shall be necessary and
not to be embittered;
To keep a few friends, but those without
capitulation—
Above all, on the same grim conditions, to
keep friends with himself—
Here is a task for all that a man has of forti-
tude and delicacy.

—ROBERT LOUIS STEVENSON

Life is a flower of which love is the honey.

—VICTOR HUGO

That best portion of a good man's life,
His little nameless unremembered acts
Of kindness and of love.

—WILLIAM WORDSWORTH

HOW—WHEN—WHERE

It is not so much WHERE you live,
As HOW, and WHY, and WHEN you live,
That answers in the affirmative,
Or maybe in the negative,
The question—Are you fit to live?

It is not so much WHERE you live,
As HOW you live, and whether good
Flows from you through your neighborhood.

And WHY you live, and whether you
Aim high and noblest ends pursue,
And keep Life brimming full and true.

And WHEN you live, and whether Time
Is at its nadir or its prime,
And whether you descend or climb.

It is not so much WHERE you live,
As whether while you live you live
And to the world your highest give,
And so make answer positive
That you are truly fit to live.

—JOHN OXENHAM

WHAT I LIVE FOR

I live for those who love me,
Whose Hearts are kind and true;
For the Heaven that smiles above me,
And awaits my spirit too;
For all human ties that bind me,
For the task by God assigned me,
For the bright hopes yet to find me,
And the good that I can do.

I live to learn their story
Who suffered for my sake;
To emulate their glory,
And follow in their wake;
Bards, patriots, martyrs, sages,
The heroic of all ages,
Whose deeds crowd History's pages,
And Time's great volume make.

I live to hold communion
With all that is divine,
To feel there is a union
'Twixt Nature's heart and mine;
To profit by affliction,
Reap truth from fields of fiction,
Grow wiser from conviction,
And fulfill God's grand design.

I live to hail that season
By gifted ones foretold,
When men shall live by reason,
And not alone by gold;
When man to man united,
And every wrong thing righted,
The whole world shall be lighted

As Eden was of old.

I live for those who love me,
 For those who know me true,
For the Heaven that smiles above me,
 And awaits my spirit too;
For the cause that lacks assistance,
For the wrong that needs resistance,
For the future in the distance,
 And the good that I can do.

—George Linnaeus Banks

THE PSALM OF LIFE

Tell me not, in mournful numbers,
 Life is but an empty dream!—
And the soul is dead that slumbers,
 And things are not what they seem.

Life is real! Life is earnest!
 And the grave is not its goal;
Dust thou art, to dust returnest,
 Was not spoken of the soul.

Not enjoyment, and not sorrow,
 Is our destined end or way;
But to act, that each tomorrow
 Find us farther than today.

Art is long, and Time is fleeting,
 And our hearts, though stout and brave
Still, like muffled drums, are beating,
 Funeral marches to the grave.

In the world's broad field of battle,
 In the bivouac of life,
Be not like dumb, driven cattle!
 Be a hero in the strife!

Trust no Future, howe'er pleasant!
 Let the dead Past bury its dead!
Act, act in the living Present!
 Heart within, and God o'erhead!
Lives of great men all remind us
 We can make our lives sublime,
And, departing, leave behind us,
 Footprints on the sands of time.
Footprints, that perhaps another,
 Sailing o'er life's solemn main,
A forlorn and shipwrecked brother,
 Seeing, shall take heart again.

Let us then be up and doing,

With a heart for any fate;
Still achieving, still pursuing,
 Learn to labor and to wait.

—Henry Wadsworth Longfellow

What a difference it makes when we are using life rather than having life use us. When we, to a marked degree, are managing our moods, controlling our emotions, making life meaningful, filling every day with the heights of Christian living, we may say with confidence that we are using life.

But when worry grips the mind and paralyzes the heart, or the dull edge of sin robs life of radiancy, or fear grips our life, rather than an abiding faith, and life runs out into a morass of doubt, disillusionment and despair, we know that life is using us.

—Frank A. Court

LIFE'S MIRROR

There are loyal hearts, there are spirits brave,
 There are souls that are pure and true;
Then give to the world the best you have,
 And the best will come back to you.

Give love, and love to your life will flow,
 A strength in your utmost need;
Have faith, and a score of hearts will show
 Their faith in your word and deed.

Give truth, and your gift will be paid in kind,
 And honor will honor meet;
And a smile that is sweet will surely find
 A smile that is just as sweet.

Give sorrow and pity to those who mourn;
 You will gather in flowers again
The scattered seeds of your thought outborne,
 Though the sowing seemed but vain.

For life is the mirror of king and slave—
 'Tis just what we are and do;
Then give to the world the best you have,
 And the best will come back to you.

—Madeline Bridges

THESE ARE THE GIFTS I ASK

These are the gifts I ask
Of Thee, Spirit serene:
Strength for the daily task,
Courage to face the road,
Good cheer to help me bear the traveler's load,
And, for the hours of rest that come between,
An inward joy of all things heard and seen.
These are the sins I fain
Would have Thee take away:
Malice and cold disdain,
Hot anger, sullen hate,
Scorn of the lowly, envy of the great,
And discontent that casts a shadow gray
On all the brightness of the common day.

—HENRY VAN DYKE

GIVING AND FORGIVING

What makes life worth the living
Is our giving and forgiving;
Giving tiny bits of kindness
That will leave a joy behind us,
And forgiving bitter trifles
That the right word often stifles,
For the little things are bigger
Than we often stop to figure.
What makes life worth the living
Is our giving and forgiving.

—THOMAS GRANT SPRINGER

GOD'S MOSAIC

An artist can take a few bits of colored glass
And fit them together with infinite pains
Into a design of symmetry.
When he is finished, his colors so blend
together:
That he has created a picture in glass.
It is a mosaic.

You are God's mosaic,
A distinctive, original design.
The way you fit each "piece" of you
togethers
Your dreams, your education,
Your lifework, and your total personality,
Will determine whether the "Design For Your
Tomorrow"
Will be the masterpiece God has in mind.

LORD, MAKE A REGULAR MAN OUT OF ME

This I would like to be—braver and bolder,
Just a bit wiser because I am older,
Just a bit kinder to those I may meet,
Just a bit manlier taking defeat;
This for the whole year my wish and my
plea—
Lord, make a regular man out of me!

This I would like to be—just a bit finer,
More of a smiler and less of a whiner,
Just a bit quicker to stretch out my hand
Helping another who's struggling to stand,
This is my prayer for the whole year to be,
Lord, make a regular man out of me!

This I would like to be—just a bit fairer,
Just a bit better, and just a bit squarer,
Not quite so ready to censure and blame,
Quicker to help every man in the game,
Not quite so eager men's failings to see,
Lord, make a regular man out of me!

This I would like to be—just a bit truer,
Less of the wisher and more of the doer,
Broader and bigger, more willing to give,
Living and helping my neighbor to live.
This for the whole year my prayer and my
plea—
Lord, make a regular man out of me!

—EDGAR A. GUEST

THE GUY IN THE GLASS

If you get what you want in struggle for self;
And the world makes you king for a day;
Then go to the mirror and look at yourself,
And see what that guy has to say.

For it isn't your father, your mother, or wife,
Who judgment on you must pass;
The fellow whose verdict counts most in your
life
Is the guy staring back from the glass.

He's the fellow to please, never mind all the
rest,
For he's with you clear to the end;
You have passed your dangerous, difficult
task,
If the guy in the glass is your friend.

You may be like Jack Horner and chisel a
    plum,
    And you think you're a wonderful guy;
But the man in the glass says: "You're a bum,"
    If you can't look him straight in the eye.

You may fool the whole world down the
    pathway of years
    And get pats on your back as you pass;
But your final reward will be heartaches and
    tears,
    If you've cheated the guy in the glass.

                —OSCAR R. GRUTER

Maybe ain't ain't so correct, but I notice that lots of folks who ain't using ain't ain't eatin'.

                —WILL ROGERS

From "IS LIFE WORTH LIVING!"?

Is life worth living? Yes, so long
    As there is wrong to right,
Wail of the weak against the strong,
    Or tyranny to fight;
Long as there lingers gloom to chase,
    Or streaming tear to dry,
One kindred woe, one sorrowing face
    That smiles as we draw nigh;
Long as a tale of anguish swells
    The heart, and lids grow wet,
And at the sound of Christmas bells
    We pardon and forget;
So long as Faith with Freedom reigns,
    And loyalty Hope survives,
And gracious Charity remains
    To leaven lowly lives;
While there is one untrodden tract
    For Intellect or Will,
And men are free to think and act
    Life is worth living still.

                —ALFRED AUSTIN

I am not bound to win, but I am bound to be true. I am not bound to succeed, but I am bound to live by the light that I have. I must stand with anybody that stands right, stand with him while he is right, and part with him when he goes wrong.

                —ABRAHAM LINCOLN

POLONIUS' ADVICE

Give thy thoughts no tongue,
Nor any unproportion'd thought his act.
Be thou familiar, but by no means vulgar.
Those friends thou hast, and their adoption
    tried,
Grapple them to thy soul with hoops of steel;
But do not dull thy palm with entertainment
Of each new-hatch'd unfledged comrade. Be-
    ware
Of entrance to a quarrel, but being in,
Bear't that the opposed may beware of thee.
Give every man thy ear, but few thy voice;
Take each man's censure, but reserve thy
    judgement.
Costly thy habit as thy purse can buy,
But not express'd in fancy; rich, not gaudy;
For the apparel oft proclaims the man,
And they in France of the best rank and sta-
    tion
Are of a most select and generous choice in
    that.
Neither a borrower nor a lender be;
For loan oft loses both itself and friend,
And borrowing dulls the edge of husbandry.
This above all: to thine own self be true,
And it must follow, as the night the day,
Thou canst not then be false to any man.

                —WILLIAM SHAKESPEARE

Health is, indeed, so necessary to all the duties as well as pleasures of life, that the crime of squandering it is equal to the folly; and he that for a short gratification brings weakness and diseases upon himself, and for the pleasure of a few years passed in the tumults of diversion and clamors of merriment, condemns the maturer and more experienced part of his life to the chamber and the couch, may be justly reproached, not only as a spendthrift of his happiness, but as a robber of the public; as a wretch that has voluntarily disqualified himself for the business of his station, and refused that part which Providence assigns him in the general task of human nature.

                —SAMUEL JOHNSON

RECIPE FOR LIVING

Some things a man must surely know,
  If he is going to live and grow:
He needs to know that life is more
  That what a man lays by in store,
That more than all he may obtain,
  Contentment offers greater gain.

He needs to feel the thrill of mirth,
  To sense the beauty of the earth,
To know the joy that kindness brings
  And all the worth of little things.
He needs to have an open mind,
  A friendly heart for all mankind,

A trust in self—without conceit—
  And strength to rise above defeat.
He needs to have the will to share,
  A mind to dream, a soul to dare,
A purpose firm, a path to plod,
  A faith in man, a trust in God.

—Alfred Grant Walton

THEIR CONSCIENCE AS THEIR KING

I made them lay their hands in mine and
  swear
To reverence the King, as if he were
Their conscience, and their conscience as
  their King,
To break the heathen and uphold the Christ,
To ride abroad redressing human wrongs,
To speak no slander, no, nor listen to it,
To honor his own words as if his God's,
To lead sweet lives of purest chastity,
To love one maiden only, cleave to her,
And worship her by years of noble deeds,
Until they won her; for indeed I knew
Of no more subtle master under heaven
Than is the maiden passion for a maid,
Not only to keep down the base in man,
But teach high thought, and amiable words
And courtliness, and the desire of fame,
And love of truth, and all that makes a man.

—Alfred Lord Tennyson

LIFE'S MEANING

These things make life worth while to me:
A sunset sky, a maple tree,
A mountain standing grim and gray
Against the skyline far away;
A baby's laugh, a summer breeze,
A roadway winding 'neath the trees;
A friend to trust, a book to read,
And work which meets some human need.
And through it all, a sense of God
Lifting my soul above the sod,
The hope and peace which He can give—
These make it worth my while to live.

One midnight deep in starlight still
I dreamed that I received this bill:
.... In account with life:
Five thousand breathless dawns all new;
Five thousand flowers fresh in dew;
Five thousand sunsets wrapped in gold;
One million snowflakes served ice cold,
Five quiet friends; one baby's love;
One white-mad sea with clouds above;
One hundred music-haunted dreams
Of moon-drenched roads and hurrying
  streams,
Of prophesying winds and trees,
Of silent stars and drowsing bees;
One June night in a fragrant wood;
One heart that loved and understood.
I wondered when I waked at day
How—how in God's name—I could pay!

—Courtland W. Sayres

THE HARDER TASK

Teach me to live! 'Tis easier far to die—
  Gently and silently to pass away—
On earth's long night to close the heavy eye,
  And waken in the glorious realms of day.

Teach me that harder lesson—how to live
  To serve Thee in the darkest paths of life.
Arm me for conflict, now fresh vigor give,
  And make me more than conqu'ror in the
  strife.

Memory

Into my heart's treasury
   I slipped a coin,
That time cannot rust
   Nor a thief purloin;
Ah, better than the minting
   Of a gold-crowned king
Is the safe-kept memory
   Of a lovely thing.

—SARA TEASDALE

UNCONSCIOUS CEREBRATION

Say not that the past is dead.
Though the Autumn leaves are shed,
Though the day's last flush has flown,
Though the lute has lost its tone—
Still within, unfelt, unseen,
Lives the life that once has been;
With a silent power still
Guiding heart or brain or will.
Lending bias, force, and hue
To the things we think and do.
Strange! how aimless looks or words
Sometimes wake forgotten chords,
Bidding dreams and memories leap
From a long unbroken sleep.

—W. E. H. Lecky

OFT, IN THE STILLY NIGHT

Oft, in the stilly night,
Ere Slumber's chain has bound me,
Fond Memory brings the light
Of other days around me,
The smiles, the tears
Of boyhood's years,
The words of love then spoken;
The eyes that shone,
Now dimmed and gone,
The cheerful hearts now broken!
Thus, in the stilly night,
Ere Slumber's chain has bound me,
Sad Memory brings the light
Of other days around me.

When I remember all
The friends, so linked together,
I've seen around me fall,
Like leaves in wintry weather;
I feel like one
Who treads alone
Some banquet-hall deserted,
Whose lights are fled,
Whose garlands dead,
And all but he departed!
Thus, in the stilly night,
Ere Slumber's chain has bound me,
Sad Memory brings the light
Of other days around me.

—Thomas Moore

MY EARLY HOME

Here sparrows build upon the trees,
And stockdove hides her nest;
The leaves are winnowed by the breeze
Into a calmer rest;
The black-cap's song was very sweet,
That used the rose to kiss;
It made the Paradise complete:
My early home was this.

The red-breast from the sweetbrier bush
Dropt down to pick the worm;
On the horse-chestnut sang the thrush,
O'er the house where I was born;
The moonlight, like a shower of pearls,
Fell o'er this "bower of bliss",
And on the bench sat boys and girls:
My early home was this.

The old house stooped just like a cave,
Thatched o'er with mosses green;
Winter around the walls would rave,
But all was calm within;
The trees are here all green agen,
Here bees the flowers still kiss,
But flowers and trees seemed sweeter then:
My early home was this.

—J. Clare

MEMORY

Music, when soft voices die,
Vibrates in the memory—
Odours, when sweet violets sicken,
Live within the sense they quicken.

Rose leaves, when the rose is dead,
Are heap'd for the beloved's bed;
And so thy thoughts, when thou art gone,
Love itself shall slumber on.

—Percy Bysshe Shelley

REMEMBER

Remember me when I am gone away,
Gone far away into the silent land;
When you can no more hold me by the
hand,
Nor I half turn to go, yet turning stay.
Remember me when no more, day by day,
You tell me of our future that you planned:
Only remember me; you understand
It will be late to counsel then or pray.
Yet if you should forget me for a while
And afterwards remember, do not grieve:
For if the darkness and corruption leave
A vestige of the thoughts that once I had,
Better by far you should forget and smile
Than that you should remember and be
sad.

—Christina Georgina Rossetti

TWENTY YEARS AGO

I've wandered to the village, Tom, I've sat
beneath the tree,
Upon the schoolhouse playground, which
sheltered you and me,
But none were there to greet me, Tom, and
few were left to know,
That played with us upon the grass some
twenty years ago.

The grass is just as green, Tom—barefooted
boys at play
Were sporting just as we did then, with spirits
just as gay;
But the "master" sleeps upon the hill, which,
coated o'er with snow,

Afforded us a sliding place, just twenty years
ago.
The old schoolhouse is alter'd some, the
benches are replaced
By new ones, very like the same our
pen-knives had defaced,
But the same old bricks are in the wall, the
bell swings to and fro,
It's music, just the same, dear Tom, 'twas
twenty years ago.

The boys were playing the same old game,
beneath the same old tree—
I do forget the name just now; you've played
the same with me
On that same spot; 'twas play'd with knives,
by throwing so and so,
The loser had a task to do, just twenty years
ago.

The river's running just as still, the willows
on its side
Are larger than they were, Tom, the stream
appears less wide.
But the grape-vine swing is ruin'd now
where once we play'd the beau,
And swung our sweethearts—"pretty girls"
—just twenty years ago.

The spring that bubbled 'neath the hill, close
by the spreading beech,
Is very low—'twas once so high that we could
almost reach;
And kneeling down to get a drink, dear Tom,
I even started so!
To see how much that I am changed since
twenty years ago.

Nearby the spring, upon an elm, you know
I cut your name,
Your sweetheart's just beneath it, Tom, and
you did mine the same—
Some heartless wretch had peel'd the bark,
'twas dying sure but slow,
Just as the one whose name was cut, died
twenty years ago.

My lids have long been dry, Tom, but tears
came in my eyes,
I thought of her I loved so well—those early
broken ties—
I visited the old churchyard, and took some
flowers to strew

Upon the graves of those we loved, some
   twenty years ago.

Some are in the churchyard laid, some sleep
   beneath the sea
But few are left of our old class, excepting
   you and me,
And when our time is come, Tom, and we
   are call'd to go,
I hope they'll lay us where we played, just
   twenty years ago.

—A. J. Gault

BREAK, BREAK, BREAK

Break, break, break,
   On thy cold gray stones, O Sea!
And I would that my tongue could utter
   The thoughts that arise in me.

O well for the fisherman's boy,
   That he shouts with his sister at play!
O well for the sailor lad,
   That he sings in his boat on the bay!

And the stately ships go on
   To their haven under the hill;
But O for the touch of a vanish'd hand,
   And the sound of a voice that is still!

Break, break, break,
   At the foot of thy crags, O Sea!
But the tender grace of a day that is dead
   Will never come back to me.

—Alfred Lord Tennyson

MEMORY

When time, which steals our years away,
Shall steal our pleasures too;
   The memory of the past will stay
And half our joys renew.

Look not mournfully into the Past. It comes not back again. Wisely improve the Present. It is thine. Go forth to meet the shadowy Future, without fear, and with a manly heart.

—Henry Wadsworth Longfellow

ROCK ME TO SLEEP

Backward, turn backward, O time in your
   flight,
Make me a child again just for to-night!
Mother come back from the echoless shore,
Take me again to your heart as of yore;
Kiss from my forehead the furrows of care,
Smooth the few silver threads out of my
   hair;
Over my slumbers your loving watch keep;—
Rock me to sleep, Mother—rock me to sleep!

Backward, flow backward, oh, tide of the
   years!
I am so weary of toil and of tears—
Toil without recompense, tears all in vain—
Take them, and give me my childhood again!
I have grown weary of dust and decay—
Weary of flinging my soul-wealth away;
Weary of sowing for others to reap;—
Rock me to sleep, Mother—rock me to sleep!

Tired of the hollow, the base, the untrue,
Mother, O Mother, my heart calls for you!
Many a summer the grass has grown green,
Blossomed and faded, our faces between:
Yet, with strong yearning and passionate pain,
Long I to-night for your presence again.
Come from the silence so long and so deep;—
Rock me to sleep, Mother—rock me to sleep!

Over my heart, in the days that are flown,
No love like mother-love ever has shone;
No other worship abides and endures—
Faithful, unselfish, and patient like yours:
None like a mother can charm away pain
From the sick soul and the world-weary brain.
Slumber's soft calms o'er my heavy lids
   creep;—
Rock me to sleep, Mother—rock me to sleep!

Clasped to your heart in a loving embrace,
With your light lashes just sweeping my face,
Never hereafter to wake or to weep;—
Rock me to sleep, Mother—rock me to sleep!

—Elizabeth Akers Allen

A man thinks with his memory.

Music

How many of us ever stop to think
Of music as a wondrous magic link
With God; taking sometimes the place of
*   prayer,*
When words have failed us 'neath the weight
*   of care?*
Music, that knows no country, race or creed;
But gives to each according to his need.

Music was a thing of the soul—a rose-lipped shell that murmured of the eternal sea—a strange bird singing the songs of another shore.

—J. C. Holland

The meaning of a song goes deep. Who is there, that, in logical words, can express the effect music has on us.

—Thomas Carlyle

Would you have your songs endure? Build on the human heart.

The most difficult of all musical instruments to learn to play is the second fiddle.

What is music? This question occupied my mind for hours last night before I fell asleep. The very existence of music is wonderful, I might even say miraculous. Its domain is between thought and phenomena. Like a twilight mediator, it hovers between spirit and matter, related to both, yet differing from each. It is spirit, but spirit subject to the measurement of time: it is matter, but matter that can dispense with space.

—Heinrich Heine

THE FINAL SONG

If I might leave behind
  Some blessing for my fellows, some fair
    trust,
To guide, to cheer, to elevate my kind
  When I am in the dust.

Might verse of mine inspire
  One virtuous aim, one high resolve impart,
Light in one drooping soul a hallowed fire
  Or bind one broken heart!

O Thou, whose touch can lend
  Life to the dead; Thy quickening grace
    supply
And grant me, swanlike, my last breath to
    spend
  In song that may not die!

In later life, when we have reached the introspective age and are prone to live in memories rather than in hopes and anticipations, association adds its mystic spell to the charm and potency of certain strains of music. The half-forgotten fragment of a line, heard or recalled by accident, is fraught with recollections sadly sweet, like flowers from the grave of dead joys. It will unlock storehouses of memory.

—Robert Love Taylor

Where words fail, music speaks.

—Hans Christian Andersen

For lo! creation's self is one great choir,
And what is Nature's order but the rhyme
Whereto the worlds keep time,
And all things move with all things from
    their prime?
Who shall expound the mystery of the lyre?
In far retreats of elemental mind
Obscurely comes and goes
The imperative breath of song, that as the
    wind
Is trackless, and oblivious whence it bows.

—William Watson

And the music's not immortal; but the world has made it sweet.

—Alfred Noyes

> May I reach
That purest heaven, be to other souls
The cup of strength in some great agony,
Enkindle generous ardor, feed pure love,
Beget the smiles that have no cruelty—
Be the good presence of a good diffused,
And in diffusion ever more intense.
So shall I join the choir invisible
Whose music is the gladness of the world.

—GEORGE ELIOT

> As they sang—
Of what I know not, but the music touched
Each chord of being—I felt my secret life
Stand open to it as the parched earth yawns
To drink the summer rain; and at the call
Of those refreshing waters, all my thoughts
Stir from their dark and secret depths, and
 burst
Into sweet, odorous flowers, and from their
 wells
Deep calls to deep and all the mystery
Of all that is, is laid open.

Life has loveliness to sell,
 Music like a curve of gold,
Scent of pine trees in the rain,
 Eyes that love you, arms that hold,
And for your spirit's still delight,
 Holy thoughts that star the night.

—SARA TEASDALE

NO FRIEND LIKE MUSIC

There is no whispering of any friend,
 No solace that can touch the quivering
 heart
In that lone hour when a sudden end
 Has captured laughter and there falls apart
A rainbow that has bridged a distant hill;
 When roses shatter on the stem, and dark
Crowds out the candle's shimmering flame
 and still
 The night creeps on with neither torch nor
 spark.

No friend like music when the last word's
 spoken

And every pleading is a plea in vain;
No friend like music when the heart is
 broken,
 To mend its wings and give it flight again;
No friend like music, breaking chains and
 bars
To let the soul march with the quiet stars!

—DANIEL WHITEHEAD HICKY

What joy to capture song from sound
and send it throbbing through the
hearts of men.

—EMILY SELINGER

THE VIOLIN

Sometimes the violin seems to me
A type of what the soul must be

When it has put aside the bark
And comes from out the friendly dark

Where wayward forest breezes run—
To lie and mellow in the sun.

The master with unerring hand
Prepares it for the spirit-land.

But ever, as the seasons roll
Their roundelay through branch and bole,—

What though its voice has come to be
The voice of immortality?—

The old, old spirit stirs within
The nature of the violin.

And so, as if some dear dead friend
A word to those behind might send,

It speaks to common human ears
Of morning blessings, evening tears:

And runs, with more than mortal art,
The gamut of the human heart.

—ROBERT HAVEN SCHAUFFLER

FOLK MUSIC

They chant their artless notes in simple
guise, They tune their hearts, by far
the noblest aim.

—ROBERT BURNS

THE BALLAD OF THE FIDDLER

He had played by the cottage fire
  Till the dancing all was done,
But his heart kept up the music
  When the last folk had gone.

So he came through the half-door softly
  And wandered up the hill,
In the glow of his heart's desire
  That was in the music still.

—SEUMAS O'SULLIVAN

ODE

We are the music makers,
And we are the dreamers of dreams,
Wandering by lone sea-breakers,
And sitting by desolate streams;
World losers and world-forsakers,
On whom the pale moon gleams:
Yet we are the movers and shakers
Of the world for ever, it seems.

With wonderful deathless ditties
We build up the world's great cities,
And out of a fabulous story
We fashion an empire's glory;
One man with a dream, at pleasure,
Shall go forth and conquer a crown;
And three with a new song's measure
Can trample an empire down.

We, in the ages lying,
In the buried past of the earth,
Built Nineveh with our singing
And Babel itself with our mirth.
And o'erthrew them with prophesying
To the old of the new world's worth;
For each age is a dream that is dying,
Or one that is coming to birth.

—ARTHUR O'SHAUGHNESSY

MUSIC

This morning the music of a brass band which had stopped under my windows moved me almost to tears. It exercised an indefinable, nostalgic power over me; it set the dreaming of another world, of infinite passion and supreme happiness. Such impressions are the echoes of Paradise in the soul; memories of ideal spheres, whose sad sweetness ravishes and intoxicates the heart. O Plato! O Phythagoras! ages ago you heard these harmonies,—surprised these moments of inward ecstasy,—knew these divine transports! If music thus carries us to heaven, it is because music is harmony, harmony is perfection, perfection is our dream, and our dream is heaven. This world of quarrels and of bitterness, of selfishness, ugliness, and misery, makes us long involuntarily for the eternal peace, for the adoration which has no limits, and the love which has no end. It is not so much the infinite as the beautiful that we yearn for. It is not being, or the limits of being, which weigh upon us; it is evil, in us and without us. It is not at all necessary to be great, so long as we are in harmony with the order of the universe. Moral ambition has no pride; it only desires to fill its place, and make its note duly heard in the universal concert of the God of love.

—HENRI-FREDERIC AMIEL

Music is well said to be the speech of angels.

—THOMAS CARLYLE

There is music in the beauty, and the silent note that Cupid strikes, far sweeter than the sound of an instrument; for there is music wherever there is harmony, order or proportion; and thus far we may maintain the music of the spheres.

—SIR THOMAS BROWNE

Melody has by Beethoven been freed from the influence of Fashion and changing Taste, and raised to an ever-valid, purely human type. Beethoven's music will be understood to all time, while that of his predecessors will, for the most part, only remain intelligible to us through the medium of reflection on the history of art.

—RICHARD WAGNER

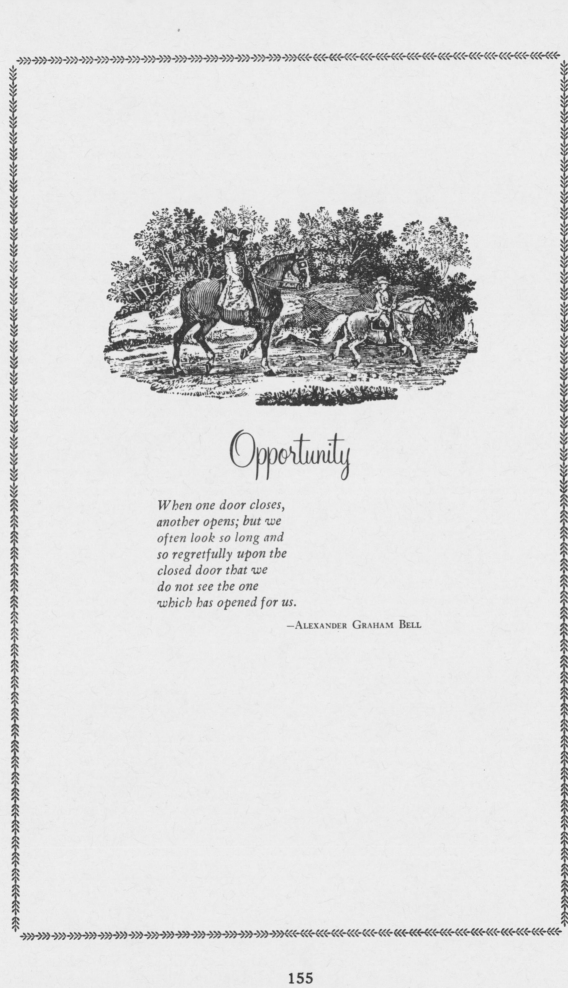

Opportunity

When one door closes,
another opens; but we
often look so long and
so regretfully upon the
closed door that we
do not see the one
which has opened for us.

—ALEXANDER GRAHAM BELL

Our doubts are traitors,
And make us lose the good we oft might win,
By fearing to attempt.

—WILLIAM SHAKESPEARE

OPPORTUNITY

They do me wrong who say I come no more
   When once I knock and fail to find you in,
For every day I stand outside your door
   And bid you wake, and rise to fight and
     win.

Wail not for precious chances passed away,
   Weep not for golden ages on the wane!
Each night I burn the records of the day;
   At sunrise every soul is born again.

Laugh like a boy at splendors that have sped,
   To vanished joys be blind and deaf and
     dumb;
My judgments seal the dead past with its
     dead,
   But never bind a moment yet to come.

Tho' deep in mire, wring not your hands and
     weep;
   I lend my arm to all who say, "I can!"
No shamefaced outcast ever sank so deep
   But yet might rise and be again a man.

Dost thou behold thy lost youth all aghast?
   Dost reel from righteous retribution's
     blow?
Then turn from blotted archives of the past
   And find the future's pages white as snow.

Art thou a mourner? Rouse thee from thy
     spell;
   Art thou a sinner? Sins may be forgiven;
Each morning gives thee wings to flee from
     hell,
   Each night a star to guide thy feet to
     Heaven.

—WALTER MALONE

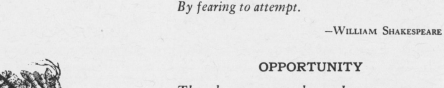

THE WAYS

To every man there openeth
A Way, and Ways, and a Way
And the High Soul climbs the High Way,
And the Low Soul gropes the Low,
And in between, on the misty flats,
The rest drift to and fro.

But to every man there openeth
A High Way, and a Low.
And every man decideth
The way his soul shall go.

—JOHN OXENHAM

NO CHANCE?

With doubt and dismay you are smitten,
You think there's no chance for you, son?
Why, the best books haven't been written,
The best race hasn't been run,
The best score hasn't been made yet,
The best song hasn't been sung,
The best tune hasn't been played yet;
Cheer up, for the world is young!

No chance? Why, the world is just eager
For things that you ought to create
Its store of true wealth is still meager,
Its needs are incessant and great;
Don't worry and fret, faint hearted,
The chances have just begun.
For the best jobs haven't been started,
The best work hasn't been done.

—BERTON BRALEY

The Moving Finger writes; and, having writ,
Moves on: nor all your Piety nor Wit
   Shall lure it back to cancel half a Line,
Nor all your Tears wash out a Word of it.

—OMAR KHAYYAM

The million little things that drop into our hands, the small opportunities each day brings He leaves us free to use or abuse and goes unchanging along His silent way.

—HELEN KELLER

There is a tide in the affairs of men,
Which, taken at the flood, leads on to fortune;
Omitted, all the voyage of their life
Is bound in shallows and in miseries;
And we must take the current when it
serves,
Or lose our ventures.

—WILLIAM SHAKESPEARE

It isn't the things that go in one ear and out the other that hurt, as much as the things that go in one ear and get all mixed up before they slip out the mouth.

To improve the golden moment of opportunity and catch the good that is within our reach, is the great art of life.

—SAMUEL JOHNSON

YOU CAN START HERE

What is this place noted for?" asked a traveler of an old-time resident.

"Why, Mister, this is the starting point for any place in the world. You can start here and go anywhere you want to."

How true!

Yet how many of us fail to realize the full richness of living because we always yearn to be somewhere else before starting seriously on our journey to the place we wish to be.

Someone should write a book about the lives that have been impoverished spiritually and materially because of the "if" which enters into most major decisions we must make—the "if" which prevents us from starting where we are and striking out directly for the goal of our hopes. It is impossible to start from some other place—we

must begin where we are, using what we have, and launch out upon our journey.

This is the starting point for any place in the world. Look under your own doorsteps to find the material you need. Then, on your mark, get set and go!

—LEO BENNETT

A NEW CHANCE

Finish every day and be done with it. You have done what you could. Some blunders and some absurdities no doubt crept in; forget them as soon as you can. Tomorrow is a new day; begin it well and serenely with too high a spirit to be cumbered with your old nonsense. This day is all that is good and fair. It is too dear, with its hopes and invitations, to waste a moment on the yesterdays.

—RALPH WALDO EMERSON

Ideals are like stars; you will not succeed in touching them with your hands, but like the seafaring man on the desert of waters, you choose them as your guides, and, following them, you reach your destiny.

—CARL SCHURZ

ISN'T IT STRANGE?

Isn't it strange
That princes and kings,
And clowns that caper
In sawdust rings,
And common people
Like you and me
Are builders for eternity?

Each is given a bag of tools,
A shapless mass,
A book of rules;
And each must make—
Ere life is flown—
A stumbling block
Or a steppingstone.

—R. L. SHARPE

A NEW CHANCE

We all have to learn, in one way or another that neither men nor boys get *second* chances in this world. We all get *new* chances till the end of our lives, but not second chances in the same set of circumstances; and the great difference between one person and another is, how he takes hold of and uses his first chance, and how he takes his fall if it is scored against him.

—THOMAS HUGHES

Bad will be the day for every man when he becomes absolutely contented with the life that he is living, with the thoughts that he is thinking, with the deeds that he is doing, when there is not forever beating at the doors of his soul some great desire to do something larger, which he knows that he was meant and made to do because he is still, in spite of all, the child of God.

—PHILLIPS BROOKS

THE SALUTATION OF THE DAWN

Listen to the Exhortation of the Dawn!
Look to this Day!
For it is Life, the very Life of Life.
In its brief course lie all the
Verities and Realities of your Existence:
  The Bliss of Growth,
  The Glory of Action,
  The Splendor of Beauty,
For Yesterday is but a Dream,
And To-morrow is only a Vision:
But To-day well-lived makes
Every Yesterday a Dream of Happiness,
And every To-morrow a Vision of Hope.
Look well therefore to this Day!
Such is the Salutation of the Dawn!

The greatest achievement of the human spirit is to live up to one's opportunities and make the most of one's resources.

—VAUVENARGUES

OPPORTUNITY

To each man's life there comes a time
    supreme;
  One day, one night, one morning, or one
    noon,
  One freighted hour, one moment
    opportune,
One rift through which sublime fullfillments
    gleam,
One space when fate goes tiding with the
    stream,
  One Once, in balance 'twixt Too Late, Too
    Soon,
  And ready for the passing instant's boon
To tip in favor the uncertain beam.
Ah, happy he who, knowing how to wait,
  Knows also how to watch and work and
    stand
  On Life's broad deck alert, and at the prow
To seize the passing moment, big with fate,
  From Opportunity's extended hand,
  When the great clock of destiny strikes
    Now!

—MARY A. TOWNSEND

There are no great and small. We fancy others greater than ourselves because they light the divine spark given them, and we do not. It is because we minimize ourselves that we do not accomplish. We do not realize the power of the positions in which we are placed.

—RALPH WALDO EMERSON

BEGIN AGAIN

Every day is a fresh beginning,
  Every morn is the world made new.
You who are weary of sorrow and sinning,
  Here is a beautiful hope for you,—
  A hope for me and a hope for you.

Every day is a fresh beginning;
  Listen, my soul, to the glad refrain,
And, spite of old sorrow and older sinning,
  And puzzles forecasted and possible pain,
  Take heart with the day, and begin again.

—SUSAN COOLIDGE

Patience

Endeavor to be patient in bearing the defects and infirmities of others, of what sort soever they be; for thou thyself also hast many failings which must be borne with by others.

—THOMAS À. KEMPIS

GOD ANSWERS

He prayed for strength that he might
*   achieve;*
He was made weak that he might obey.
He prayed for wealth that he might do
*   greater things;*
He was given infirmity that he might do
*   better things.*
He prayed for riches that he might be happy;
He was given poverty that he might be wise.
He prayed for power that he might have the
*   praise of men;*
He was given infirmity that he might feel
*   the need of God.*
He prayed for all things that he might enjoy
*   life;*
He was given life that he might enjoy all
*   things.*
He had received nothing that he asked for
*   —all that he hoped for;*
His prayer was answered—he was most
*   blessed.*

SAY NOT THE STRUGGLE NAUGHT AVAILETH

Say not the struggle naught availeth,
*   The labour and the wounds are vain,*
The enemy faints not, nor faileth,
*   And as things have been they remain.*

If hopes were dupes, fears may be liars;
*   It may be, in you smoke concealed,*
Your comrades chase e'en now the fliers,
*   And, but for you, possess the field.*

For while the tired waves, vainly breaking,
*   Seem here no painful inch to gain,*
Far back, through creeks and inlets making,
*   Comes silent, flooding in, the main.*

And not by eastern windows only,
*   When daylight comes, comes in the light,*
In front, the sun climbs slow, how slowly,
*   But westward, look, the land is bright!*

—A. H. Clough

Patience is bitter, but its fruits sweet.

—Jean J. Rousseau

LEARN TO WAIT

Learn to wait—life's hardest lesson
*   Conned, perchance, through blinding tears;*
While the heart throbs sadly echo
*   To the tread of passing years.*
Learn to wait—hope's slow fruition;
*   Faint not, though the way seems long;*
There is joy in each condition;
*   Hearts through suffering may grow strong.*
Thus a soul untouched by sorrow
*   Aims not at a higher state;*
Joy seeks not a brighter morrow;
*   Only sad hearts learn to wait.*

A little more patience, a little more charity for all, a little more devotion, a little more love; with less bowing down to the past, and a silent ignoring of pretended authority; a brave looking forward to the future with more faith in our fellows, and the race will be ripe for a great burst of light and life.

—Elbert Hubbard

Not so in haste, my heart!
Have faith in God and wait;
Although He linger long,
He never comes too late.

He that is slow to anger is better than the mighty; and he that ruleth his spirit than he that taketh a city.

—Proverbs 16:32

UNANSWERED

I thank Thee, Lord, for mine unanswered
  prayers,
  Unanswered, save Thy quiet kindly "Nay,"
Yet it seemed hard among my heavy cares
  That bitter day.

I wanted joy: but Thou didst know for me
  That sorrow was the lift I needed most,
And in its mystic depths I learned to see
  The Holy Ghost.
I wanted health; but Thou didst bid me
    sound
  The secret treasures of pain,
And in the moans and groans my heart oft
    found
  Thy Christ again.

I wanted wealth; 'twas not the better part;
  There is a wealth with poverty oft given,
And Thou didst teach me of the gold of
    heart,
  Best gift of Heaven.

I thank Thee, Lord, for these unanswered
  prayers,
  And for Thy word, the quiet, kindly
  "Nay,"
'Twas Thy withholding lightened all my
    cares
  That blessed day.

Sweet are the thoughts that savor of content, The quiet mind is richer than a crown—A mind content, both crown and kingdom is.

—Robert Greene

Faith takes up the cross, love binds it to the soul, patience bears it to the end.

—Bonard

YOUR PLACE

Is your place a small place?
Tend it with care:
He set you there.

Is your place a large place?
Guard it with care:
He set you there.

What'er your place, it is
Not yours alone, but His
Who set you there.

—John Oxenham

Twelve Things to Remember—1. The value of time. 2. The success of perseverance. 3. The pleasure of working. 4. The dignity of simplicity. 5. The worth of character. 6. The power of kindness. 7. The influence of example. 8. The obligation of duty. 9. The wisdom of economy. 10. The virtue of patience. 11. The improvement of talent. 12. The joy of originating.

—Marshall Field

SONNET ON HIS BLINDNESS

When I consider how my light is spent
  Ere half my days, in this dark world and
    wide,
  And that one talent, which is death to hide,
Lodged with me useless, though my soul
    more bent
To serve therewith my Maker, and present
  My true account, lest He, returning, chide:
  "Doth God exact day labor, light denied?"
I fondly ask; but Patience, to prevent
  That murmur, soon replies, "God doth not
    need
    Either man's work, or His own gifts;
      who best
Bear His mild yoke, they serve Him best.
    His state
  Is kingly. Thousands at His bidding speed,
    And post o'er land and ocean without
      rest;
They also serve who only stand and wait."

—John Milton

THE BEST WE CAN

Face your deficiencies and acknowledge them, but do not let them master you. Let them teach you patience, sweetness, insight.

When we do the best we can, we never know what miracle is wrought in our own life or in the life of another.

—HELEN KELLER

When earnest labor brings you fame and
    glory,
    And all earth's noblest ones upon you smile,
Remember that life's longest, grandest story
    Fills but a moment in earth's little while:
"This, too, shall pass away."

—LANTA WILSON SMITH

The life of man is made up of action and endurance; the life is fruitful in the ratio in which it is laid out in noble action or in patient perseverance.

—CANON LIDDON

BE PATIENT

They are such dear familiar feet that go
Along the path with ours—feet fast or slow
But trying to keep pace; if they mistake
Or tread upon some flower that we would
    take
Upon our breast, or bruise some reed,
Or crush poor hope until it bleed,
We must be mute;
Not turning quickly to impute
Grave fault: for they and we
Have such a little way to go, can be
Together such a little while upon the way—
We must be patient while we may.

So many little faults we find.
We see them, for not blind
Is love. We see them, but if you and I
Perhaps remember them, some by and by,
They will not be
Faults then, grave faults, to you and me,
But just odd ways, mistakes, or even less—

Remembrances to bless.
Days change so many things, yes, hours;
We see so differently in sun and showers!
Mistaken words tonight
May be so cherished by tomorrow's light—
We shall be patient, for we know
There's such a little way to go.

—GEORGE KLINGLE

No road is too long to the man who advances deliberately and without undue haste; and no honors are too distant for the man who prepares himself for them with patience.

—BRUYÈRE

If we wish to be just judges of all things, let us first persuade ourselves of this: that there is not one of us without fault; no man is found who can acquit himself; and he who calls himself innocent does so with reference to a witness, and not to his conscience.

—SENECA

THE LOWEST PLACE

Give me the lowest place; not that I dare
    Ask for that lowest place, but thou hast
      died
That I might live and share
    Thy glory by thy side.

Give me the lowest place; or if for me
    That lowest place too high, make one more
      low
Where I may sit and see
    My God, and love thee so.

—CHRISTINA G. ROSSETTI

And I believe the devil's voice
    Sinks deeper in our ear
Than any whisper sent from Heaven,
    However sweet and clear.

—ADAM LINDSAY GORDON

Patriotism

A thoughtful mind ...
sees not the flag alone,
but the nation itself ...
the principles, the truths,
the history.

—HENRY WARD BEECHER

From "STANZAS ON FREEDOM"

*Men! whose boast it is that ye
Come of fathers brave and free,
If there breathe on earth a slave,
Are ye truly free and brave?
If ye do not feel the chain,
When it works a brother's pain,
Are you not base slaves indeed,
Slaves unworthy to be freed? ...*

*Is true freedom but to break
Fetters for our own dear sake,
And, with leathern hearts, forget
That we owe mankind a debt?
No! true freedom is to share
All the chains our brothers wear,
And, with heart and hand, to be
Earnest to make others free!*

*They are slaves who fear to speak
For the fallen and the weak;
They are slaves who will not choose
Hatred, scoffing, and abuse,
Rather than in silence shrink
From the truth they needs must think;
They are slaves who dare not be
In the right with two or three.*

—JAMES RUSSELL LOWELL

LOVE OF COUNTRY

*Breathes there the man, with soul so dead,
Who never to himself hath said,
  This is my own, my native land!
Whose heart hath ne'er within him burn'd,
As home his footsteps he hath turn'd
  From wandering on a foreign strand?
If such there breathe, go, mark him well;
For him no minstrel raptures swell;
High though his titles, proud his name,
Boundless his wealth as wish can claim,—
Despite those titles, power, and pelf,
The wretch, concentred all in self,
Living, shall forfeit fair renown,
And, doubly dying, shall go down
To the vile dust from whence he sprung,
Unwept, unhonor'd, and unsung.*

—SIR WALTER SCOTT

*Lord, let war's tempest cease,
Fold the whole world in peace
Under Thy wings.
Make all the nations one,
All hearts beneath the sun,
Till Thou shalt reign alone,
Great King of Kings.*

—HENRY WADSWORTH LONGFELLOW

I only regret that I have but one life to give for my country.

—NATHAN HALE

America is God's crucible, the great Melting-Pot where all the races of Europe are melting and reforming! Here you stand, good folk, think I, when I see them at Ellis Island, here you stand in your fifty groups, with your fifty languages and histories, and your fifty blood hatreds and rivalries. But you won't be long like that, brothers, for these are the fires of God you've come to—these are the fires of God. A fig for your feuds and vendettas! Germans and Frenchmen, Irishmen and, Englishmen, Jews and Russians—into the Crucible with you all! God is making the American. The real American has not yet arrived. He is only in the crucible, I tell you—he will be the fusion of all races, the common superman.

—ISRAEL ZANGWILL

Gold is good in its place, but living, brave, patriotic men are better than gold.

—Abraham Lincoln

AMERICA FOR ME

'Tis fine to see the Old World, and travel up
      and down
Among the famous palaces and cities of
      renown,
To admire the crumbly castles and the statues
      of the kings,—
But now I think I've had enough of
      antiquated things.

   So it's home again, and home again, America
      for me!
   My heart is turning home again, and there I
      long to be
   In the land of youth and freedom beyond
      the ocean bars,
   Where the air is full of sunlight and the flag
      is full of stars.

Oh, London is a man's town, there's power
      in the air;
And Paris is a woman's town, with flowers
      in her hair;
And it's sweet to dream in Venice, and it's
      great to study Rome,
But when it comes to living, there is no
      place like home.

I like the German fir-woods, in green
      battalions drilled;
I like the gardens of Versailles with flashing
      fountains filled;
But, oh, to take your hand, my dear, and
      ramble for a day
In the friendly western woodland where
      Nature has her way!

I know that Europe's wonderful, yet
      something seems to lack!
The Past is too much with her, and the
      people looking back.
   But the glory of the Present is to make the
      Future free,—
   We love our land for what she is and what
      she is to be.

   Oh, it's home again, and home again,

America for me!
I want a ship that's westward bound to
      plough the rolling sea,
To the blessed Land of Room Enough
      beyond the ocean bars,
Where the air is full of sunlight and the
      flag is full of stars.

—Henry van Dyke

MEMORIAL DAY

From out our crowded calendar
      One day we pluck to give;
It is the day the Dying pause
      To honor those who live.

—McLandburgh Wilson

America is a willingness of the heart.

F. Scott Fitzgerald

CONCORD HYMN

By the rude bridge that arched the flood,
   Their flag to April's breeze unfurled,
Here once the embattled farmers stood,
   And fired the shot heard round the world.

The foe long since in silence slept;
   Alike the conqueror silent sleeps;
And Time the ruined bridge has swept
   Down the dark stream which seaward
      creeps.

On this green bank, by this soft stream,
   We set today a votive stone;
That memory may their deed redeem,
   When, like our sires, our sons are gone.

Spirit, that made those spirits dare
   To die, and leave their children free,
Bid Time and Nature gently spare
   The shaft we raise to them and thee.

—Ralph Waldo Emerson

For what avail the plow or sail,
Or land or life, if freedom fail?

—Ralph Waldo Emerson

Far dearer, the grave or the prison,
Illumed by one patriot name,
Than the trophies of all who have risen
On Liberty's ruins to fame.

—THOMAS MOORE

Two Voices are there; one is of the sea;
One of the mountains; each a mighty Voice,
In both from age to age thou didst rejoice,
They were thy chosen music, Liberty!

—WILLIAM WORDSWORTH

I'm glad to be dying for England. Other women are sacrificing more—husbands, brothers, sons. I have only my own life to give.

—EDITH CAVELL

A nation can survive its fools, and even the ambitious. But it cannot survive treason from within. An enemy at the gates is less formidable, for he is known and he carries his banners openly. But the traitor moves among those within the gate freely, his sly whispers rustling through all the alleys, heard in the very halls of government itself. For the traitor appears no traitor; he speaks in the accents familiar to his victims, and he wears their face and their garments, and he appeals to the baseness that lies deep in the hearts of all men. He rots the soul of a nation; he works secretly and unknown in the night to undermine the pillars of a city; he infects the body politic so that it can no longer resist. A murderer is less to be feared.

—CICERO

The sheet-anchor of the Ship of State is the common school. Teach, first and last, Americanism. Let no youth leave the school without being thoroughly grounded in the history, the principles, and the incalculable blessings of American liberty. Let the boys be the trained soldiers of constitutional freedom, the girls the intelligent lovers of freemen.

—CHAUNCEY M. DEPEW

THE GETTYSBURG ADDRESS
November 18, 1863

Four score and seven years ago our fathers brought forth on this continent a new nation, conceived in liberty, and dedicated to the proposition that all men are created equal.

Now we are engaged in a great civil war, testing whether that nation, or any nation so conceived and so dedicated, can long endure. We are met on a great battlefield of that war. We have come to dedicate a portion of that field as a final resting place for those who here gave their lives that that nation might live. It is altogether fitting and proper that we should do this.

But in a larger sense we cannot dedicate, we cannot consecrate, we cannot hallow this ground. The brave men, living and dead, who struggled here, have consecrated it far above our poor power to add or detract. The world will little note nor long remember what we say here, but it can never forget what they did here. It is for us, the living, rather, to be dedicated here to the unfinished work which they who fought here have thus far so nobly advanced. It is rather for us to be here dedicated to the great task remaining before us—that from these honored dead we take increased devotion to that cause for which they gave the last full measure of devotion; that we here highly resolve that these dead shall not have died in vain; that this nation, under God, shall have a new birth of freedom; and that government of the people, by the people, and for the people, shall not perish from the earth.

—ABRAHAM LINCOLN

Whoever serves his country well has no need of ancestors.

—VOLTAIRE

O Lord, forgive us for being so sensitive about the things that do not matter— and so insensitive to the things that do! Amen.

HOW SLEEP THE BRAVE

*How sleep the brave, who sink to rest
By all their country's wishes blest!
When Spring, with dewy fingers cold,
Returns to deck their hallowed mould,
She there shall dress a sweeter sod
Than Fancy's feet have ever trod.*

*By fairy hands their kneel is rung;
By forms unseen their dirge is sung;
There Honour comes, a pilgrim grey,
To bless the turf that wraps their clay;
And Freedom shall awhile repair
To dwell, a weeping hermit, there!*

—WILLIAM COLLINS

A good newspaper and Bible in every home, a good schoolhouse in every district, and a church in every neighborhood, all appreciated as they deserve, are the chief support of virtue, morality, civil liberty and religion.

—BENJAMIN FRANKLIN

Americans spend seven billion dollars a year on games of chance. And, mind you, this doesn't include weddings, starting up in business, and holding elections.

—THE OPTIMETER

*We cross the prairies as of old
The Pilgrims crossed the sea,
To make the West as they the East
The homestead of the Free.*

Great men are they who see that spiritual is stronger than any material force, that thoughts rule the world.

Man is neither master of his life nor of his fate. He can but offer to his fellowmen his efforts to diminish human suffering; he can but offer to God his indomitable faith in the growth of liberty.

—VICTOR HUGO

THE SHIP OF STATE

*Thou, too, sail on, O Ship of State!
Sail on, O Union, strong and great!
Humanity with all its fears,
With all the hopes of future years,
Is hanging breathless on thy fate!
We know what Master laid thy keel,
What Workmen wrought thy ribs of steel,
Who made each mast, and sail, and rope,
What anvils rang, what hammers beat,
In what a forge, and what a heat
Were shaped the anchors of thy hope!
Fear not each sudden sound and shock,
'Tis of the wave and not the rock;
'Tis but the flapping of the sail,
And not a rent made by the gale!
In spite of rock and tempest's roar,
In spite of false lights on the shore,
Sail on, nor fear to breast the sea!
Our hearts, our hopes, are all with thee,
Our hearts, our hopes, our prayers, our tears,
Our faith triumphant o'er our fears,
Are all with thee—are all with thee!*

—HENRY WADSWORTH LONGFELLOW

FOUR THINGS

*Four things in any land must dwell,
If it endures and prospers well:
One is manhood true and good;
One is noble womanhood;
One is child life, clean and bright;
And one an altar kept alight.*

No man is worth his salt who is not ready at all times to risk his body, to risk his well-being, to risk his life, in a great cause.

—THEODORE ROOSEVELT

If my people, which are called by my name, shall humble themselves, and pray, and seek my face, and turn from their wicked ways; then will I hear from Heaven, and will forgive their sin, and will heal their land.

—II CHRONICLES 7:14

THE FRONTIERSMAN

The suns of summer seared his skin;
The cold his blood congealed;
The forest giants blocked his way;
The stubborn acres' yield
He wrenched from them by dint of arm,
And grim old Solitude
Broke bread with him and shared his cot
Within the cabin rude.
The gray rocks gnarled his massive hands;
The north wind shook his frame;
The wolf of hunger bit him oft;
The world forgot his name;
But mid the lurch and crash of trees,
Within the clearing's span
Where now the bursting wheat-heads dip,
The Fates turned out—a man!

—RICHARD WIGHTMAN

RECESSIONAL

God of our Fathers, known of old—
    Lord of our far-flung battle line—
Beneath Whose awful hand we hold
    Dominion over palm and pine—
Lord God of Hosts, be with us yet,
    Lest we forget—lest we forget!

The tumult and the shouting dies;
    The captains and the kings depart:
Still stands Thine ancient Sacrifice,
    An humble and a contrite heart.
Lord God of Hosts, be with us yet,
    Lest we forget—lest we forget!

Far-called, our navies melt away;
    On dune and headland sinks the fire:
Lo, all our pomp of yesterday
    Is one with Nineveh and Tyre!
Judge of the Nations, spare us yet,
    Lest we forget—lest we forget!

If, drunk with sight of power, we loose
    Wild tongues that have not Thee in awe—
Such boasting as the Gentiles use
    Or lesser breeds without the Law—
Lord God of Hosts, be with us yet,
    Lest we forget—lest we forget!

For heathen heart that puts her trust
    In reeking tube and iron shard—

All valiant dust that builds on dust,
    And guarding, calls not Thee to guard—
For frantic boast and foolish word,
    Thy mercy on Thy people, Lord!
Amen.

—RUDYARD KIPLING

Rapine, avarice, expense,
This is idolatry; and these we adore:
Plain living and high thinking are no more:
The homely beauty of the good old cause
Is gone.

—WILLIAM WORDSWORTH

God grant that not only the love of liberty but a thorough knowledge of the rights of man may pervade all the nations of the earth, so that a philosopher may set his foot anywhere on its surface and say: "This is my country."

—BENJAMIN FRANKLIN

Blessed is the generation in which the old listen to the young; and doubly blessed is the generation in which the young listen to the old.

—THE TALMUD

Patriotism depends as much on mutual suffering as on mutual success. It is by that experience of all fortunes and all feelings that a great national character is created.

—BENJAMIN DISRAELI

The true test of a civilization is, not the census, nor the size of cities, nor the crops—no, but the kind of man the country turns out.

People hardly ever make use of the freedom they have, for example, freedom of thought; instead they demand freedom of speech as a compensation.

—SOREN KIERKEGAARD

Religion

I do not ask for any crown
  But that which all may win;
Nor try to conquer any world
  Except the one within.
Be Thou my guide until I find
  Led by a tender hand,
The happy kingdom in myself
  And dare to take command.

—Louisa May Alcott

Like the kind of a church you like.
Put off your guile and put on your best smile,
  And hike, my brother, just hike,
To the work in hand that has to be done—
  The work of saving a few.
It isn't the church that is wrong, my boy;
  It isn't the church—IT'S YOU.

Not forsaking the assembling of ourselves together, as the manner of
some is."

                    —HEBREWS 10:25

THE CHURCH YOU WANT

If you want to have the kind of a church
  Like the kind of a church you like,
You needn't slip your clothes in a grip
  And start on a long, long hike.
You'll only find what you left behind,
  For there's nothing really new
It's a knock at yourself when you knock
    the church;
  It isn't the church—IT'S YOU.

When everything seems to be going wrong,
  And trouble seems everywhere brewing;
When prayer-meeting, young people's meet,
  and all,
  Seems simmering slowly—stewing,
Just take a look at yourself and say,
  "What's the use of being blue?"
Are you doing your "bit" to make things
  "hit"?
  It isn't the church—IT'S YOU.

It's really strange sometimes, don't you know,
  That things go as well as they do,
When we think of the little—the very small
  mite—
  We add to the work of the few;
We sit, and stand around, and complain of
  what's done.
  And do very little but fuss.
Are we bearing our share of the burdens to
  bear?
  It isn't the church—IT'S US.

So if you want to have the kind of a church

Praise God, from whom all blessings flow!
Praise Him, all creatures here below!
Praise Him above, ye heavenly host!
Praise Father, Son, and Holy Ghost!

                    —THOMAS KEN

THIS IS MY CHURCH

It is composed of people like me. We make
  it what it is.
It will be friendly, if I am.
Its pews will be filled, if I help to fill them.
It will do great work, if I work.
It will make generous gifts to many causes, if
  I am a generous giver.

It will bring other people into its worship and
  fellowship if I bring them.
It will be a church of loyalty and love, of
  fearlessness and faith, and a church with
  a noble spirit—if I, who make it what it is,
  am filled with these.
Therefore, with the help of God, I shall
  dedicate myself to the task of being all the
  things that I want my church to be.

A world without a Sabbath would be like
a man without a smile, like a summer
without flowers, and like a homestead without a garden. It is the joyous day of the
whole week.

                  —HENRY WARD BEECHER

NO TIME FOR GOD

*You've time to build houses, and in them
    dwell.*
    And time to do business—to buy and to sell;
*But none for repentance, or deep earnest
    prayer;*
    *To seek your salvation you've no time to
    spare.*

*You've time for earth's pleasures, for frolic
    and fun,*
    *For her glittering treasures, how quickly
    you run;*
But care not to seek the fair mansion above,
    The favor of God or the gift of His love.

You've time to take voyages over the sea,
    And time to take in the world's jubilee;
*But soon your bright hopes will be lost in
    the gloom*
    *Of the cold, dark river of death and the
    tomb.*

*You've time to resort to the mountain and
    glen;*
    *And time to gain knowledge from books
    and from men;*
Yet no time to search for the wisdom of God,
    *But what of your soul when you're under
    the sod?*
For time will not linger when helpless you lie,
    *Staring death in the face, you will take time
    to die.*
*Then, what of the judgment—pause, think,
    I implore!*
    For time will be lost on eternity's shore.

THE LAYMAN

*Leave it to the ministers, and soon the church
    will die;*
*Leave it to the womenfolk; the young will
    pass it by;*
*For the church is all that lifts us from the
    coarse and selfish mob,*
*And the church that is to prosper needs the
    layman on the job.*
*Now, a layman has his business, and a layman
    has his joys;*
*But he also has the training of his little girls
    and boys;*

*I wonder how he'd like it if there were no
    churches here*
*And he had to raise his children in a godless
    atmosphere.*

*It's the church's special function to uphold
    the finer things,*
*And to teach the way of living from which
    all that's noble springs;*
*But the minister can't do it single-handed
    and alone,*
*For the laymen of the country are the church's
    corner-stone.*

*When you see a church that's empty, though
    its doors are open wide,*
*It's not the church that's dying; it's the laymen
    who have died;*
*For it's not by song or sermon that the
    church's work is done;*
*But by the laymen of the country who for
    God must carry on.*

—Edgar A. Guest

COUNTRY CHURCH

*A country church seems close to God
In its simplest way—
Its white spire shining in the sun
As we kneel to pray—
Its tombstoned yard encircling
The peaceful quiet walls—
The church bells sweetly ringing
Their Sunday morning calls.
Here love wears a cotton dress,
And friendly faces glow . . .
Jesus loved the simple things . . .
True faith lives here I know.*

—Ethel Bailey

THERE IS STRENGTH

*—In silence, that speech does not know.
—In faith, that bluster can never imitate.
—In love, that hate can never realize.
—In quiet, that noise never understands.
—In prayer, that comes in no other way.*

EVERY-DAY GOODNESS

Christianity—is not a voice in the wilderness, but a life in the world. It is not an idea in the air but feet on the ground, going God's way. It is not an exotic to be kept under glass, but a hardy plant to bear twelve months of fruits in all kinds of weather. Fidelity to duty is its root and branch. Nothing we can say to the Lord, no calling Him by great or dear names, can take the place of the plain doing of His will. We may cry out about the beauty of eating bread with Him in His kingdom, but it is wasted breath and a rootless hope, unless we plow and plant in His kingdom here and now. To remember Him at His table and to forget Him at ours, is to have invested in bad securities. There is no substitute for plain, every-day goodness.

—BABCOCK

STEWARDSHIP

I bought gasoline; I went to the show;
I bought some new tubes for my old radio;
I bought candy and peanuts, nut bars and
*   ice cream;*
While my salary lasted, life sure was a scream.

It takes careful spending to make money go
*   round;*
One's methods of finance must always be
*   sound.*
With habits quite costly, it's real hard to
*   save;*
My wife spent ten "bucks" on a permanent
*   wave.*

The church came round begging. It sure
*   made me sore!*
If they'd let me alone, I'd give a lot more.
They have plenty of nerve! They forgot all
*   the past!*
I gave them a quarter the year before last.

The study of God's word, for the purpose of discovering God's will, is the secret discipline which has formed the greatest characters.

—J. W. ALEXANDER

SOME KEEP THE SABBATH

Some keep the Sabbath going to church;
*   I keep it staying at home,*
With a bobolink for a chorister,
*   And an orchard for a dome.*

Some keep the Sabbath in surplice;
*   I just wear my wings;*
And instead of tolling the bell for church,
*   Our little sexton sings.*

God preaches—a noted clergyman—
*   And the sermon is never long;*
So instead of getting to heaven at last,
*   I'm going all along!*

—EMILY DICKINSON

MY CHURCH

On me nor Priest nor Presbyter nor Pope,
*   Bishop nor Dean may stamp a party name;*
But Jesus, with his largely human scope,
*   The service of my human life may claim.*
Let prideful priests do battle about creeds,
*   The church is mine that does most*
*   Christlike deeds.*

THE CHURCH IN THE WILDWOOD

There's a church in the valley by the
*   wildwood*
*   No lovelier place in the dale;*
No spot is so dear to my childhood
*   As the little brown church in the vale.*

How sweet on a clear, Sabbath morning
*   To list to the clear-ringing bell,*
Its tones so sweetly are calling:
*   O, come to the church in the vale.*

There, close by the church in the valley,
*   Lies one that I loved so well;*
She sleeps, sweetly sleeps, 'neath the willow;
*   Disturb not her rest in the vale.*

There, close by the side of that loved one,
*   'Neath the tree where the wild flowers*
*   bloom,*
When the farewell hymn shall be chanted,
*   I shall rest by her side in the tomb.*

—WILLIAM S. PITTS

OUT OF THIS LIFE

Out of this life I'm unable to take
*   Things of silver and gold I make.*
All that I cherish and hoard away,
*   After I leave, on earth must stay.*
All that I gather, and all that I keep,
*   I must leave behind when I fall asleep.*
And I wonder often what I shall own
*   In that other life, when I pass alone.*
What shall they find and what shall they see
*   In the soul that answers the call for me?*
Shall the great judge learn, when my task
*   is through*
*   That my spirit has gathered some riches,*
*   too?*
Or shall at the last it be mine to find
*   That all that I'd worked for I'd left behind.*

A PREACHER'S PRAYER

I do not ask
That crowds may throng the temple,
That standing room be priced;
I only ask that as I voice the message
They may see the Christ.

I do not ask
For churchly pomp or pageantry,
Or music such as wealth can buy;
I only pray that as I voice the message
He might be nigh.

I do not ask
That men may sound my praise,
Or headlines spread my name abroad;
I only ask that as I voice the message
Hearts may find God.

—RALPH S. CUSHMAN

The minister is to be a live man, a real man, a true man, a simple man, great in his love, great in his life, great in his work, great in his simplicity, great in his gentleness.

—JOHN HALL

We have committed the Golden Rule to memory; let us now commit it to life.

—EDWIN MARKHAM

RELIGIOUS UNITY

Yes, we do differ when we most agree,
For words are not the same to you and me,
And it may be our several spiritual needs
Are best supplied by seeming different
*   creeds.*
*   And, differing, we agree in one*
*   Inseparable communion,*
If the true life be in our hearts; the faith
*   Which not to want is death;*
*   To want is penance; to desire*
*   Is purgatorial fire;*
To hope is paradise; and to believe
Is all of heaven that earth can e'er receive.

—HARTLEY COLERIDGE

The University of the People is the Sunday School.

—DAVID LLOYD GEORGE

FAITH SHALL BUILD A FAIRER THRONE

The waves unbuild the wasting shore;
*   Where mountains towered, the billows*
*   sweep,*
Yet still their borrowed spoils restore,
*   And build new empires from the deep.*
So while the floods of thought lay waste
*   The proud domain of priestly creeds,*
Its heaven-appointed tides will haste
*   To plant new homes for human needs.*
Be ours to mark with hearts unchilled
*   The change an outworn church deplores;*
The legend sinks, but Faith shall build
*   A fairer throne on new found shores.*

—OLIVER WENDELL HOLMES

Who has not found the heaven below
*   Will fail of it above.*
God's residence is next to mine,
*   His furniture is love.*

—EMILY DICKINSON

I find the doing of the will of God leaves me no time for disputing about his plans.

—G. MACDONALD

GIVING

God gives us joy that we may give;
   He gives us joy that we may share;
Sometimes He gives us loads to lift
   That we may learn to bear.
For life is gladder when we give,
   And love is sweeter when we share,
And heavy loads rest lightly too
   When we have learned to bear.

SACRIFICE

When he has more than he can eat
To feed a stranger's not a feat.
When he has more than he can spend
It isn't hard to give or lend.
Who gives but what he'll never miss
Will never know what giving is,
He'll win few praises from the Lord
The widow's mite to heaven went
Because real sacrifice is meant.

              —EDGAR A. GUEST

No man really gives unless the things he gives could be of use to himself. The more useful it is and the more desirable, the greater becomes its value. He who gives such things that he doesn't value or has no use for, in reality gives nothing.

              —EARL E. MARQUISS

Money Measures Men—their capacity and their consecration. In some instances money masters men. They become its slaves. In many instances money multiplies men. Through the ministry of the money he earns and gives, a Christian labors on every continent, preaches in a thousand pulpits, teaches and trains tomorrow's leaders. He ministers to multitudes in the name of Christ.

A loving heart is the truest wisdom.

              —CHARLES DICKENS

ALL CAN BE FAITHFUL

God does not give to everyone the same abilities. There are those with one talent, those with three and those with five. Some gained the advantage in heritage, in training or through opportunities.

God, however, did give to each the ability to be dependable. He requires of a steward that he be found faithful over that to which he is entrusted.

Our churches have their troubles with those who are undependable. They are the ones who find it easier to accept a responsibility than to announce by words, instead of later actions, that they will not give the required performance.

God will reward the person who did the best with his given talents. He will bless the one who accepted responsibility and was loyal to it. But, in none of his teachings do we find leniency for those not found faithful.

God's church depends upon his people being faithful. The responsibility is theirs.

HE PRAYETH BEST
(From "The Rime of the Ancient Mariner," Part VII)

O sweeter than the marriage-feast,
'Tis sweeter far to me,
To walk together to the kirk
With a goodly company!—

To walk together to the kirk,
And all together pray,
While each to his great Father bends,
Old men, and babes, and loving friends,
And youths and maidens gay!

Farewell, farewell! but this I tell
To thee, thou Wedding-Guest!
He prayeth well, who loveth well
Both man and bird and beast.

He prayeth best, who loveth best
All things both great and small;
For the dear God who loveth us,
He made and loveth all.

             —SAMUEL TAYLOR COLERIDGE

God builds no churches. By His plan
That labor has been left to man.
No spires miraculously arise,
No little mission from the skies
Falls on a bleak and barren place
To be a source of strength and grace.
The church demands its price
In human toil and sacrifice.

The humblest spire in mortal ken,
Where God abides, was built by men,
And if the church is still to grow,
Is still the light of hope to throw
Across the valleys of despair,
Man still must build God's house of prayer.
God sends no churches from the skies,
Out of our hearts they must arise.

ANGEL

If after kirk ye bide a wee,
There's some would like to speak to ye;
If after kirk ye rise and flee,
We'll all seem cold and stiff to ye.
The one that's in the seat wi' ye,
Is stranger here than you, may be;
All here hae got their fears and cares—
Add you your soul unto our prayers;
Be ye our angel unawares.

Oft have I seen at some cathedral door
A laborer, pausing in the dust and heat,
Lay down his burden, and with reverent feet
Enter, and cross himself, and on the floor
Kneel to repeat his paternoster o'er;
Far off the noises of the world retreat;
The loud vociferations of the street
Become an undistinguishable roar.
So, as I enter here from day to day,
And leave my burden at this minster gate
Kneeling in prayer, and not ashamed to pray,
The tumult of the time disconsolate,
To inarticulate murmurs dies away,
While the eternal ages watch and wait.

Sunday is the golden clasp that binds together the volume of the week.

—HENRY WADSWORTH LONGFELLOW

WANT TO BE HAPPY?

Yes, I know you do. For the desire for happiness is present in every human heart. And we seek happiness, each one of us, in our own way. We think "if I can do certain things, if I can get to such a place, if I can reach such a position, if I can get possession of so much money, then, I will be perfectly happy." But when we reach the goal we have set before us, too often we find nothing but disappointment. For these things do not, and cannot bring happiness in themselves. Happiness is an intangible thing that comes, not through possession, but through qualities of mind and heart. The Master of Life gives us the only rule for the attainment of happiness in the Beatitudes, and they are so plain that we can understand them. Why not try His way?

"If ye know these things, happy are ye if ye do them."

I am quite certain that there is nothing which draws so good, or at least so large, a congregation as a fight in the pulpit.

—BOLTON HALL

PRAYER

Lord, what a change within us one short
*   hour*
Spent in thy presence will prevail to make!
What heavy burdens from our bosoms take,
What parched grounds refresh as with a
*   shower!*
We kneel, and all around us seems to lower;
We rise, and all, the distant and the near,
Stands forth in sunny outline brave and clear;
We kneel, how weak! we rise, how full of
*   power!*
Why, therefore, should we do ourselves this
*   wrong,*
Or others, that we are not always strong,
That we are ever overborne with care,
That we should ever weak or heartless be,
Anxious or troubled, when with us is prayer,
And joy and strength and courage are with
*   thee!*

—RICHARD TRENCH

It's good to have money and the things that money can buy, but it's good, too, to check up once in a while and make sure you haven't lost the things that money can't buy.

—George Horace Lorimer

GOD'S ALTAR

There is in all the sons of men
A love that in the spirit dwells,
That panteth after things unseen,
And tidings of the future tells.

And God hath built his altar here
To keep this fire of faith alive,
And sent his priests in holy fear
To speak the truth—for truth to strive.

—Ralph Waldo Emerson

Enter this door
As if the floor
Within were gold,
And every wall
Of jewels all
Of wealth untold;
As if a choir
In robes of fire
Were singing here.
Nor shout, nor rush,
But hush . . .
For God is here.

Religion is meant to be bread for daily use, not cake for special occasions.

My soul, be on thy guard;
Ten thousand foes arise;
The host of sin are pressing hard,
To draw thee from the skies.

O watch, and fight, and pray;
The battle ne'er give o'er;
Renew it boldly every day,
And help divine implore.

—George Heath

THE MAN WITH THE CONSECRATED CAR

He couldn't speak before a crowd;
He couldn't teach a class.
But when he came to Sunday School,
He brought the folks "enmassee."
He couldn't sing to save his life;
In public he couldn't pray.
But always his "jalopy" was just
Crammed on each Lord's Day.
And although he could not sing,
Nor teach, nor lead in prayer,
He listened well, he had a smile, and
He was always there.
With all the others whom he brought,
Who lived both near and far—
And God's work prospered—for he
Had a consecrated car.

THE BIBLE

We search the world for truth. We cull
The good, the true, the beautiful,
From graven stone and written scroll,
And all old flower-fields of the soul;
And, weary seekers of the best,
We come back laden from our quest,
To find that all the sages said
Is the Book our mothers read.

—John Greenleaf Whittier

And should my soul be torn with grief
Upon my shelf I find
A little volume, torn and thumbed,
For comfort just designed.
I take my little Bible down
And read its pages o'er,
And when I part from it I find
I'm stronger than before.

—Edgar A. Guest

Religion is the spice which is meant to keep life from corruption.

—Francis Bacon

Struggle

Man's extremity is God's opportunity. Extremities are a warrant for importunities. A man at his wit's end is not at his faith's end.

—Matthew Henry

And you never can tell how close you are,
It may be near when it seems afar;
So stick to the fight when you're hardest hit—
It's when things seem worst that you
    mustn't quit.

The way we are facing has a lot to do with
our destination.

This old world we're livin' in
Is mighty hard to beat;
You get a thorn with every rose,
But ain't the roses sweet!

—FRANK L. STANTON

Amid my list of blessings infinite, Stands
this the foremost, "That my heart has
bled."

—EDWARD YOUNG

Light is the task when many share the
toil.

—HOMER

Just about any dream
    Grows stronger
If you hold on
    A little longer.

—MARGO GINA HART

DON'T QUIT

When things go wrong, as they sometimes
    will,
When the road you're trudging seems all up
    hill,
When the funds are low and the debts are
    high,
And you want to smile, but you have to sigh,
When care is pressing you down a bit,
Rest, if you must—but don't you quit.

Life is queer with its twists and turns,
As everyone of us sometimes learns,
And many a failure turns about
When he might have won had he stuck it out;
Don't give up, though the pace seems slow—
You might succeed with another blow.

Often the goal is nearer than
It seems to a faint and faltering man,
Often the struggler has given up
When he might have captured the victor's
    cup.
And he learned too late, when the night
    slipped down,
How close he was to the golden crown.

Success is failure turned inside out—
The silver tint of the clouds of doubt—

KEEP A-GOIN'

If you strike a thorn or rose,
    Keep a-goin'!
It it hails or if it snows,
    Keep a-goin'!
'Taint no use to sit an' whine
When the fish ain't on your line;
Bait your hook an' keep a-tryin'—
    Keep a-goin'!

When the weather kills your crop,
    Keep a-goin'!
Though 'tis work to reach the top,
    Keep a-goin'!
S'pose you're out o' ev'ry dime,
Gittin' broke ain't any crime;
Tell the world you're feelin' prime—
    Keep a-goin'!

When it looks like all is *up*,
    Keep a-goin'!
Drain the sweetness from the cup,
    Keep a-goin'!
See the wild birds on the wing,
Hear the bells that sweetly ring,
When you feel like sighin', sing—
    Keep a-goin'!

                  —FRANK L. STANTON

Be not dismayed nor be surprised
    If what you do is criticized.
Mistakes are made, I'll not deny
    But only made by those who try.

Every man is said to have his peculiar ambition. Whether it be true or not, I can say, for one, that I have no other so great as that of being truly esteemed of my fellow-men, by rendering myself worthy of their esteem. How far I shall succeed in gratifying this ambition is yet to be developed. I am young and unknown to many of you. I was born, and have ever remained, in the most humble walks of life. I have no wealthy or popular relations or friends to recommend me. My case is thrown exclusively upon the independent voters of the country; and, if elected, they will have conferred a favor upon me for which I shall be unremitting in my labors to compensate • •

But, if the good people in their wisdom shall see fit to keep me in the background, I have been too familiar with disappointments to be very much chagrined.

                  —ABRAHAM LINCOLN
(to the People of Sangamon, March 9, 1832)

DON'T TROUBLE TROUBLE

Don't you trouble trouble till trouble troubles you.
Don't you look for trouble; let trouble look for you.
Who feareth hath forsaken the heavenly Father's side;

What He hath undertaken He surely will provide.

The very birds reprove thee with their happy song;
The very flowers teach thee that fretting is a wrong.
"Cheer up," the sparrow chirpeth; "Thy Father feedeth me;
Think how much He careth, oh, lonely child, for thee."

"Fear not," the flowers whisper; "since thus He hath arrayed
The buttercup and daisy, how canst thou be afraid?"
Then don't you trouble trouble till trouble troubles you;
You'll only double trouble, and trouble others too.

                  —MARK GUY PEARSE

GOD SEES THE SCARS

When some friend has proved untrue—betrayed your simple trust;
Used you for his selfish ends and trampled in the dust
The past, with all its memories and all its sacred ties,
The light is blotted from the sky—for something in you dies.

Bless your false and faithless friend, just smile and pass along.
God must be the judge of it; He knows the right from wrong.
Life is short, don't waste the hours by brooding on the past;
His great laws are good and just; Truth conquers at the last.

Red and deep our wounds may be—but after all the pain
God's own finger touches us and we are healed again.
With faith restored, and trust renewed—we look toward the stars.
The world will see the smiles we have—but God will see the scars.

HAVING HARD TIMES?

There is a certain businessman who, whenever someone comes into his office bemoaning his misfortunes in business, love, or life in general, takes him aside and invites him to study a framed handlettered sign hanging on the wall. It reads:

"Failed in business—'31
Defeated for Legislature—'32
Failed in business again—'33
Elected to Legislature—'34
Sweetheart died—'35
Suffered nervous breakdown—'36
Defeated for Speaker—'38
Defeated for Elector—'40
Defeated for Congress—'43
Elected to Congress—'46
Defeated for Congress—'48
Defeated for Senate—'55
Defeated for Vice President—'56
Defeated for Senate—'58
Elected President of the United States —'60

And the name beneath this record of misfortune, crowned by final success?
ABRAHAM LINCOLN.

THE SENSIBLE WAY

There's nothing so bad
  That it could not be worse;
There's little that time may not mend,
  And troubles, no matter how thickly they
    come,
Most surely will come to an end.

You've stumbled—well so have we all in our
    time.
Don't dwell over much on regret,
For you're sorry, God knows, we'll leave it at
    that
Let past things be past, and forget.
Don't despond, don't give up, but just be
    yourself—
The self that is highest and best,
Just live every day in a sensible way,
And then leave to God all the rest.

Point thy tongue on the anvil of truth.

—Pindar

OBSTACLES

There are few positions in life in which difficulties have not to be encountered. These difficulties are, however, our best instructors, as our mistakes often form our best experience. We learn wisdom from failure more than from success. We often discover what will do by finding out what will not do. Horne Tooke used to say that he had become all the better acquainted with the country from having had the good luck sometimes to lose his way. Great thoughts, discoveries, inventions have very generally been nurtured in hardship, often pondered over in sorrow and established with difficulty.

—Paxton Hood

FRIENDLY OBSTACLES

For every hill I've had to climb,
  For every stone that bruised my feet,
For all the blood and sweat and grime,
  For blinding storms and burning heat,
My heart sings but a grateful song—
These were the things that made me strong!

For all the heartaches and the tears,
  For all the anguish and the pain,
For gloomy days and fruitless years,
  And for the hopes that lived in vain,
I do give thanks, for now I know
These were the things that helped me grow!

'Tis not the softer things of life
  Which stimulate man's will to strive;
But bleak adversity and strife
  Do most to keep man's will alive.
O'er rose-strewn paths the weaklings creep,
But brave hearts dare to climb the steep.

JUDGE NOT

Pray, find no fault with the man who limps,
Or stumbles along the road;
Unless you have worn the shoes he wears
Or struggled beneath his load.

There may be tacks in his shoes that hurt,
Though hidden away from view;

Or the burdens he bears, placed on your back
Might cause you to stumble, too.

Don't sneer at the man who's down today
Unless you have felt the blow
That caused his fall, or felt the shame
That only the fallen know.

You may be strong, but still the blows
That were his, if dealt to you,
In the selfsame way at the selfsame time,
Might cause you to falter too.

Don't be too harsh with the man who sins,
  Or pelt him with words or stones,
Unless you be sure, yea doubly sure,
  That you have no sins of your own.
For you know perhaps if the tempter's voice
  Should whisper as softly to you
As it did to him when he went astray,
  It would cause you to falter too.

COURAGE

It's knowing the worst—and discovering that, in God's world, the very worst can't really hurt you.

And when God, who sees all and who wishes to save us, upsets our designs, we stupidly complain against Him, we accuse His Providence. We do not comprehend that in punishing us, in overturning our plans and causing us suffering, He is doing all this to deliver us, to open the Infinite to us.

—Victor Hugo

GIVE 'EM BOTH BARRELS

Hold to the course, though the storms are
    about you;
Stick to the road where the banner still flies;
Fate and his legions are ready to rout you—
  Give 'em both barrels—and aim for their
    eyes.

Life's not a rose bed, a dream or a bubble,

A living in clover beneath cloudless skies;
And Fate hates a fighter who's looking for
    trouble,
So give 'em both barrels—and shoot for the
    eyes.
Fame never comes to the loafers and sitters,
  Life's full of knots in a shifting disguise;
Fate only picks on the cowards and quitters,
  So give 'em both barrels—and aim for the
    eyes.

—Grantland Rice

Thank God every morning when you get up that you have something to do which must be done, whether you like it or not. Being forced to work, and forced to do your best, will breed in you temperance, self-control, diligence, strength of will, content, and a hundred other virtues which the idle never know.

—Charles Kingsley

The great tests of life reveal character; it is not until winter comes that we know the pine is an evergreen.

DESTINY

We shape ourselves the joy or fear
  Of which the coming life is made,
And fill our future's atmosphere
  With sunshine or with shade.

The tissue of the life to be
  We weave with colors all our own,
And in the field of destiny
  We reap as we have sown.

—John Greenleaf Whittier

THE SACRAMENT OF WORK

Upon thy bended knees, thank God for
  work,—
Work—once man's penance, now his high
  reward!
For work to do, and strength to do the work,
  We thank Thee, Lord!

Since outcast Adam toiled to make a home,
The primal curse a blessing has become,
Man in his toil finds recompense for loss,
A workless world had known nor Christ nor
    Cross.

Some toil for love, and some for simple greed,
Same reap a harvest past their utmost need,
More, in their less find truer happiness,
And all, in work, relief from bitterness.

Upon thy bended knees, thank God for work!
In workless days all ills and evils lurk.
For work to do, and strength to do the work,
    We thank Thee, Lord!

                   —JOHN OXENHAM

From "BISHOP BLOUGRAM'S APOLOGY"

When the fight begins within himself,
A man's worth something. God stoops o'er his
    head,
Satan looks up between his feet—both tug—
He's left, himself, i' the middle; the soul
    wakes
And grows. Prolonging that battle through
    his life
Never leave growing till the life to come!

             —ROBERT BROWNING

He cannot heal who has not suffered much,
For only Sorrow sorrow understands;
They will not come for healing at our touch
Who have not seen the scars upon our hands.

        —EDWIN McNEILL POTEAT

THE LOOM OF TIME

Man's life is laid in the loom of time
  To a pattern he does not see,
While the weavers work and the shutties fly
  Till the dawn of eternity.

Some shuttles are filled with silver threads
  And some with threads of gold,
While often but the darker hues
  Are all that they may hold.

But the weaver watches with skillful eye
  Each shuttle fly to and fro,
And sees the pattern so deftly wrought
  As the loom moves sure and slow.

God surely planned the patterns
  Each thread, the dark and fair,
Is chosen by His master skill
  And placed in the web with care.

He only knows its beauty,
  And guides the shuttles which hold
The threads so unattractive,
  As well as the threads of gold.

Not till each loom is silent,
  And the shuttles cease to fly,
Shall God reveal the pattern
  And explain the reason why

The dark threads were as needful
  In the weaver's skillful hand
As the threads of gold and silver
  For the pattern which He planned.

PARADOX

It is in loving—not in being loved,—
  The heart is blest;
It is in giving—not in seeking gifts,—
  We find our quest.

If thou art hungry, lacking heavenly food,—
  Give hope and cheer.
If thou art sad and wouldst be comforted,—
  Stay sorrow's tear.

Whatever be thy longing and thy need,—
  That do thou give;
So shall thy soul be fed, and thou indeed,
  Shalt truly live.

Help me the slow of heart to move
By some clear, winning word of love;
Teach me the wayward feet to stay
And guide them in the homeward way.

Encouragement is oxygen to the soul! No one ever climbed spiritual heights without it. No one ever *lived* without it.

Success

No one has success until he has the abounding life. This is made up of the many-fold activity of energy, enthusiasm and gladness. It is to spring to meet the day with a thrill at being alive. It is to go forth to meet the morning in an ecstasy of joy. It is to realize the oneness of humanity in true spiritual sympathy.

—LILLIAN WHITING

"Men were born to succeed, not to fail."

—HENRY DAVID THOREAU

GREATNESS

A man is as great as the dreams he dreams,
  As great as the love he bears;
As great as the values he redeems,
  And the happiness he shares.
A man is as great as the thoughts he thinks,
  As the worth he has attained;
As the fountains at which his spirit drinks
  And the insight he has gained.
A man is as great as the truth he speaks,
  As great as the help he gives,
As great as the destiny he seeks,
  As great as the life he lives.

—C. E. FLYNN

Success in life is relative. In my judgment, success means making the most of such ability, personality, and physique as you have. Don't measure your success against others, but aganist your own potentialities. Never fret because somebody else has done better. If you become imbued with that philosophy of life and sincerely try to do the best you can, and achieve the sincere feeling that you are doing the best you are capable of, you have attained as much success as any man can attain. More than that, you will go on that basis just as far as you can go.

For every man who has lost God because of a great sorrow, there are a thousand who have lost him because of great success.

THAT'S SUCCESS!

It's doing your job the best you can
And being just to your fellow man;
It's making money—but holding friends
And being true to your aims and ends;
It's figuring how and learning why
And looking forward and thinking high

And dreaming a little and doing much.
It's keeping always in closest touch
With what is finest in word and deed;
It's being thorough, yet making speed;
It's daring blithely the field of chance
While making labor a brave romance;

It's going onward despite defeat
And fighting stanchly, but keeping sweet;
It's being clean and its playing fair;
It's laughing lightly at Dame Despair;
It's looking up at the stars above
And drinking deeply of life and love.

It's struggling on with the will to win
But taking loss with a cheerful grin;
It's sharing sorrow and work and mirth,
And making better this good old earth;
It's serving, striving through strain and stress;
It's doing your noblest—that's Success!

—BERTON BRALEY

He has achieved success who has lived well, laughed often and loved much; who has gained the respect of intelligent men and the love of little children; who has filled his niche and accomplished his task; who has left the world better than he found it, whether by an improved poppy, a perfect poem or a rescued soul; who has never lacked appreciation of earth's beauty or failed to express it; who has looked for the best in others and given the best he had; whose life was an inspiration; whose memory is a benediction.

—MRS. A. J. STANLEY

IT COULDN'T BE DONE

Somebody said that it couldn't be done,
*   But he with a chuckle replied*
That "maybe it couldn't," but he would be
*   one*
*   Who wouldn't say so till he'd tried.*
So he buckled right in with the trace of a grin
*   On his face. If he worried he hid it.*
He started to sing as he tackled the thing
*   That couldn't be done, and he did it.*
Somebody scoffed: "Oh, you'll never do that;
*   At least no one ever has done it";*
But he took off his coat and he took off his
*   hat,*
*   And the first thing we knew he'd begun it.*
With a lift of his chin and a bit of a grin,
*   Without any doubting or quiddit,*
He started to sing as he tackled the thing
*   That couldn't be done, and he did it.*

There are thousands to tell you it cannot be
*   done,*
*   There are thousands to prophesy failure;*
There are thousands to point out to you, one
*   by one,*
*   The dangers that wait to assail you.*
But just buckle in with a bit of a grin,
*   Just take off you coat and go to it;*
Just start to sing as you tackle the thing
*   That "cannot be done," and you'll do it.*

—Edgar A. Guest

Then, welcome each rebuff
That turns earth's smoothness rough,
Each sting that bids nor sit nor stand but go!

THE WILL TO WIN

If you want a thing bad enough
To go out and fight for it,
Work day and night for it,
Give up your time and your peace and your
*   sleep for it,*
If only desire of it
Makes you quite mad enough
Never to tire of it,
Makes you hold all other things tawdry and
*   cheap for it.*

If life seems all empty and useless without it
And all that you scheme and you dream is
*   about it,*
If gladly you'll sweat for it,
Fret for it,
Plan for it,
Lose all your terror of God or man for it,
If you'll simply go after that thing that you
*   want,*
With all your capacity,
Strength and sagacity,
Faith, hope and confidence, stern pertinacity,
If neither cold poverty, famished and gaunt,
Nor sickness nor pain
Of body and brain
Can turn you away from the thing that you
*   want,*
If dogged and grim you besiege and beset it,
*   You'll get it*

—Berton Braley

Trifles make perfection—and perfection is no trifle.

THE BLESSINGS OF WORK

If you wake up in the morning
*   With your hardest job to do,*
Don't start the day with grumbling—
*   That won't help you see it through.*
Be glad for work that's difficult,
*   For tasks that challenge you.*
Workers find a thousand blessings
*   The idle never knew.*

RECIPE FOR SUCCESS

Bite off more than you can chew,
*   Then chew it.*
Plan more than you can do,
*   Then do it.*
Point your arrow at a star,
*   Take your aim, and there you are.*

Arrange more time than you can spare,
*   Then spare it.*
Take on more than you can bear,
*   Then bear it.*
Plan your castle in the air,
*   Then build a ship to take you there.*

MEASURE OF SUCCESS

When sunset falls upon your day
And fades from out the west,
When business cares are put away
And you lie down to rest,
The measure of the day's success
Or failure may be told
In terms of human happiness
And not in terms of gold.

Is there beside some hearth tonight
More joy because you wrought?
Does some one face the bitter fight
With courage you have taught?
Is something added to the store
Of human happiness?
If so, the day that now is o'er
Has been a real success.

It is not he that enters upon any career, or starts in any race, but he that runs well and perseveringly that gains the plaudits of others, or the approval of his own conscience.

—ALEXANDER CAMPBELL

The Margin of Success: Make good! Don't complain! Do the things you are expected to do—and more. Don't waste time in giving reasons why you didn't, or couldn't, or wouldn't The less you do, the more you complain. Efficiency—keep that word in your heart. Get to saying that word in your sleep. Do your work a little better than anyone else does it. That is the margin of success.

Nothing great was ever achieved without enthusiasm.

—RALPH WALDO EMERSON

The darkest hour in any man's life is when he sits down to plan how to get money without earning it.

—HORACE GREELEY

Use the talents you have, and you will not feel so keenly your need of more talents.

The cash interpretation put upon the word "success" is our national disease.

—WILLIAM JAMES

SUCCESS

How do you tackle your work each day?
Are you scared of the job you find?
Do you grapple the task that comes your way
With a confident, easy mind?
Do you stand right up to the work ahead
Or fearfully pause to view it?
Do you start to toil with a sense of dread
Or feel that you're going to do it?

You can do as much as you think you can;
But you'll never accomplish more;
If you're afraid of yourself, young man,
There's little for you in store.
For failure comes from the inside first,
It's there if we only knew it,
And you can win, though you face the worse,
If you feel that you're going to do it.

SUCCESS! It's found in the soul of you,
And not in the realms of luck!
The world will furnish the work to do,
But you must provide the pluck.
You can do whatever you think you can,
It's all in the way you view it.
It's all in the start you make, young man;
You must feel that you're going to do it.

—EDGAR A. GUEST

REWARD OF SERVICE

The sweetest lives are those to duty wed,
Whose deeds both great and small
Are close-knit strands of an unbroken thread,
Where love enables all.
The world may sound no trumpets, ring no
* bells,*
The Book of Life the slurring record tells.

Thy love shall chant its own beatitudes,

After its own like working. A child's kiss
Set on thy singing lips shall make thee glad;
A poor man served by thee shall make thee
  rich;
A sick man helped by thee shall make thee
  strong;
Thou shalt be served thyself by every sense
Of service which thou renderest.

—Elizabeth Barrett Browning

Success in business starts not only with teamwork, but with the establishment of common goals implemented by business planning. A plan is a system to make something happen that might otherwise not happen. And a goal in business is measured by time and money. Tomorrow I want five dollars; next year I want a million dollars. The plan is the system whereby the goal is realizable.

Success is rooted in reciprocity. He who does not benefit the world is headed for bankruptcy on the high-speed clutch.

—H. H. Rogers

DO YOUR BEST

It takes a little courage
  And a lot of self-control,
And some given determination,
  If you want to reach a goal.

It takes a deal of striving,
  And a firm and stern set chin;
No matter what the battle,
  If you're really out to win.

There is a rule in life to guide you,
  As you see Prosperity:
Never put your wishbone
  Where your backbone ought to be.

—Florence Koba

When the high heart we magnify,
  And the clear vision celebrate,
And worship greatness passing by,
  Ourselves are great.

—John Drinkwater

I have learned that success is to be measured not so much by the position that one has reached in life as by the obstacles which he has overcome while trying to succeed.

—Booker T. Washington

Why should we be in such desperate haste to succeed, and in such desperate enterprises? If a man does not keep pace with his companions, perhaps it is because he hears a differest drummer.

—Henry David Thoreau

LUCK

Do you believe in luck? I should say I do. It's a wonderful force. I have watched the careers of too many lucky men to doubt its efficacy.

You see some fellow reach out and grab an opportunity that the other fellow standing around had not realized was there. Having grabbed it, he hangs on it with a grip that makes the jaws of a bulldog seem like a fairy touch. He calls into his play his breadth of vision. He sees the possibility of the situation, has the ambition to desire it, and the courage to tackle it.

He intensifies his strong points, bolsters his weak ones, cultivates those personal qualities that cause other men to trust him and cooperate with him. He sows the seeds of sunshine, of good cheer, of optimism, of unstinted kindness. He gives freely of what he has, both spiritual and physical things.

He thinks a little straighter, works a little harder and a little longer; travels on his nerve and enthusiasm; he gives such service as his best efforts permit. He keeps his head cool, his feet warm, his mind busy. He doesn't worry over trifles.

He plans his work and then sticks to it, rain or shine. He talks and acts like a winner, for he knows in time he will be one. And then—LUCK does all the rest.

YOU HAVE IMPORTANT WORK TO DO

You have a contribution to make to the world that you alone can make. No one else can take your place. No matter who you are, or where you are, you are important.

Our happy friend, William L. Stidger, tells us that once Walter Damrosch stopped his orchestra, when apparently everything was going smoothly, and asked, "Where is the seventh flute? Where is the seventh flute?"

Mr. Stidger says his call was not for the first flute, or the second—but the seventh. Even the seventh flute had an important place in creating the harmony Conductor Damrosch desired.

"We may feel inferior, untalented, not even beautiful, and some of us uneducated," comments Mr. Stidger, "but each of us has a part to play and should play it well."

He tells how he used to watch the man who plays the triangle in the Radio City Orchestra. Often he would sit through the entire number, watchful, eager, waiting. Then, toward the close of the piece, he would, with perfect timing, deftly touch the instrument and bring forth a melody which put just the right ending on the entire number.

So, whatever your job, do it well. It is important.

—THOMAS DREIER

ISN'T IT TRUE?

Isn't it true that a lot of us blame the road when it's really just a pebble in our shoe? We think the whole road is rough And, looking back over something that seemed extremely hard and rough, we wonder how we got through it so easily. The mental pebbles that we put in our shoes make the job hard—not the job itself. Once we get rid of the mental obstacle, our whole attitude is different.

IF YOU SMILE

Here's a bit of homely guidance
    That is worth a pile of gold
If you use it in your going for a while.
It's the wisdom of the ages
    Given alike for young and old—
Your work will be more welcome if you
    smile!

You may be old and trembling,
    Or you may be young and strong,
And folks may praise your efforts or revile;
But you quickly learn the lesson
    As you win your way along
That your work will be more welcome if you
    smile!

I know the cynics sneer at this
    And call it silly stuff,
And seek with "deeper wisdom" to beguile;
But you'll find it serves the purpose
    When the way is dark or rough,
And you make your work more welcome
    with a smile!

—LEIGH M. HODGES

Life becomes tragic to him who has plenty to live on but little to live for.

Try not to become a man of success but rather try to become a man of value.

—ALBERT EINSTEIN

HIGH RESOLVE

I'll hold my candle high, and then
Perhaps I'll see the hearts of men
Above the sordidness of life,
Beyond misunderstandings, strife.
Though many deeds that others do
Seem foolish, rash and sinful too,
Just who am I to criticize
What I perceive with my dull eyes?
I'll hold my candle high, and then,
Perhaps I'll see the hearts of men.

Youth

Equipped? Why, the poorest young man is equipped as only the God of the whole universe could afford to equip him.

—T. DeWitt Talmage

A skill that the world shall admire
Strength that the world shall employ
And faith that shall burn as a fire
Are what may be found in a boy.

He with his freckles of tan,
He with that fun-loving grin,
May rise to great heights as a man
And many a battle win;
Back of the slang of the streets
And back of the love of a toy,
It may be a great spirit beats—
Lincoln once played as a boy.

DEDICATE YOUR LIFE

See families wrecked by liquor;
For their sakes—dedicate your life.
See soldiers marching to kill;
For their sakes—dedicate your life.
See church members indifferent and careless;
For their sakes—dedicate your life.
See children dying from hunger;
For their sakes—dedicate your life.
See girls selling their bodies for dollars;
For their sakes—dedicate your life.
See share-croppers living in shanties;
For their sakes—dedicate your life.
See rich men groping in the dark;
For their sakes—dedicate your life.

—Samuel F. Pugh

THE BOY

A possible man of affairs,
A possible leader of men,
Back of the grin he wears
There may be the courage of ten;
Lawyer or merchant or priest,
Artist or singer of joy,
This, when his strength is increased,
Is what may become of a boy.

Heedless and mischievous now,
Spending his boyhood in play,
Yet the glory may rest on his brow
And fame may exalt him some day;

You can never have a greater or a less dominion than that over yourself.

—Leonard da Vinci

OUR HEROES

Here's a hand to the boy who has courage
  To do what he knows to be right;
When he falls in the way of temptation,
  He has a hard battle to fight.
Who strives against self and his comrades
  Will find a most powerful foe.
All honor to him if he conquers.
  A cheer for the boy who says "No!"

There's many a battle fought daily
  The world knows nothing about;
There's many a brave little soldier
Whose strength puts a legion to rout.
And he who fights sin singlehanded
  Is more of a hero, I say,
Than he who leads soldiers to battle
  And conquers by arms in the fray.

Be steadfast, my boy, when you're tempted,
  To do what you know to be right
Stand firm by the colors of manhood,
  And you will o'ercome in the fight.
"The right," be your battle cry ever
  In waging the warfare of life,
And God, who knows who are the heroes,
  Will give you the strength for the strife.

—Phoebe Cary

The man who trims himself to suit everybody will soon whittle himself away.

—HUGH MURR

When, at sixteen, I was vain because
someone praised me, my father said:
"They are only praising your youth. You
can take no credit for beauty at sixteen. But
if you are beautiful at sixty, it will be your
own soul's doing. Then you may be proud
of it and be loved for it."

—MARIE STOPES

"There's nothing so sweet as a girl—
Dainty and tender and whimsical, too
Loving and lovable, eager to please
Questioning, longing, expectant and true
No flower ever fairer than is one of these
There's nothing so sweet as a girl—
Unless it's a boy!

There's nothing so fine as a boy—
Sturdy and lovable, valiant and strong
Noisy and mischievous, daring and bold
Loyal and faithful to his right or wrong
Caveman and savage, and then knight of old
There's nothing so fine as a boy—
Unless it's a girl!"

I saw a sweet young thing,
With carmine cheek and nyloned leg
Draped over the arm of a rocking chair
Yapping about self-expression.
Self-expression, Bah!
The chattering monkeys and the laughing
hyenas,
Have self-expression in full measure,
And they remain monkeys and hyenas,
While man, through self-denial
Has gained some semblance of the divine.

—EDWIN DOANE ROBINSON

The nicest words I know are these:
"Excuse me," "Thank you," "If you
please."

—JAMES W. FOLEY

A BOY'S SONG

Where the pools are bright and deep,
Where the grey trout lies asleep,
Up the river and over the lea,
That's the way for Billy and me.

Where the blackbird sings the latest,
Where the hawthorn blooms the sweetest,
Where's the nestlings chirp and flee,
That's the way for Billy and me.

Where the mowers mow the cleanest,
Where the hay lies thick and greenest,
There to track the homeward bee,
That's the way for Billy and me.

Where the hazel bank is steepest,
Where the shadow falls the deepest,
Where the clustering nuts fall free,
That's the way for Billy and me.

Why the boys should drive away
Lttle sweet maidens from the play,
Or love to banter and fight so well,
That's the thing I never could tell.

But this I know, I love to play
Through the meadows, among the hay;
Up the water and over the lea,
That's the way for Billy and me.

—JAMES HOGG

From "VOLUNTARIES"

In an age of fops and toys,
Wanting wisdom, void of right,
Who shall nerve heroic boys
To hazard all in Freedom's fight—
Break sharply off their jolly games,
Forsake their comrades gay
And quit proud homes and youthful dames
For famine, toil, and fray?
Yet on the nimble air benign
Speed nimbler messages,
That waft the breath of grace divine
To hearts in sloth and ease.
So nigh is grandeur to our dust,
So near is God to man,
When Duty whispers low, Thou must
The youth replies, I can.

—RALPH WALDO EMERSON

THE "OLD, OLD SONG"

When all the world is young, lad,
And all the trees are green;
And every goose a swan, lad,
And every lass a queen;
Then hey for boot and horse, lad,
And round the world away;
Young blood must have its course, lad,
And every dog its day.
When all the world is old, lad,
And all the trees are brown;
And all the sport is stale, lad,
And all the wheels run down:
Creep home, and take your place there,
The spent and maim'd among:
God grant you find one face there
You loved when all was young.

—CHARLES KINGSLEY

EVERY YOUTH

Every youth has a quest to make
For life is the King's Highway;
A joyous heart is the script we take
On the road to Everyday.
Every youth has his gift to guard,
As he fares to a far off goal
A body pure, and a mind unmarred,
And the light of a lovely soul.
Every youth has a task of his own
For the Father has willed it so,
Youth seeks the way, and He alone,
Can show him the path to go.
Every youth has a lovely Guide,
From the vale to the mountain crest,
For the Unseen Friend who walks beside
Is the Way and the End of the quest.

The best thing to give to your enemy is forgiveness; to an opponent, tolerance; to a friend, your heart; to your child, a good example; to a father, deference; to your mother, conduct that will make her proud of you; to yourself, respect; to all men, charity.

—LORD BALFOUR

NO MIDDLE WAY

None of us can escape the importance of choice. We may think that we can set our lives in the direction of a middle way by trying to make the best of both worlds. If so, we may as well know at once that we cannot have what is often called the best of both worlds. When we want something from both of them, we finally get the worst of both and never the best.

Moreover, there is no best in evil, for by its very character evil must be the worst of all. No one can sit on the fence for long. He will finally land on one side or the other. So when we pitch the tent of our lives we ought to be careful regarding the direction in which it is facing.

THE FLIGHT OF YOUTH

There are gains for all our losses.
There are balms for all our pain:
But when youth, the dream departs
It takes something from our hearts,
And it never comes again.

We are stronger, and are better,
Under manhood's sterner reign:
Still we feel that something sweet
Followed youth, with flying feet,
And will never come again.

Something beautiful is vanished,
And we sigh for it in vain;
We behold it everywhere,
On the earth, and in the air,
But it never comes again!

—RICHARD HENRY STODDARD

EQUIPMENT

Figure it out for yourself, my lad,
You've all that the greatest of men have had,
Two arms, two hands, two legs, two eyes
And brain to use if you would be wise.
With this equipment they all began,
So start for the top and say, "I can."

Look them over, the wise and great,
They take their food from a common plate,

And similar knives and forks they use,
With similar laces they tie their shoes,
The world considers them brave and smart,
But you've all they had when they made their
    start.

You can triumph and come to skill,
You can be great if you only will.
You're well equipped for what fight you
    choose,
You have legs and arms and a brain to use,
And the man who has risen great deeds to do
Began his life with no more than you.

You are the handicap you must face,
You are the one who must choose your place,
You must say where you want to go,
How much you will study the truth to know.
God has equipped you for life, but He
Lets you decide what you want to be.

Courage must come from the soul within,
The man must furnish the will to win.
So figure it out for yourself, my lad.
You were born with all the great have had,
With your equipment they all began
Get hold of yourself, and says "I can."

                —Edgar A. Guest

A YOUTH'S PRAYER

To build a life that's clean, upright, secure,
God's temple that will through the years en-
    dure;
To walk courageously, steadfast and sure;
    This is my prayer.
To teach a war-torn world the fruits of peace;
To plead that cruelty and hate must cease,
That earth might see goodwill and love in-
    crease;
    This is my prayer.
To dedicate my life, my youth, my all
To Christ, and then in answer to his call,
Be faithful to each task—the large, the small;
    This is my prayer.

              —George W. Wiseman

Mud thrown is ground lost.

MY CHUM

He stood at the crossroads all alone,
    With the sunrise in his face;
He had no fear for the path unknown;
    He was set for a manly race.
But the road stretched east, and the road
    stretched west;
There was no one to tell him which way was
    the best;
So my chum turned wrong and went down,
    down, down,
Till he lost the race and the victor's crown
And fell at last in an ugly snare,
Because no one stood at the crossroads there.

Another chum on another day
    At the selfsame crossroads stood;
He paused a moment to choose the way
    That would stretch to the greater good.
And the road stretched east, and the road
    stretched west;
But I was there to show him the best;
So my chum turned right and went on and on,
Till he won the race and the victor's crown;
He came at last to the mansions fair,
Because I stood at the crossroads there.

Since then I have raised a daily prayer
That I be kept faithful standing there.
To warn the runners as they come,
And save my own or another's chum.

MASTER OF MEN.

"There is a young lad, Master,
With two small fish," they said.
"Five barley loaves he carries, too,
But little use they'd be to you
With thousands wanting bread."

And then the Master saw him,
A slender, growing lad,
Who with impetuous, boyish grace
Turned to His own a wistful face
And offered all he had.

At dusk the lad walked homeward.
What though the stars were dim?
A light within his soul he bore—
He'd not be lonely any more—
The Master needed him.

COME CLEAN!

When the game is on and your friends about,
And you could put your rival out
By a trick that's mean but wouldn't be seen,
Come clean, my lad, come clean!

When exams are called and you want to pass,
And you know how you could lead your class,
But the plan's not square, you know its mean;
Come clean, my lad, come clean!

With the boss away, you've a chance to
shirk,
Not lose your pay—not have to work,
He'll neither fire you nor vent his spleen;
Come clean, my lad, come clean!

When you're all alone and no one about,
And not a soul could find it out,
And you're tempted to do a thing that's
obscene;
Come clean, my lad, come clean!

For a home awaits, and a girl that's true,
And a church and state have need of you,
They must have your best—on you they lean,
Come clean, my lad, come clean!

KEEP A-TRYING!

You may never reach the summit of the mountain of your dreams, where so long ago you built your castles airy; you may never stand upon the height that beckons with its gleams; you may end your days a-fighting fates contrary. You may find the load too heavy, you may fail at every plan, you may meet with disappointment and with sighing; but it's just as well to plod along and meet them like a man; and it isn't any harm to keep a-trying.

You may see the swifter pilgrim forge along and take the lead, and the careless world may laugh at you for failing; but the thing for you to do is just to make your best old speed; it is better far than quitting or bewailing.

Keep a-going, keep a-trying; you may fall and be forgotten in the climbing; you may never get your name inscribed upon the glory roll, you may never hear the victor bells a-chiming. But if you can play a losing game and keep your manly grit, and if you can keep your flag unfurled and flying, you will know your brow is worthy for the laurel crown to fit; you're a winner if you only keep a-trying.

—William T. Card

ALADDIN

When I was a beggarly boy,
And lived in a cellar damp,
I had not a friend nor a toy,
But I had Aladdin's lamp;
When I could not sleep for cold,
I had fire enough in my brain,
And builded, with roofs of gold,
My beautiful castles in Spain!

Since then I have toiled day and night,
I have money and power good store,
But I'd give all my lamps of silver bright,
For the one that is mine no more;
Take, Fortune, whatever you choose,
You gave, and may snatch again;
I have nothing 'twould pain me to lose,
For I own no more castles in Spain!

—James Russell Lowell

ULTIMA VERITAS

I know that right is right
And givers shall increase;
That duty lights the way
For the beautiful feet of peace;
That courage is better than fear
And faith is truer than doubt

And fierce though he fiends may fight
And long though the angels hide,
I know that truth and right
Have the universe on their side,
And that somewhere beyond the stars
Is a Love that is stronger than hate.
When the night unlocks her bars
I shall see Him and I will wait.

—Washington Gladden

Go serenely, go boldly, go augustly;
Who can withstand thee then?

ABBOTT, WENONAH STEVENS 79
Above yon sombre swell of land 32
ADAMS, GEORGE MATTHEW 31
ADAMS, SARAH FLOWER 49
ADDISON, JOSEPH 25, 57, 77, 119
A Dieu! And Au Revoir 81
Adoration, Praise and Thanksgiving 114
After Work 80
Age is a quality of mind 74
À KEMPIS, THOMAS 159
Aladdin 194
ALCOTT, LOUISA MAY 169
ALEXANDER, JOSEPH ADDISON 30
ALFORD, HENRY 107
ALIGHIERI, DANTE 26
All Can Be Faithful 174
All honor to him who shall win the prize 88
ALLEN, ELIZABETH AKERS 150
ALLEN, JAMES L. 65
Alternatives 38
Am I a Builder? 32
America for Me 165
Amid the cares of married strife 127
AMIEL, HENRI-FREDERIC 26, 38, 48, 154
And I said to the man 68
And should my soul be torn 176
And the voice that was calmer than silence 98
ANDERSEN, HANS CHRISTIAN 20
Angel 175
Angry Word, An 128
Any Wife or Husband 130
Apparent Failure 14
ARISTOTLE 56
ARNOLD, EDWIN 42
ARNOLD, MATTHEW 56
Arrow and the Song, The 44
Artist can take a few bits, An 144
As a fond mother 76
As a Man Soweth 34
As I Grow Old 10
As I grow old, the winds of life 12
As long as mortals have the nerve 69
As through the land at eve we went 126
As We Grow Older 10
As you love me 81
Aspiration 56
At Christmas 72
AUGUSTINE, SAINT 96
AUSTIN, ALFRED 145
AUTERMONT, HARRIETT du 92

BABCOCK, MALTBIE DAVENPORT 34, 172
Backward, turn backward 150
BACON, FRANCIS 24, 77
Bad Times 121
BAILEY, BERTHA 18
BAILEY, ETHEL 171
BAILEY, MARGARET 66
BAILEY, PHILIP JAMES 104
BAKER, BONNIE WHITE 136
BAKER, KARLE WILSON 9, 61
BALFOUR, LORD 192
Ballad of the Fiddler, The 154
BANGS, JOHN KENDRICK 47, 115
BANKS, GEORGE LINNAEUS 143
BARBAULD, ANNA LETITIA 75
BARR, AMELIA E. 118
Barter 60
BARTON, BRUCE 94, 100, 141
BAXTER, RICHARD 29
Be Patient 162
Be Strong 34
Be Strong 134
Be strong to hope 134
Be True 43

BEAUMONT, JOSEPH 121
Beautiful Thoughts 18
Beauty 18
Beauty of Jesus in Me, The 17
Beauty they thought was dead 17
Because I could not stop for death 76
Because You Care 128
Because you love me 105
BECKER, CHARLOTTE 57, 87, 121
Bedrock 121
BEECHER, HENRY WARD 25, 102, 103, 112, 163
Before I knew how cruel 41
Begin Again 158
Believe me, if all those endearing young charms 111
BELL, ALEXANDER G. 155
BENNETT, LEO 157
Best We Can, The 162
Beyond, The 90
Beyond the Farthest Horizon 132
Beyond the last's horizon's rim 82
Bhagavad-Gita, The 80
BILLINGS, JOSH 125
Bishop Blougram's Apology 182
Bite off more than you can chew 185
BLAKE, KATHERINE D. 57
Blessings of Work, The 185
BLOCK, MARY 64
BOLTON, SARAH KNOWLES 89
BONAR, HORATIUS 43
Books 23
Books on strange things 22
Boomerang, The 102
Boy, The 34
Boy, The 190
Boy's Song, A 191
BRAINARD, MARY GARDNER 91
BRALEY, BERTON 99, 103, 156, 184, 185
Break, Break, Break 150
Breathes there the man 164
BREEDING, JOSEPHINE STONE 50
Bride's Prayer, A 126
Bridge Builder, The 38
BRIDGES, MADELINE 109, 143
Bridle Your Tongue 32
Brief life is here our portion 11
BRONTË, EMILY 65, 80
BROOKS, PHILLIPS 158
BROWNE, SIR THOMAS 154
BROWNING, ELIZABETH BAR-RETT 24, 25, 32, 60, 106, 110, 187
BROWNING, ROBERT 11, 14, 79, 182
BRUNER, MARGARET E. 51, 81, 107, 128
BRYANT, WILLIAM CULLEN 46, 76
BUCHANAN, ROBERT 19
Build a little fence of trust 59
Build on resolve, and not upon regret 140
Build thee more stately mansions 33
BUNYAN, JOHN 83, 138
BURKE, EDMUND 44
BURNS, ROBERT 114, 138
BURROUGHS, JOHN 12
BURTON, HENRY 101
Bustle in a House, The 79
But I think the king of that country 74
Butterfly, The 83
BUTTS, MARY FRANCES 59
By the rude bridge that arched the flood 165
BYRON, LORD 60, 89

Calm Soul of All Things 56
CAMPBELL, ANNE 107, 128, 140
CARD, WILLIAM T. 35

CARDOZO, ELIZABETH C. 88
Careless word may kindle strife, A 112
CARLETON, EMMA 96
CARLETON, WILL 32
CARLYLE, THOMAS 64, 71, 122
CARRUTH, WILLIAM HERBERT 94
CARTER, ROSALIE 101
CARUTHERS, MAZIE V. 125
CARY, PHOEBE 190
CATO 13
CELLINI, BENVENUTO 26
CHALMERS, PATRICK REGINALD 23
CHALMERS, THOMAS 58
CHANNING, WILLIAM ELLERY 18
Character of a Happy Life 118
CHENEY, ELIZABETH 93
CHENEY, JOHN VANCE 138
CHESTERTON, GILBERT K. 52, 134
CHILD, L. M. 17
CHOLMONDELEY, HESTER H. 42
Choose Carefully 112
CHURCHILL, WINSTON 125
Church in the Wildwood, The 172
Church You Want, The 170
CICERO 13, 166
CLARK, ESTHER M. 122
CLARK, MARTHA HASKELL 55
CLARK, THOMAS CURTIS 90
CLARKE, J. 148
CLEMMER, MARY 112
Closing the Doors 92
CLOUGH, A. H. 160
COATES, FLORENCE EARLE 89
COLERIDGE, HARTLEY 173
COLERIDGE, SAMUEL TAYLOR 104, 174
COLLIER, JEREMY 63
COLLINS, WILLIAM 167
Come Clean 194
Coming Child, The 71
Companionship 107
Concord Hymn 165
CONFUCIUS 22
Conscience 40
Convictions 29
COOKE, EDMUND VANCE 90
COOLIDGE, SUSAN 158
CORNELIUS, MAXWELL N. 46
CORY, DAVID 108
Count each affliction, whether light or grave 50
Country Church 171
Country church seems close to God, A 171
Courage 61
Courage 63
Courage 65
Courage 181
Courage is armor 61
Courage isn't a brilliant dash 63
COURT, FRANK A. 143
Coward 43
COWPER, WILLIAM 111, 136
CRANE, FRANK 125, 128
CRASHAW, RICHARD 71
CRAVEN, ELIZABETH 114
CRAWFORD, CAPT. JACK 102
Crossing the Bar 81
CURTIS, G. W. 25
CUSHMAN, RALPH S. 173

Daffodils, The 54
Dare to Do Right 65
Dauntless 64
DAVIES, MARY CAROLYN 102, 112
Day Is Done, The 47
Daylight is gone, the 100

Days grow shorter, The 14
DAWSON, GRACE STRICKER 99
Dear, do not weep 140
Dear friend, I pray thee 101
Death Be Not Proud 81
Death Stands Above Me 84
Death takes our loved ones 81
Dedicate Your Life 190
DEEMS, CHARLES F. 49
Defeat may serve as well as victory 85
DEKKER, THOMAS 58
DEPEW, CHAUNCEY M. 166
DeSALES, ST. FRANCIS 64
Destiny 181
DeVERE, SIR AUBREY 50
Devil, The 175
DICKENS, CHARLES 48
DICKINSON, EMILY 19, 22, 76, 79, 86, 116, 172
Did you tackle that trouble 90
Distance nor death, shall part us 109
Divine Law 119
Do the work that's nearest 31
Do you know that your soul is of my soul a part 68
Do Your Best 187
DOBBS, HOYT M. 43
DOBSON, AUSTIN 106
DONNE, JOHN 81
Don't Give Up 86
Don't Quit 178
Don't Trouble Trouble 179
Doomed Man, The 30
Doubts Are Traitors 63
Dream That Comes True, The 95
DREIER, THOMAS 26, 188
DROMGOOLE, WILL ALLEN 38
DRYDEN, JOHN 66
DYER, EDWARD 54

Each in His Own Tongue 94
Earth yields nothing more divine, The 88
Easter 83
Easter Morning 68
East London 133
Easy roads are crowded, The 65
EDGEWORTH, MARIA 30
ELIOT, GEORGE 49, 88, 153
EMERSON, RALPH WALDO 15, 20, 22, 25, 40, 49, 55, 58, 64, 79, 116, 138, 157, 158, 165, 176, 191
Emphasis 110
End of the Rope, The 62
ENNIS 104
Enter this door 176
EPICTITUS 57
Equipment 192
ERICK, LULA 58
Eternal Hope 134
Every-Day Goodness 172
Every day is a fresh beginning 158
Every Youth 192

Faith 46
Faith Shall Build a Fairer Throne 173
Fame is vapor 43
FARLEY, ROBERT E. 118
Fear Death?—to feel the fog in my throat 79
Fellowship 98
Fidelis 111
FIELD, FRANKLIN 11
FIELD, MARSHALL 161
FIELDS, JAMES T. 119
Figure it out for yourself, my lad 192
Final Song, The 152
Fire mist and a planet, A 94
FLETCHER, JOHN 24
FLETCHER, LOUISA 52
Flight of Youth, The 192
FLINT, ANNIE JOHNSON 48
FLORIO, J. 22
Flower unblown, a book unread, The 11

Flowers 17
FLYNN, C. E. 184
Foe Within, The 40
For age is opportunity no less 10
For all things beautiful 16
For every hill I've had to climb 180
For life that lends me happiness 116
For One Lately Bereft 51
For Those Who Fail 88
Force of Prayer, The 47
Fortitude 62
FOSDICK, HARRY EMERSON 11
FOSS, SAM WALTER 95
Four Things 167
Four things in any land must dwell 167
FRANCIS, SAINT 96
FRANK, EDGAR 59
FRANKLIN, BENJAMIN 30
FREE, SPENCER MICHAEL 97
FREEMAN, JAMES DILLET 120
Friend 100
Friend, may you keep your luggage light, 120
Friend Who Stands By, The 103
Friendly Obstacles 180
Friendship 100
FRITSCH, H. S. 74
Frontiersman, The 168
FULLER, ETHEL ROMIG 94
Funny Thing, A 103

GARFIELD, JAMES A. 56
Gate at the End of Things, The 41
GATES, JESSIE ROSE 46
GAULT, A. J. 150
Gettysburg Address, The 166
GILKEY, JAMES GORDON 49
GILLILAN, STRICKLAND 42, 133
GILLOM, ARTHUR L. 108
Give 'em Both Barrels 181
Give me the lowest place 162
Give thy thoughts no tongue 145
Giving 174
Giving and Forgiving 144
GLADDEN, WASHINGTON 140, 194
Glorious Court, A 24
Go, bury thy sorrow 48
Go, little book and wish to all 25
God Answers 160
God bless all those who labor with their hands 70
God Bless You 122
God builds no churches 175
God built and launched this year 95
God gave my world to me 139
God gives us joy 174
God Is Beautiful 19
God keep my heart attuned to laughter 10
God Keep You 109
God—Let Me Be Aware 44
God made a wonderful mother 68
God of our fathers, known of old 168
God Sees the Scars 179
GODE, MARGUERITE 126
God's Altar 176
God's Mosaic 144
GOETHE, JOHANN W. von 34
GOETHE, WOLFGANG von 124
Goldenrod is yellow, The 74
GOLDSMITH, OLIVER 133, 140
Good Company 22
Good Impulses 96
Good Thanksgiving, A 73
GORDON, ARMISTEAD 46
Goshen! 59
Gospel of Labor, The 74
GRAFFIN, MARGARET JOHNSTON 68
Grandest Prize, The 35
Gratitude 116
GRAYSON, DAVID 121
Great Heart 28

Greatness 184
GREELEY, HORACE 43
GREEN, J. WHITFIELD 43
GREENBIE, MARJORIE BARSTOW 12
GRENVILLE, R. H. 70
GRISWOLD, ALFRED WHITNEY 24
GROVER, EDWIN OSGOOD 93
Grow old along with me 11
Growing Old 14
Growing Older 13
GRUTER, OSCAR R. 145
GUEST, EDGAR A. 38, 40, 42, 64, 65, 66, 72, 124, 144, 171, 174, 176, 185, 186, 193
Guilty 31
Guy in the Glass, The 144

HALL, BOLTON 175
HALL, MARY LEE 74
Happiest Heart, The 138
Happiness 119
Happiness is like a crystal 119
Happy the Man 120
Happy the man, and happy he alone 66
Harder Task, The 146
Harsh words, like chickens, love to stray 33
HASKINS, M. LOUISE 68
Have we not all, amid life's petty strife 30
Have you had a kindness shown? 101
HAVERGAL, FRANCES RIDLEY 48
Having Hard Times 180
HAWTHORNE, LAWRENCE 56
HAWTHORNE, NATHANIEL 119, 120
HAYNES, CAROL 130
He couldn't speak before a crowd 176
He had played by the cottage fire 154
He Is Not Dead 83
He knows, he loves, he cares 31
He may be six kinds of a liar 103
He prayed for strength 160
He Prayeth Best 174
He sang for joy 89
He sendeth sun, he sendeth shower 49
He stood at the crossroads all alone 193
He that is down needs fear no fall 138
He was caught in the whirl 20
HEATH, GEORGE 176
Heaven 76
HEINE, HEINRICH 152
HENLEY, WILLIAM ERNEST 80
HENRY, MATTHEW 177
HERBERT, GEORGE 115
Here sparrows build upon the trees 148
Here's a bit of homely guidance 188
Here's a hand to the boy 190
HICKY, DANIEL WHITEHEAD 153
High Resolve 188
HILL, LESLIE 139
Hills of Rest, The 82
His Faults 128
HODGES, LEIGH M. 188
HOENE, R. H. 32
HOGG, JAMES 191
Hold Fast to Dreams 36
Hold to the course 181
HOLLAND, J. G. 96, 112
HOLMES, OLIVER WENDELL 12, 33, 173
Home 124
Homemaker's Prayer, The 126
Home's not merely four square walls 125
HOOD, PAXTON 180
Hope 134
Hope 140
Hope, like a gleaming taper's light 133
Hope we not in this life only 69
Horse can't pull while kicking, A 31
Horse Sense 31
HORTON, THEODORE 96

House is built of logs and stones, A 124
House of Christmas, The 52
How can you live in Goshen? 59
How Did You Die? 90
How Do I Love Thee 106
How do you tackle your work each day? 186
How happy is he born and taught 118
How many of us ever stop to think 151
How often for some trivial wrong 107
How Old Are You? 74
How Sleep the Brave? 167
How to Build a House 125
How Troublesome Is Day 72
How—When—Where 142
HUBBARD, ELBERT 132, 160
HUGHES, LANGSTON 36
HUGHES, THOMAS 158
HUGO, VICTOR 77, 96, 120, 124, 181
Humility 135
Humility 140
HUNT, LEIGH 16
Hyacinths to Feed Thy Soul 59
HYDE, WILLIAM DeWITT 24

I am done with the years that were 10
I bargained with Life for a penny 10
I Believe 93
I believe the poets 24
I bought gasoline, I went to the show 172
I cannot say 83
I Died for Beauty 19
I do not ask 173
I do not ask for any crown 169
I have closed the door on doubt 92
I have hoped, I have planned 89
I have only just a minute 34
I have to live with myself 38
I know that right is right 194
I like the man who fears what he must 89
I live for those who love me 142
I Love You 99
I made them lay their hands in mine 146
I need a strength to keep me true 96
I never cut my neighbor's throat 31
I Never Knew a Night 47
I never saw a moor 76
I Never Thought to Offer Thanks 116
I Resolve 55
I sat alone with my conscience 40
I saw a sweet young thing 191
I seek in prayerful words 122
I shall not mind 12
I shall wear laughter on my lips 133
I sheath my sword 89
I sing the hymn of the conquered 87
I thank thee, God, that I have lived 114
I thank Thee, Lord, for mine 161
I think that God will never send 101
I wandered lonely as a cloud 54
I want to remember lovely things 58
I Want You 108
I watched them tearing a building down 32
I will go forth among men 88
I Will Not Doubt 92
I will not think of treasures lost 64
I will start anew this morning 44
I wish there were some wonderful place 52
I would empty the chalice of heartache 100
I'd rather see a sermon than hear one any day 66
If 35
If after kirk ye bide a wee 175
If I am tempted to reveal 36
If I Had Known 102
If I had time to find a place 162
If I might leave behind 152
If I should die and leave you 74

If I stoop into a dark, tremendous sea 11
If love should count you worthy 109
If radio's slim fingers 94
If there be some weaker one 93
If with pleasure you are viewing 98
If You Are Ever Going to Love Me 104
If you are impatient 96
If You But Knew 110
If you get what you want 144
If you hear a kind word spoken 102
If you should go before me 78
If You Smile 188
If you strike a thorn 178
If you think you are beaten, you are 28
If you want a thing bad enough 185
If you want to have the kind of a church 170
If you woke up in the morning 185
If you'd move to a bygone measure 23
I'll hold my candle high 188
Immortality 82
Immortality in Books 22
In an age of fops and toys 191
In Anger 39
In Memoriam 93
In silence, that speech does not know 171
In summing up the things to praise 35
In the bitter waves of woe 46
Indispensable Man, The 136
Inevitable, The 89
Influence 39
INGERSOLL, ROBERT G. 26, 127
Insight 55
Into my heart's treasure 147
Intreat me not to leave thee 109
Inward Peace 57
Io Victus 87
IRVING, WASHINGTON 24, 35
Is Life Worth Living 145
Is your place a small place? 161
Isn't It Strange? 157
Isn't It True? 188
It ain't the failures he may meet 29
It Couldn't Be Done 185
It is composed of people 170
It is in loving 182
It is not growing like a tree 55
It is not much where you live 142
It isn't that we talk so much 107
It isn't the thing you do 96
It seemeth such a little way 90
It takes a heap o' living in a house 124
It takes a little courage 187
It Takes Courage 64
It's a risk to have a husband 95
It's doing your job 184
It's easy to sit in the shine 90
It's part of a man when his skies are blue 64
It's Up to You 32
It's wiser being good than bad 14
I've dreamed many dreams that never came true 62
I've wandered to the village 149
I've shut the door on yesterday 59
IZZARD, WES 125

JACKSON, ANDREW 63
JACKSON, HELEN HUNT 74
Jesus, stand beside them 73
JOHNSON, SAMUEL 145
JONES, LLOYD 87
JONSON, BEN 55
JORDAN, DAVID STARR 29
Journey, The 90
Judged by One's Company 44
Judge Not 180
Just a Minute 34
Just stand aside and watch 42
Just Think 82

KEATS, JOHN 16
Keep a brave spirit and never despair 131
Keep a'Goin' 178
Keep a'Trying 194
Keep Going 58
Keep Your Own Gate 32
KELLER, HELEN 60, 96, 162
KHAYYAM, OMAR 156
KILMER, ALINE 89
KILMER, JOYCE 54, 115
Kindest and the happiest pair, The 111
KINGSLEY, CHARLES 19, 23, 31, 71, 132, 181, 192
KIPLING, RUDYARD 35, 77, 168
KISER, S. E. 89
KLINGLE, GEORGE 162
Knowledge and wisdom 136
KNOX, WILLIAM 137
KOBA, FLORENCE 187
KROEBER, THEODORA 78

Land of Beginning Again, The 52
Land of Magic, The 23
LANDOR, WALTER SAVAGE 84, 100
LANG, ANDREW 24
Last Lines 80
LATHROP, LENA 127
Laugh, and the world laughs with you 62
LAW, WILLIAM 113
LAWRENCE, BROTHER 139
Layman, The 171
Lead, *Kindly Light* 84
Learn to Wait 160
Leave it to the minister 171
LECKY, W. E. H. 148
L'envoi 77
LEONARD, PRISCILLA 57, 119
LEO THE GREAT 56
Let me but live my life from year to year 56
Let Me Die Working 84
Let me grow lovely 9
Let me not shut myself within myself 103
Let me not stumble blindly 44
Let My Life Sing 112
Let nothing disturb thee 49
Let Others Cheer the Winning Man 88
Let Something Good Be Said 102
Let us be guests in one another's house 130
Letters 100
Life 141
Life 77
Life Beyond 79
Life did not bring me silken gowns 55
Life has loveliness to sell 60
Life! I know not what 75
Life is a leaf of paper white 29
Life is too short for grievances 110
Life's Meaning 146
Life's Melody 36
Life's Mirror 143
Lifting and Leaning 33
Like Mother, Like Son 68
LINCOLN, ABRAHAM 37, 73, 145, 166, 179, 180
LIN YUTANG 11
Listen to the exhortation of the dawn 158
Little more tired at the close of day, A 13
Little Te Deum, A 16
LONGFELLOW, HENRY WADSWORTH 10, 39, 44, 46, 47, 49, 60, 76, 82, 94, 109, 143, 150, 164, 167
Looking Forward 59
Loom of Time, The 182
Lord, let war's tempest cease 164
Lord, Make a Regular Man Out of Me 144

Lord, make me an instrument of thy peace 96
Lord, may there be no moment in her life 125
Lord of all pots and pans 126
Lord, when thy seest that my work 80
Lord, who am I to teach the way 139
LOVE, ADELAIDE 78
Love and Hate 109
Love of Country 164
Love That Gives 111
Love that is hoarded 36
Love That Wilt Not Let Me Go 78
Love Thyself Last 139
LOVELACE, RICHARD 50
Love's Lantern 54
Love's Strength 106
LOWELL, JAMES RUSSELL 24, 29, 30, 35, 94, 98, 164, 194
Lowest Place, The 162
Loyalty 103
Luck 187
LUTHER, MARTIN 41
LYSAGHT, SIDNEY ROYCE 109, 132

MACAULAY, THOMAS B. 22
MACKAY, CHARLES 43, 78
MAETERLINCK, MAURICE 119
Make It Up 110
Make me too brave to lie or be unkind 112
Make new friends but keep the old 99
MALLOCH, DOUGLAS 12
MALONE, WALTER 156
MANCROIX 55
Man is as great, A 184
Man is dear to man, the poorest poor 59
Man must live, A 87
Man with the consecrated car, The 176
MANN, HORACE 23
Man's life is laid in the loom of time 182
MARKER, ANDREW R. 34
MARKHAM, EDWIN 10, 85
MARQUIS, DON 90
MARTIN, MARGARET NICKERSON 62
MASON, WALT 31
MASSIEU, J. B. 114
Master of Men 193
MATHESON, GEORGE 78
MAUGHAM, W. SOMERSET 10
May I reach 153
May sorrow pass you by 136
McCULLOUGH, MARY E. 69
McKEEHAN, IRENE PETTIT 92
McNEILL, DON 14
Means to Attain Happy Life, The 122
Measure of Success 186
Measure thy life by loss, not gain 106
Memorial Day 165
Memory 147
Memory 149
Memory 150
Men don't believe in the devil 175
Men! whose boast it is 164
MERCER, ERNESTINE 49
MEREDITH, ANDREW 129
MEZQUIDA, ANNA BLAKE 133
Mile with Me, A 34
MILLER, J. R. 36
MILLER, JOAQUIN 88
MILLER, WILLIAM L. 36
MILTON, JOHN 42, 76, 161
Mine be a cot beside the hill 58
Minor Prophet, A 88
Miss You 108
MONTGOMERY, ROBERT 18
MOORE, THOMAS 100, 111, 148
MORELY, CHRISTOPHER 22
More things are wrought by prayer 94
Morning Prayer 30
MORTENSON, ALICE HANSCHE 17
MORTON, DAVID 17

Most glorious Lord of life 68
Mother's Wrinkled Hands 70
MOULTON, LOUISE CHANDLER 18
MURRAY, ANDREW 139
Music 151
Music 154
Music when soft voices die 149
My Chum 193
My Church 172
My Creed 40
My Early Home 148
My God, I thank Thee who has made 115
My hand is lonely for your clasping, dear 107
My Life Closed Twice 116
My life is but a working day 58
My Life Touched Yours 17
My Mind to Me a Kingdom Is 54
My Prayer 93
My Purpose 58
My soul, be on thy guard 176
My Task 142
My Wage 10
My World 139
Myself 38

NAPOLEON 39
NESBIT, WILBUR D. 25
Never Old, The 10
New Chance, A 157
New Chance, A 158
New Start, A 44
New Year Prayer, A 69
NEWMAN, CARDINAL 76
NEWMAN, JOHN HENRY 84
No Chance? 156
No coward soul is mine 80
No Friend Like Music 153
No Funeral Gloom 83
No Great, No Small 138
No man can choose what coming hours may bring 57
No Middle Way 192
No Star Is Ever Lost 30
No Time for God 171
No vision and you perish 92
Noblest Men, The 71
Noblest men that live on earth, The 71
Nobody Else But You 36
None but you can harm you 39
Not Growing Old 10
Not in Vain 69
Not now, but in the coming years 47
Not what we have, but what we use 121
Nothing Shall Part Us 109
Nothing Worthwhile Is Free 29
NUSBAUM, CYRUS S. 100

O for a book and a shadie nook 21
O happy home where thou art loved 123
O happy world today if we could know 69
O Master Let Me Walk with Thee 140
O sweeter than the marriage feast 174
O what a glory doth this world put on 60
Obedience 32
Obstacles 180
Ode 154
Oft, in the Stilly Night 148
Often when it seemed I found 55
Oh, there is never sorrow of heart 47
Oh, who will walk a mile with me 34
Oh! Why Should the Spirit of Mortal Be Proud? 137
Old man going a lone highway, A 38
Old, Old Song, The 192
Old Stoic, The 65
On Death, 76
On me nor Priest nor Presbyter 172

Once to every man and nation 35
One prayed in vain to paint the vision blest 90
One ship drives east and another drives west 28
Opportunity 156
Opportunity 158
O'REILLY, PAT 68
OSBORNE, EDITH D. 23
OSLER, WILLIAM 53, 92
O'SHAUGHNESSY, ARTHUR 154
O'SULLIVAN, SEUMAS 154
Our Heroes 190
Our Prayer 115
Out of the Past 112
Out of This Life 173
Out of this life I'm unable to take 173
Overheard in an Orchard 93
OVERSTREET, BONARO W. 27
OXENHAM, JOHN 16, 28, 80, 81, 104, 121, 142, 156, 161, 182

PAINE, ALBERT BIGELOW 82
PAINE, THOMAS 40
PALMER, ALICE FREEMAN 83
Paradox 182
PARKER, THEODORE 39
PARRY, JOSEPH 99
Pass It On 101
PAYER, S. H. 133
Peace 57
Peace After Sorrow 46
PEACOCK, THOMAS LOVE 72
PEARSE, MARK GUY 179
PEIFER, MRS. ROY L. 130
Penalty of Love, The 109
PENN, WILLIAM 82
Petition to Time, A 13
PETROVA, OLGA 128
PHELPS, ELIZABETH STUART 80
PHELPS, WILLIAM LYON 129, 130
PICKFORD, MARY 86
PIETY, CHAUNCEY R. 139
Pilgrim's Progress, The 83
PITTS, WILLIAM S. 172
Plea, A 122
Pleasant Thoughts 58
PLINY 124
Plough, The 32
Poem for the Living 78
POLLOCK 106
Polonius' Advice 145
POPE, ALEXANDER 59, 120, 132
PORTER, JANE 117
Possible man of affairs, A 190
POWERS, HORATIO NELSON 67
Pray, find no fault with the man 180
Prayer 94
Prayer for Veterans' Day 70
Prayer of a Husband 125
Preacher's Prayer, A 123
Prescription for You, A 96
PROCTOR, ADELAIDE A. 30, 111, 115, 134
PROCTOR, BRYAN WALLER 10, 13
Profanity 41
Prospice 79
Psalm of Life, The 143
PUGH, SAMUEL F. 190

Quitter, The 29

Rainy Day, The 49
Real Test, The 86
Recessional 168
Recipe for Living 146
Recipe for Success 185
Red Geraniums 55
REESE, LIZETTE WOODWORTH 51
Religion 169
Religious Unity 173
Remember 149
Remember me when I am gone 149